EPIPHANIES,
THEORIES,
and Downright Good Thoughts…

EPIPHANIES, THEORIES,

and Downright Good Thoughts…

…made while being single.

J.C.L. FALTOT

iUniverse, Inc.
Bloomington

Epiphanies, Theories, and Downright Good Thoughts...
...made while being single.

iUniverse books may be ordered through booksellers or by contacting:

iUniverse
1663 Liberty Drive
Bloomington, IN 47403
www.iuniverse.com
1-800-Authors (1-800-288-4677)

ISBN: 978-1-4759-7538-3 (sc)
ISBN: 978-1-4759-7539-0 (ebk)

Printed in the United States of America

iUniverse rev. date: 04/03/2013

This book is dedicated to my girlfriend . . .
. . . wherever she may be.

Contents

Intro

I've spent a good portion of my life being single. There, I said it. It's not an easy thing to be, I'll tell you that much. Especially after you reach a certain age and everyone is trying to shack up with that special someone. If I had to list some of my fonder memories, I would definitely . . . without question . . . without reservation . . . never mention the time that I was single. Life is so much better when you have a spouse, friend, family member, pet—whatever to come home to. Heck, I'd even throw in an aloe plant as being decent company.

Ok, so maybe an aloe plant is a little bit of a stretch, but hey, let me tell you why you may consider such an outrageous concept in the first place.

My experiences with living alone can best be summed up in one word: "island-i-ous." This particular word cannot be found in any English dictionary but here's a translation: an island unto one's self. This is not exactly a chosen state of existence but could be considered as such. For if one does not find someone else to live with (or you have zero friends) then yes, island-i-ous can be forced upon you. If your situation *is* a forced one, then you may find ways out of this predicament. However, if you choose to not flee, then you will continue onward in isolation. The island that you inhabit (the island being "you") will then begin to change. The girth of your island amasses in middle areas you never thought possible and the backside of your island fills out in a manner best left to the Kardashians to be proud of. Your island changes to the point where you worry no one will ever vacation on your island ever again and thus, you start a full scale cleaning on your island (I trust you are seeing the metaphor here).

You hire experts to purge the ever-increasing mass on said island (personal trainers).

You begin to ration food even though you have access to plenty (diet changes).

And you may even entertaining trimming certain woods and forests on parts of your island that you hadn't thought of before. I wouldn't recommend this action, but do as your heart pleases. Understand that when you're through, you will live with the consequences of your decision and remain hopeful that your woods grow back in the same fashion they had originally grown in.

Before we go any further, I should probably ask if you read the latest rendition of Epiphanies, Theories and Downright Good Thoughts. Yes? No? Well, if you were lucky enough to read the first book (Epiphanies, Theories, and Downright Good Thoughts . . . made while playing video games), then the answer to your question is 'yes', this is the sequel to that book. Here's an obvious fact: playing too many video games is liable to leave you single. That's a truth, my friends. Not to say that's always been the case for me but it's certainly a contributing factor.

Leading a life as a single person allows for certain behaviors to persist. In my case, it's been a plethora of things: video games, strange smells, and dumping laundry in seven different places throughout the apartment are just a few of those. If you're lucky enough to have a large space to live in, you'll find odd things to hoard in your spare bedrooms. Old clothes? That elliptical you bought but never use? How about trinkets from your exes? You may deliberate over what to do in that multi-purpose room, but in the end, you find that it will forever be the all-purpose station until you eventually find someone to share your life with.

That is, if you ever find someone.

Now, I don't mean to sound like a Debbie Downer or a Pessimistic Pete, but there are certain realities we must live with. One of them is that we are all not meant to be married folk. That's a harsh truth. Some of us are meant to lead an existence that encompasses a very singular focus. There isn't necessarily anything wrong with that, it's just harder to do when society and culture expects you to perform otherwise. I have a family that's large so they highly recommend continuing the namesake.

That's quite a pickle to be in, let me tell you.

I didn't exactly grow up an only child. No, far from it actually. I have five brothers; three older and two younger, but I still managed to get my alone time when I wanted it. For hours I would sit and listen to music, do my homework like a good kid, or consider leaving to go play video games (of course). Yes, I did mix in some socializing but point is, I'm used to having that "me time." I can handle it. It ain't so bad, but those were the days where you could just open your bedroom door and go downstairs to see the rest of your family. If I were to do the same while living in my apartment . . . well, it wouldn't exactly have the same results. I'd probably have the cops called on me and rightfully be carted away.

How does one go about dealing with this new situation then? You know, the balancing of alone time with appropriate social interaction? Well, let me enlighten you as best I can. At first, you reach out to those who are your closest of friends. You call on these relationships because they're a) familiar and b) you genuinely enjoy their company. Here's the catch: that only lasts for so long. These friends, who were once inseparable from you, either grow up or grow *out* in life. This is not to say that everyone will abandon you—it's just that some friends move on while others stick around. This is the natural flow of things and is not to be hated nor reviled. We can't exactly control the zip code that our friends choose to inhabit for the rest of our lives. And if they've found a partner for life, then that partner becomes more important than you, sorry to say.

Once you've exhausted the friendship circle, you will move on to another group: your coworkers. They're semi-normal, right? You see them every day so you have a basic understanding of their quirks and ticks. Let me tell you something though: NO. Run away. As fast as you can. Ok, I'm being a little overdramatic but here are some inevitable truths. Taking a job means that you are *working*. If you happen to find some close friends while at work (or even a mate) then kudos to you. However, do not throw caution to the wind because the people you work with are not always the ones who you should be hanging out with. And if you do, you'll discover some things about them that you may have been better off just not knowing. Alas, I don't say that this is for everyone, but I'm just giving you a proper forewarning.

Ok, so the friendship circle is shrinking and the coworkers are a little crazy, so what's left? Ah yes, community organizations. Your local church or religious sector, perhaps? That seems like a good start. And for many people, it's just the right spot to build some communion. If you find the right one, it's really easy to stay plugged in. Funny thing is, when you're 20something and you find other 20somethings going to church, you discover another interesting truth: people are going there to find a likely husband or wife. Holy crap, right? My dad always told me that if I wanted to find a 'nice girl', then I should go to church. I never thought he was serious until I came face-to-face with others who were receiving similar advice from their fathers. A simple church service could turn into "Hey, would you like to meet my family next week?" To which I'd reply with, "Um, we just met last Sunday . . . ."

Well, that was a bust.

So maybe the church thing won't work out as well as you had hoped. On the upside, you can still go—just beware of the stage five clingers looking to wed you as early as next Sunday. Church is still as fine a place as any to meet good people, I've found. Please do not forsake this knowledge I bestow upon you. The common perception is that church is only for crazy folks and ultra-conservatives but that's a stereotype you really just need to put to the wayside. Yes, church-goers are crazy, but at least they are open in their craziness. It's those "normal" people you have to watch out for.

But once again, here we are. Old friends? No. Coworkers? Not likely. Church-organization-looking-for-quick-love? Nay; and don't go back unless you're going for the right reasons. Other than pursuing a life of crime ala Bonnie and Clyde style, the options are limited. This is when I realized something: you have to get back in touch with your *family*. Really? My family? Is there no other way? Well, I suppose I can try that and see how it goes.

It's shocking how we tend to distance ourselves from the one thing that brought us into this world. For many, the choice is made before they even have an opportunity to fall back with family, but I still find that everyone (and I mean everyone) has someone they consider to be family: be it blood or otherwise. You may have waited years to get away from those who governed your very existence, but when you're out of alternatives, you find yourself inevitably running back. Your family's here to stay and you may as well get accustomed to that fact.

Once I knew this, I wondered how many other people have had to face the truth. You know—either move back home or continue the search for a soulmate to end their lonely bachelor or bachelorette days. Like a good boy, I did my research. I checked on the U.S. census statistics to find out who was getting hitched and who wasn't. So are you ready for this? According to 2010's U.S. census data, 62.2% of all men ages 25-29 have never been married, with 47.8% of women being in that same category. The reason why I reference this age group is for two reasons: 1) it's the median age where people typically get married and 2) it's about that time where your parents start dropping you hints that they'd like you to consider loving someone other than yourself. As any attentive son would, I took heed of my parents' choice words, but I planned to continue on my own terms. Yes, I wanted them to be grandparents someday, but I also wanted someone really special to convince me to leave the life of a single man. How long does that venture take though? Well, in my short life, it's taken a long time.

My immediate family knows me better than most. We're not a perfect unit by any stretch of the imagination and we have our faults, but we understand each other on deeper levels than merely knowledge of a favorite dessert or sports team. Some families are more dysfunctional than others, but at the end of the day, the common theme is this: everyone may not like each other, but family is family. Well, at least it *should* be that way, right? I fully understand that many families don't have that consideration. Broken homes, broken families, broken hearts; it's terrible all the way through. That's why it's so important to find proper support. Friends can become family, coworkers can become family, or even the church becomes your family. One way or another, we are always searching for some place that we can call *home*.

Home is usually defined by the presence of more than just one's own self. In my personal quest to find another home, I've taken some serious spills and had some serious thrills (more spills I'd say than anything). So with that in mind I invite you to another compilation of epiphanies, theories, and downright good thoughts. This time I'm revolving my stories around a time that is tumultuous, ridiculous, and loaded with self-discovery. Or if you prefer, I suppose the more appropriate title could be "Failures, letdowns, and redemptions . . . made while living alone in an apartment."

Yes, that might be more accurate.

Epiphany: The single guy's apartment is a place of refuge . . .

. . . for those who are not single.

This is probably the best place to start. When I finally got my first full-time gig as a working man, I packed up and headed for my new domicile: a one bedroom/one bath/one kitchen apartment. Where I was headed was a good two hours from where I called home. Far enough away to feel like I was on my own but close enough in proximity to return as necessary. My degree had landed me what one might call the "big boy" job; financially I could sustain myself. Daunting but I accepted my newfound fate and greeted it with open arms.

This wasn't the most important thing to me though. What I was *really* looking forward to was a place to call my own. I could come and go as I pleased, sleep on a couch that was mine, and drink right from the milk carton (which seems like an outdated comment these days but hey, I could still do it if I wanted to). This was going to be my own personal paradise and nobody could tell me otherwise. This is not to say that I despised my parent's place; I just wanted my space as an adult. Plain and simple.

Probably one of the first things I did was establish a working order of the apartment. Television? Check. Bed? Check. Futon? Check, but damn it, that thing's got to go if I'm ever going to date somebody. Nothing says "I'm still living the college life" like a futon in your apartment. Come to think of it, I had a nice setup minus the whole futon debacle. I even had an old school entertainment center complete with two speakers and an FM radio (yes, an FM radio); the kind where you have to turn a knob the size of an apple to get a signal. Ah yes, life was good. Then someone had the bright idea of a "guy's night." You know, the one night dedicated to just us dudes hanging out in my bachelor pad.

Sounded like a really glorious concept so why the heck not, right?

Most of my closest friends were either engaged or on a path to be married soon. Since so many of them are old school (much props), they elected to live apart from their future spouse until the big wedding day. Despite what common culture deems acceptable, I will be doing the same. More couples tend to stay together if they wait to move in together after they're engaged or married. And if you don't believe me, then here's a nice little statistic for you—the National Center for Health Statistics (sounds legit, does it not?) concluded in 2010 that the rate for which couples "split up" after living together before marriage increased by 6 percent. And since stats don't lie, the perception I get is that young couples still believe they are immune to this aforementioned fact. Unfortunately that's true of anybody who is young. You're invincible until you get caught in the crossfire of a statistic. That's a harsh truth to become acquainted with.

Anyway, I wasn't living with anyone else and figured this "guy's night" would be fun. My friends were in the same mode of thinking. We picked a day during the week, plotted out food arrangements, and holed up at my abode for a few hours around evening time. The typical guy's night consisted of pizza, a few drinks, and video games (and if you read the latest Epiphanies book then you would know that this is not outside the norm for my friends and me). And no, there wasn't any weed, green leaves, or special substances to make us get high. There was plenty of coke though. The really good kind, Diet Coke, to be exact. Some guys gotta watch their figure, ya know?

The weeks went on and we had our good times. I felt like it was a great opportunity to continue the whole keeping-in-touch thing going. Even my newly acquired friends would join so it wasn't always such a college reunion. Life was swimming along quite nicely. My friends bantered at me with great appeal for our "guy's nights."

"Man, why didn't we think of this sooner?!"

Truthfully, why didn't we? We could have had a giant man-cave dedicated to a fifth year of college. We had enjoyed our last year of college in a house off campus and the word that best describes the experience is this: pureawesomeness. And yes, I'm creating a word because the sheer magnitude of the situation calls for it. What type of fun can be had when your best friends are all centralized to a single locale? Well, the best kind actually.

"Dude, we should have got a house together. We could do this every weeknight!"

Once again, this was something we could have done in hindsight. In college I had lived with three of my closest friends. But what if that had been five, six, hell, *seven* of us? It was totally feasible if you could find the proper housing arrangements. And though it has the makings of a Real World spin-off, the idea of seven guys living under one roof could also give rise to accusations of a fraternity house. History has taught us that this could totally happen though (the movie Old School, anyone?). Oh well—opportunity wasted.

"Why don't we get poker games started too?"

Sure, I thought. Why not?! I mean, I didn't have much space but if I could somehow accommodate my friends, then that'd be great. That way we could always have games over at my place. We'd never be short of something to do. Whether it was video games, poker, pizza, whatever . . . my quaint little shack would be the fortress of solitude for all those who were welcome . . .

. . . but as we all know, things change. Most notably, people move on with their lives and the hands of time pull you forward faster than you have time to think. My once large group of seven dudes slowly began to trickle to five. Then four . . . then three . . . then the extremely awkward night where it was just me and one other guy. The evening was culminated by a conversation which involved one of us asking the other if it were alright if we didn't have another "guy's night" next week. I recall that being a very sad day. And just a little bit weird to boot.

I contemplated the marriages that were all around me. Fret not, my friends, marriage is not meant for everybody. Even more important, marriage should not be taken lightly if you persist in ignoring the bigger picture. I'm no registered psychologist or relationship counselor but I have noticed that very rarely do marriages last when the bride and groom are more fixated on the "day" rather than the journey of marriage itself. Marriage is intended as a freedom to protect you from outside forces—it is not a prison; and marriage is not meant to be treated like a birthday where you celebrate it once a year, it is a life-long commitment. My words may seem filled with fluff or even sales-like, but I've *seen* good marriages in action. That's powerful enough to make you believe what marriage is for and what it's defined as.

Clearly, I wasn't in a place yet to be thinking about this. Rumor on the street is that you need a lady first in order to make a marriage possible. That's just what I hear, of course.

This unknown territory of having married friends would be enlightening for me. Big SPOILER ALERT! coming up first—married people love to hang out with other married people. Single folks though? Eh, not so much. The only way that happens is one of two reasons. Either a) you're a relative or b) you're a close friend that still hasn't got your life together but your presence is still tolerable. The point I'm trying to get to is that you shouldn't feel obligated to fulfill these fantasies as set forth by your friends. Yeah, their lives may be different now that they're married, but you don't have to live up to some stereotype as attached to single people like yourself. No, I suggest doing something that's actually even sweeter: being *mysterious*.

In my travels as a singleton, I tried to live up to the iconic "ideal single guy" image. I wanted to go out and make memories so grotesque that I'd want to forget them as soon as I retold the tale. Trouble is, I didn't have too many of those nights to begin with. And once those lonely nights began to add up, I really started to look inward. And when I looked inward, I came to some rather hefty epiphanies of my own. The most pertinent one being that you can either continue trying to impress others, or you can live by impressing yourself. Instead of leading a life that others want, you can instead create your own mystery of *you*. When asked how your life is going, say things such as the following:

"Well, it was a crazy weekend . . . . I wish I could remember most of the incredibly awesome things I did, but hey, when you're me, who has time to keep up and record this stuff?"

Or . . .

"You should have seen this place I was at . . . I don't really remember though. I was too busy being awesome to really recall."

Or . . .

"If you had been there, you'd probably think differently about the way you view me. Not that you don't think I'm incredibly awesome already, but still . . . ."

Sure, people may ask you follow-up questions about these ambiguous answers but you really don't have to respond. You know you're awesome so having to answer to anybody else would just be absurd. Just brush off their offensive with a topic-changer and go about your business. Eventually people may begin to wonder if you're a moonlighting as a hero or vigilante. Like Bruce Wayne is the Batman, Peter Parker is Spider-Man, or if they think you're a villain, you may be a character sent to destroy social standards like the Octo-Mom. Either way, people will begin to question if you're leading some sort of dual life layered with secrecy and excitement. Their appeal for you will actually *increase* since they'll know less about you. And that's a really great thing because now you'll be able to live your own life without having to appease others. Sound like a good plan? Well it is because I've done it.

An acquaintance of mine may know me but they also don't *know* me. That's for my closest friends, my family, and my (eventual) wife to know. Nobody need have access to what really transpires on Friday or Saturday nights at my abode. Sure, I may have been playing Dance Central on my Kinect for three hours, but to my coworkers on Monday morning, I was romancing a tall brunette at an expensive winery, taste-testing the finest reds and whites this side of the Mississippi. Where the fabled relationship will go from there, I'm not sure, but if I don't beat Usher's "Scream" on Hard soon, I'll give up Dance Central and go back to Just Dance.

I will warn any young apprentice that there is a delicate balance in this scenario. You may be formulating these great tales about yourself, but be mindful of the mini-legend you're becoming. What we tell people we are and who we *really* are is a double-edged sword of problematic proportions. Know that the mystery will never outweigh who and what you want to be. And do not become a product of the growing façade you've put yourself in. It is only meant as a shield to protect you from social pressures. Nothing more and nothing less. So when your acquaintances grow tired of asking about your exploits, you can have much more meaningful conversations. Like how their family is doing or if they've talked to that estranged relative lately. That's more important than building your own pretend kingdom of singlehood while you pursue a life worth living.

So as I was saying, the following Wednesday came and for the first time (in a long while), I sat alone in seclusion. I stared at the big screen television I bought to allow for optimal viewing. I surveyed the entertainment center I had upgraded to listen to music while we all played poker. I rubbed my hand upon the recliner (ever so gently) I had received which allowed me to pass out once the night was over. It was at this critical moment when I realized something: I needed a fish tank. A really nice fish tank. I'd always wanted small trout or one of those cool axolotl things so the fish tank was inevitable. If you are unfamiliar with the unique axolotl, then I suggest looking the critters up online. You may want one or be inclined to make your best "eww" face at the sight of these little guys.

Truthfully, I had several epiphanies that night (the fish tank was not the only one). I was positive that I had triumphed in creating the perfect den for the bachelor. The only thing missing (besides my fish tank) was a good poster/calendar of some half-naked chicks. Tacky, yes, but tasteful if you can find the right compilation of gals. I'd seen it done in most dorm rooms so I figured I'd give it a whirl, but after sifting through enough Twilight posters of Edward and Bella to make me vomit, I decided that I was past that "poster phase."

I soon became aware that I had also made a workable party zone for any occasion. I had some nifty wine coolers, some shot glasses, and a gallery of mementos I had accumulated from the various bachelor parties I'd been to. Each had its own set of memories attached to it. There was the impromptu Dave and Buster's gathering, a camp outing, the Canada trip (twice taken) and the party-we-all-thought-might-be-lame-but-turned-out-great in a parent's backyard. All were fond moments, frozen in time, and still fresh enough for me to reminisce on. But now these memories were all I had.

Don't worry, there'll be a pity party after the book reading, I assure you.

In a matter of a year, my place had transformed into the "Single Man's Cave"; the "Bachelor's Oasis"; or if you prefer, the "Lion's Den" (as some people liked to call it; and personally I liked that one the best despite its ridiculousness). There was just me here now and no one was going to visit. I sighed often, maybe even shed a tear from time to time but I kept my chin up. You know that period in your life where everyone says "live it up and enjoy it while it lasts"? Well, that all seemed to pass before I even had time to freaking think about what was happening!

I was determined not to mope about my predicament any longer. I took action. The company of my friends had come and passed but I was determined to make the most of this situation. I decided that I was going to make my apartment the best damn apartment possible. That way my friends would *want* to abandon their wives for the night and come back. That'll show them. There would be no fortress like my fortress in all the land; a fortified pillar of singleness that would stand the test of time. And most of all, it would represent the one great goal of every man: freedom.

Oh, I just got tingles.

I quickly invited everyone back for a guy's night. I bought pizza, beer, rented old WCW/WWE wrestling DVDs to reclaim the good ol' days . . . I did it all. There was no way that my friends could resist this kind of entertainment. The only thing missing was another surge protector to allow for multi-television gaming (though I knew full well that this would not be advisable). Soon, the invite went out and I waited.

And waited.

And waited.

And waited still.

I waited until I decided that I needed to eat my frozen pizza before it got too old. I returned the DVDs of professional wrestling to the library that were two months overdue (that late fee was a real b-otch). And I gave away my beer at another party I was invited to. What a buzzkill. I didn't even get to spend the items the way I had intended. Through it all, I was hoping for some kind of sign. The type that would tell me 'hey, it's gonna be ok'; a sign that told me my efforts were not in vain. That it was alright for me to try and fight for the olden days of "just the boys." Sadly, this sign never really came but I did continue to search though. I searched high and low for quite some time.

I'd read my horoscope in the local newspaper—

"Today you are feeling energetic. However, there is something that you feel amiss and you are longing for. Tonight: write down your thoughts to help get clarity on the situation. Number of stars: four."

Wow, that was helpful. Ok, I'll write down my angst and see what happens. Wait, isn't that what I'm doing right now? Maybe tomorrow's will yield more answers . . . .

"Today you are still feeling energetic. You have a greater sense of clarity with your personal dealings and are willing to move forward. Tonight: Reconnect with an old friend. Numbers of stars: five"

Really? Ok, that was just dumb. No, I did *not* resolve all my problems in 24 hours and no, I am *not* having a "five star" day. And for the record, are there ever two or three star days? I don't think I've ever seen a horoscope that gave anyone less than three stars. And you know what; it's probably because the nut that sees he's having a less-than-three-star-day might jump off a cliff. Sure, that sounds a tad bit extreme, but here I am getting just as worked up over a stupid horoscope! Give me four and five star days, but please, oh please great horoscope gods—do not give me a "less than average" kind of day. That's just cruel.

Alright, so horoscopes were clearly the wrong place to look for answers. So where to go next? How about my coworkers? Surely they could vouch and tell me that I needed to bring my friends back down to Earth. Make them realize what they were missing out on. There's got to be some encouragement, right? The answers were less than uplifting:

"You know, they're just in a different place now. I'm sure they'll want to come by at some point."
Or . . .
"It's only natural, you know? They have more than themselves to look after now. It's just not about them anymore, but two people."
Or . . .
"Owning a house is a big deal. It's a large investment so they are probably just busy with making the house look nice."

Man, that last one stung the most. I can deal with people having other commitments, but to tell me that a house was an ordeal all in its own was something else entirely. It transformed my Buckingham Palace into the Poor Man's Garage overnight. A house? I didn't even consider this. Why would anyone want to visit someone who merely owned an apartment when they had a house? It was blasphemy.

For starters, a house has more than one level. You can go upstairs if you so desire or you can go downstairs. You also have an actual kitchen that doesn't necessarily share space with your living room. Therefore if you spill something, you only need to use a paper towel since it fell on a wooded floor and not the carpet from your living room. You can even take your dinner to the living room too. Options, man! Options!

I started to make a list of all the features houses had that my apartment lacked. This list was longer than I anticipated. A garage for my car; neighbors who wouldn't make noise directly above or below; a mailbox, an actual mailbox for getting mail without the need of a 4-digit pin code—this was adding up fast. A basement? True, some houses don't have basements, but all of my friends had basements! The basement could very well be your *own* man-cave. It's as if they knew all along! Complete with old college banners, pictures, and accolades that you can sit in and talk over. And why not add a fridge down there while you're at it?! Put food, beer, the whole shebang right there. Forget the fridge at my apartment. That thing is only good for storing spoiled milk and empty pizza boxes.

I tried to rebuttal with some reasons as to why apartments were better than houses, but I just couldn't find any. I was losing the battle on paper, but maybe it wasn't about what was on paper? My friendship alone accounted for something, did it not? I had spent so much energy on the tangibles, but very little on the intangibles. My hope was renewed but I was still unsettled. I had recorded all the usual materials that made a house a house, but even then, I felt like I was missing something. As if I had overlooked some crucial detail but that detail hadn't exposed itself quite yet.

Well, that detail eventually came to light—and in a big way.

These houses, for all their glory, were inhabited by something both tangible and intangible in nature. Something so oppositional to my world that its mere presence would turn my bachelor pad to dust. No, it was not the big screen TVs, the wrestling tapes or even the fish tanks. These houses, for all their special features and additional space, had one very special element keeping me from enjoying the fruits of male bonding: a female companion. Not just any female companion though; a *wife*. I was up against the stiffest of competition imaginable. As much as I didn't want to admit it, I had to. This last piece of the puzzle was the game-changer. No other way around it. How was I supposed to compete with that?! I certainly wasn't going to offer up any spooning opportunities (that ended in college) and I certainly wasn't contemplating a change of scenery to the area below my belly button. That was out of the question entirely. So there I was: stuck in the world of the single man's apartment. Just I, my big screen, my poker table, my hefty entertainment center, and the empty space reserved for that fish tank I may never own, but openly covet.

Woe is me, right?

I decided to have a chat with somebody that I figured might be able to help me out. You're probably correct in assuming who I turned to. Yes, it was my Xbox. I had more than once come upon the answers I was looking for in front of a gaming console. And so, I spent several nights battling zombies, saving princesses, and conquering creepy dungeons all in hopes of coming to some resolution on what to do next. Then, as things normally played out, an answer came to me whilst punishing a group of newbs in an online game of Halo: why not ask God for help?

In my life, I reserve the really hard questions for the big guy upstairs. Questions such as: which video game to purchase next or how my Pirates were going to perform in the spring, but this situation warranted an even more serious take on things. And so, I prayed about my growing isolation. I prayed to see the silver lining in my bachelor pad. I prayed that my friends would recognize that I still had a rockin' sweet place to hang out at. And I prayed that I wouldn't have to be completely isolated every other night of my life. I prayed good and long and long and good and when I was done, God gave me an answer as He so often does.

His first order of business was for me to give part of my wardrobe to the Salvation Army. I recall waking up one day, looking down at my floor, and seeing nothing but clothes scattered about the room. My bedroom was no small place, but when one cannot see their own floor, you certainly have a clutter problem. I shuddered as the show "Hoarders" came to mind. Was I one of them? Had I slipped into the world of hoarding? No, not really. Apparently a true hoarder has so much needless crap lying around that the entrance ways and exits become blocked in their homes. The only thing I'd done was neglect to fold my laundry from the night before; thus, I feel like I'm safe.

You see, I had adopted this method of dropping my newly dried clothes right at the foot of my bed. I knew I'd run into them on my way to slumber (thus reminding me to fold those damn things at some point). Otherwise, they'd sit in my dryer for another day or two becoming ever more wrinkled. Probably not the most effective method for folding one's clothes, but hey, it worked for me.

Decision made, I gathered up the items I didn't need and stuffed them in big trash bags. Old coats, t-shirts, everything but old underwear got the ax as I parted with my old belongings. I then meandered on down to a local drop point and ditched my trash bags full of clothes. I felt pretty good about what I'd done so I became curious as to how the whole concept of the Salvation Army started in the first place. Well, I'll tell you as I'm sure you're wondering now.

Turns out the guys who founded this whole Salvation Army thing did it over 150 years ago. And it was done under the principles of a Protestant church no less. My research on the charity yielded some pretty unimpressive things though as I Google-searched my way through their history. There were articles on internal controversies that had racked the organization for the past decade, even so far back as 40-50 years. It was disappointing to read about, but I feel like the idea was good in its execution.

There was a story on administrators embezzling charity money under "administrative expenses." A court case about kids who were sexually abused while under the care of Salvation Army homes for the homeless. There was even a complaint about how the Salvation Army discriminated against gays; essentially not allowing gays to work for the charity.

You might say my newfound knowledge of the Salvation Army left me feeling disappointed. Wow, who ordered the buzzkill, right? Weren't we just discussing my bachelor pad a few moments ago? Well, walk with me a little while longer.

My investigation into the Salvation Army left me feeling ill. Very rarely do we find an organization that is completely squeaky clean in all of its dealings. The problem is that everyone looks to these organizations to uphold the standards of what the place was built upon. One bad move and you face years of repairing an image that has been stained by the selfish or twisted actions of just a few individuals. One person may think it's wrong but collectively, people will make dumb decisions, so what can you do? Well, I've since found that the most important thing is knowing that what you did *was* good and it's that peace of mind that's worth your effort. My bachelor pad's extreme change was not necessarily bad in nature because its intentions were good. I wanted to see my friends more so I took the actions I felt were necessary to make that happen. I'm sure that when the Salvation Army was founded, they didn't dream that years later, their successors would abuse the inner workings of the organization. In fact, what they probably wished for was a longstanding service to humanity.

And hey, that's what I was after when it came to my friends—building an environment that could stand the test of time, at least for as long as it could. A man only needs so much space and the rest is just for kicks and giggles. I needed to get rid of some things I didn't need anymore and by golly, my old clothes was one of them.

The second order of business God told me to handle was not so subtle. It's true that I had gotten rid of my old clothes, but what about the overall tidiness of my apartment space? I've always been relatively clean (both personally and within my domicile) but if there's one thing I neglect more than anything, it's gotta be dusting. Dusting is just a huge time-waster in my eyes. I mean, I could be using that valuable time to do something more constructive like . . . I don't know . . . play a video game or two? And if I were still in school, I could probably use that time to study or finish homework. Yeah, not the biggest fan of dusting right here. That much is true.

I suppose it's all necessary though. The moment of truth came when I was moving some furniture around (in order to get my laundry ironically enough) and came across the biggest dust bunny I'd ever seen in my life. It may have actually had eyes on it and teeth sticking out. If I uttered a scream at all, I don't remember it but I truly might have. Before I swept that bad boy up, I did some research on what the heck makes up a dust bunny (surprised at all?).

The results were downright shocking and disgusting.

According to my dictionary findings, and I'll paraphrase here, dust is the culmination of uprooted soil, pollen in the air, ash from volcanoes (ok, that's cool) and pollution (ok, not so cool) in the atmosphere. That's just the stuff on the *outside* of your home. What's on the *inside* of your home is really disturbing. Dust can be made up of all the above but is more likely containing the following: paper fibers, textile fibers, human hair, mites, and . . . wait for it . . . human skin cells.

Now that's just awesome.

I was basically staring at a giant ball of my own skin cells mixed with tiny little bugs. Unless you're some kind of weirdo, the mixture that I just described can't be the most appealing thing to imagine. And ladies, if you ever meet a guy who has this kind of a dust ball just lying around his place, do yourself a favor and consider telling him what's up. Or just say that you'd rather not sit in a room that's filled with his skin cells (or something to that effect). Just sayin . . . .

Dust needed to be a thing of the past for this guy. Not since I'd lived at home or even at college had I seen so much dust. I mean, the homes I'd lived in had dust bunnies, but none the size of softballs. Come to think of it, the types of dust balls we had in college were somewhat similar to the one I was now facing in my own apartment. And if one of the girls were here now, I know exactly what they'd be saying.

"You realize you have large balls of dust in your corners, right?"
"Ew, there's a huge ball of dust by your TV."
"You need a feather duster like NOW."

I could hear their voices then and I can hear their voices now. I needed to ditch the dust bunnies and do it fast if I was going to get my buddies back. I went out and got the finest feather duster that Target could provide and got to work. My efforts made me feel like an FBI agent trying to find fingerprints at the scene of a crime. Sure, there was no murder to solve, but my place felt much cleaner. I soaked up my newfound cleanliness with a deep breath, but started hacking immediately afterward. Then the sneezing started. Then about six hours later I had a sinus infection. What the heck, bro?! I guess it'll take more than one quick dusting to get rid of everything, huh?

With an aloe-coated Kleenex in hand, I pulled out my laptop, did the Google search thing and found what I had feared: feather dusters don't actually dust. They just *move* the little human hairs and bugs around your room. Oh, that's just fantastic. I was coughing and hacking because I had roused the dust mites and now they were fluttering around my apartment. I was better off when they were all congregated in one place!

Instead of getting really angry, I turned to another alternative. Ok, first it was a good game of Halo, but right after that, I bought some dust wipes. Oh, baby, do I love my dust wipes. With dust wipes, you can actually *feel* the dust being collected beneath your fingertips. A few good dabs of these wonderful dust collectors and your furniture looks brand new.

And boy, did it ever look new.

I could breathe again too. That was a major bonus if I do say so. I had finally conquered the dust in my apartment so I took a moment (again) to revel in my accomplishment. This time I didn't hack or cough. I surveyed all that I had done and felt relieved.

And it was *good*.

The apartment was clean and for once, it was more than a "single guy lives here clean." There was freshness in the air of renewed life; not of aloneness or decay. I had experienced this kind of cleanliness before. I didn't recognize this at first, but a few more breaths and I knew: it was a memory of my mother. She was notorious, nay famous, for turning the dirtiest of places into pristine chapels of sanitation. This skill, whether innately honed or learned, made her darn good at what she did. Her circumstance likely contributed to this talent of hers. When you rear six boys (seven if you include my father . . . and by all rights, I should) you learn a thing or two about cleaning.

Men, if left alone to their own devices, are never really that clean. We're always running through mud, getting our hands dirty, and eating the kinds of food that would make a dumpster diver cringe. It's in our DNA, I suppose. No ifs, ands, or buts about it. And though I was clearly of the stereotype, I had taken the time to properly alter my apartment. It was no longer an escape made specifically for bachelors; it was a world where all forms of life could cohabitate. Weird how it took me so long to realize this, but I got there nonetheless.

I think I took some pictures that day and saved them to my computer. Then while I was on the old laptop, I sent out a Facebook message to my buddies (and their wives) explaining how I'd like to have some people over to commemorate my cleaned castle. The responses came back quickly, which gave me great elation since I wouldn't have to keep up this clean thing for more than a week. Seven days was all I needed for the 'ok' from my friends and their spouses.

A week came and went and the big moment was finally here. My friends visited and to my delight, the ladies were impressed. They commented on how nice things were and how I had finally seemed to settle into where I was. I even had a veggie tray for everyone to pick off of because let's be honest, having a veggie tray at a party says "I'm clean" and "I'm socially conscious of other people's tastes" too.

I decidedly bragged a little here and there, told of my battle with the dust mites and even cracked a joke or two about how I'd need to find more clothes since I gave half of mine away. Again, I was met with more credibility points for my efforts. Things were really going my way. I got the thumbs up from a few of my friends and we talked about reviving Guy's Night in the near future. Even the wives were on board for the idea.

Hallelujah, the plan was a success! Thank you, God, for giving me the resources that I so desperately craved. I was so overjoyed yet calmed by the experience. I slept well that night; very well. Probably one of the better sleeps I had in recent memory. The days of pizza, beer, and poker were going to return very soon and I couldn't have been happier.

That is, until the next night came around.

I had been seeing a girl for a little while and she stopped over to see my place. It was her first time there so I made extra certain that my place would have all the dust, clothes, and items in order. If I could get a married woman's approval, just imagine what a single girl might think, right?

This guy sure has it together. He's definitely a keeper.

Oh yes, that's what I knew she'd be thinking. Anything else just wouldn't make sense. Well, we had dinner just as planned, talked a bit and then I threw in a movie to culminate the night. Dinner and a movie is always a good choice; a killer combination that works every time to break the tension. She curled up underneath my arm as I turned on a personal favorite of mine from the '90s, the movie Tombstone starring Kurt Russell and Val Kilmer. Not very romantic, I agree, but our relationship had finally reached the point where a make out session was in order. Before that even occurred, she sat up and looked me dead in the eye. I was a little confused by this move (I thought she was conservative like me), but I was prepared to put the brakes on if things got too out of hand. Then, she said it.

"You know, your place is like, really *clean*."

"Thanks," I replied, thinking that this was the right and appropriate response. To my chagrin, this was *not* the appropriate response.

"No, it's almost like *too* clean. You're not gay or something, are you?"

You know, there are times in a man's life where he has more than just an epiphany, theory, or downright good thought. Sometimes he has a revelation so subtle yet so powerful that he has no viable way of ever discerning its arrival.

"No," I said. "I'm not, but I don't clean very often. I just did this because I knew you were coming over."

She laughed, I cringed and we didn't touch each other the rest of the night. And when she left, I don't believe she ever returned. How could she? The next day I pulled out my feather duster and rubbed that sucker all through every nook and cranny in my apartment. This action was followed by the intentional dropping of laundry conveniently on my bedroom floor without ever being folded. I even spilled some tea on my carpet for good measure. *There's a stain that no one will ever be able to explain*, I thought and I smiled at its glory. Then my phone rang. It was my buddy, Mitch, who was calling to catch up.

"Hey man," he said. "Susie and I are stopping by for a minute. She forgot her food container from the other night."

I immediately got a visual in my head: a small container, sitting idly, somewhere near the back of my fridge. I couldn't remember what was in it but I knew they had brought it to the party a few days before.

"Yeah, man. When will you be here?"

"We are just pulling in now. Be up soon."

Rather than ask that he be the only one stopping up, I said 'ok', hung up the phone, and looked at my apartment. "Guys Night" was most assuredly over now. That much was true. I took solace in knowing what my place now stood for: a messy, stained, full-of-wrinkled-shirts-desperately-needing-to-be-ironed refuge of bachelorhood. When Adam and Eve were cast out of the Garden, it may have looked something like this. Chaos reigned; there was no place for tidiness here.

I couldn't have felt more at home though. Mitch came to my front door, minus Susie, and I gave him their missing Tupperware. Susie didn't need to be there; nor did Mitch. I was ok with where I was. I didn't need the eyes of a friend or a stranger to let me know how I felt. I was fine with this place I dwelled within, no need for impressing others.

The next get-together came around and one of my girl-space-friends (friend that is a girl I am not currently dating or trying to date) couldn't help but call out a tea stain on my floor. She pointed to the black stain positioned next to the leg of my couch.

"Hey, you should probably get this cleaned, you know. Don't want any ladies to see this," she said with a smirk on her face.

My jaw dropped in disbelief.

You can't win with women, I thought. You just can't win. Perhaps this was the first *real* lesson I had on living alone: you'll always be alone if you're trying to too hard to *not* be alone. Life has a divine way of opening doors that are ready to be opened, but if you're so eager to look for one that is, you're bound to walk through one that's not ready for you yet. In my life, I've done more than just jiggle the handle—I've knocked down doors (sometimes literally) just to get what I was after. I used to perceive this as confidence or having direction, but a fool's errand is a fool's errand. The fool will always be left wondering *why* when the deed is done rather than asking *when*. So when the time is right for the bachelor pad to cease, I'll be ready.

It just won't be till this book is done.

Theory: There are dog people and there are cat people . . .

. . . and there are fish people and gerbil people and chicken people and . . . .

Living single doesn't always entail you being *completely* single. There are opportunities for companionship other than someone of the opposite sex. Aside from living in a fantasy where Yvonne Strahovski (or Ryan Gosling for you ladies) may one day knock on your door, you can still find something to help you face those lonely nights. I'm talking about pets, of course. Beautiful, cute, expensive little pets. You may not have that special someone to call your own, but you can darn well cough up some cash to buy a pet if you feel the nerve to do so.

But let me caution you first by saying this: once you decide to check out the local shelter or pet mart—you're toast. When you stare into the eyes of three dozen or so desperate faces, your knees will grow weak. You may decide at that very moment how you'll save as many furry critters as you possibly can; regardless of the financial or emotional burden associated with this task.

Good luck.

I've since come to the realization that not everyone needs or deserves a pet. Some people just aren't cut out for the task. That even includes married couples. I've had friends who have gotten pets then turned around and given them back in two weeks time since the commitment was too great. Imagine my shock when a month later I hear that the couple is pregnant and expecting. Can't give this one back guys! But hey, it all happens for a reason, right?

I've sometimes wondered where I fall along the spectrum of suitable pets. I grew up with a dog in my family. And what a lovely animal she was. A half-breed, Morgan was the perfect dog. Not just because she was my first pet; no, she was much more. She was a stray that wandered into our yard like a lost traveler who needed a place to camp for the night. But a few hot dogs later and a couple nice pats on the head, she's all ours. I wouldn't have had it any other way. She was half German shepherd, half retriever and about 65 pounds tops. At least that's what the vet told us. And though the shepherd in her sounds intimidating, she was actually quite docile. Well, if you were female or a child anyway. It was the men she despised the most, which made us wonder if she'd been abused in her prior life. We'll never know for sure, but it's something I wish I would have.

For the better part of 10 years, Morgan watched over our house. She was a faithful watch dog and a wonderful friend. My brothers were barely tall enough to see over a kitchen counter back then and when they stood next to Morgan, they could literally look her straight in the eye. But that dog, intimidating size and everything, wouldn't have hurt a fly unless commanded to. I remember watching my youngest brother lay his head upon her belly while she slept on the back porch, never minding the pint-sized child trying to snuggle up. Yes, she was a great dog; a real treasure to have in a family full of young boys. She'd even let you complain about a rough day if you needed to vent. True, she was only a dog, but when I told her about my day I could sense her understanding. Her eyes had a way of saying, "Sure, I know you're angry so just let it all out."

As with any pet, Morgan didn't live forever. When her time came, I was distraught beyond all measure. She passed away one morning (likely during the night) right in the middle of our family room. My dad had rushed upstairs to wake me and inform me of the situation. Obviously he could have waited but my dad has never been one to hold back his impulse emotions. We all loved Morgan equally, even my dad despite his constant complaints about her, so her passing was not handled easily. The same day she died, I spent the entire morning and mid-afternoon digging her grave in the front yard. Yes, it's as sad as it sounds. And all the while, I had to argue with my younger brother about whether or not we'd go see the Hulk movie like I had promised. Well, long story short, we went and saw that movie, but I didn't remember much due to the tragedy that morning. What I do remember is persistently digging a doggy-sized grave whilst I wept over Morgan's memory. Ironically, Morgan passed a few weeks after I was graduated from high school. It's as if she somehow knew I was leaving for good and I wouldn't be around to see her anymore. Strange how an animal can sense these things. Yes, it all could have been a coincidence but I don't believe in coincidences. Morgan's life was no coincidence so how was her passing a coincidence? That line of questioning doesn't sit well with me.

My family had other animals after Morgan, but none seemed to stack up. They were either too clumsy, too high maintenance, or even too dumb in comparison to our first family pet. We gave cats a try; even hermit crabs, but nothing seemed to work. The cat ran away after about three months and when Sebastian the III perished from complications still unknown to this day, we settled on the understanding that there was simply no valid replacement for Morgan. My family was in a state of worry, but I trudged on through college and eventually into the "real world" without too much concern for what was happening back at my parent's house. It was then, years later and sitting alone on my couch, that I realized how much I missed my Morgan. I wanted a "new" Morgan if that were possible; a little buddy to come home to. Not too much to ask, right?

My search started off by asking questions. I needed to know how other single folk handled a pet. And though you may think that this was step was beneficial, I actually found it to be quite the opposite. For what I found was not I was expecting.

For starters, people told me I was a "dog person." They'd say that I "fit the description" of a dog person and that a canine would suit me best. But honestly, what the heck does that mean anyway? Ok, so I'm a "dog person." Care to elaborate on what that entails? Well, some of my cohorts explained that I needed a pet that was active, engaging and eager to learn things from me. At that point I'd retort with "this is why I need a girlfriend" but when I knew that was a longshot, I'd return to the dog concept. At least with a dog I could purchase the darn thing and own it for a while.

So I looked into getting a dog. At first, I went for the smaller breeds. This was due to my confined space at the apartment, but in my heart I knew what I really wanted: a German Shepherd. Sleek, regal, elegant—all the traits of my late dog, Morgan. I didn't want to just settle for any old dog; I wanted the best.

My very particular taste did not yield positive results. The shepherds I encountered were nothing like Morgan and when I looked at the smaller breeds, I still found myself drifting back to the big dogs. They were all nice dogs, I'm sure, but none of them had that "I'm the one for you, man" written upon their tiny little snouts. Distraught, my mind and body wandered to another section of the animal shelter.

And so, I decided to check on the cats. Now cats are completely different from dogs. As you know, we had one cat when I was kid but I never liked that guy. "Leo" was his name and he was as cocky and arrogant as a cat with that name could be. He was one-fifth the mass of everyone else yet he acted as though he owned the place. Um, hello, little guy but *we* are the ones who feed *you.* It's not the other way around. Somehow though, cats tend to think that they rule the roost wherever they stay. And of course, their masters allow that type of behavior to continue. Shame on you, cat owners of the world. You've reinforced character traits that will take generations to rid ourselves of.

But let's be real here, cats will always be jerks. And they'll always have a chip on their shoulder. Ever see a cat move out of the way when you're parking your car? Yeah, they don't move for you, *you* have to move for them. My parent's cat, Leo, did that quite frequently. I could have taught the feline an eternal lesson by just rolling over top of his lounged body, but I figure the years of guilt associated with my act would have haunted me for sure. Then again, I was probably more worried about how I'd explain the circumstances of a flattened cat in our garage.

So as I stood there, reminiscing on my past experiences with cats, I found myself in doubt. I somehow knew I couldn't substitute my dog-loving days for cat-filled nights. Another sad reality, but I had to move on. I knew there was a pet out there that needed me. Onward I went with high hopes and a new resolve to not settle for second best (but mostly not to settle for a cat).

Well, what about fish? I was heading right down the food chain with this next alternative. Fish could be flashy in a sparkling tank, but what else are they good for? I found myself questioning their interactive qualities. I could feed them, clean their tank, and repeat this process but that was it. There was nothing beyond that endless cycle of food and cleanliness. The only way I'd benefit is to house a lobster, a few crabs, and maybe a salmon. At least that way I could make a meal of them if I didn't feel like tidying up the tank anymore.

So fish were out.

How about gerbils? Or maybe hamsters? No, they both smell and if one ever got loose in my apartment I'd probably mistake it for a rat and trample the darned thing with an army boot. Oversized rodents are off the prospect list. How's about a bird then? Oh sure; an animal that not only squawks annoyingly but smells like feces on a daily basis. Yeah, I could definitely see myself owning one of those creatures. It's too bad the Komodo dragon is beyond domestication. Sure, my fantasy pet is a giant, deer-eating lizard but how cool would that be? For example, having one would provide some fun conversation at parties.

"Hey, why is that one door closed all the time?"

"Oh, my pet Komodo dragon is in there."

"Pet Komodo dragon?!"

"Yeah, man. Don't open that door if you know what's good for you."

"Cool, bro."

"Yeah . . . way cool. Did you know that a single bite contains hundreds of bacteria that'll kill potential prey in less than 24 hours!?"

"No way, bro."

"Yeah, bro. *Way* . . . ."

Oh yes—an awesome pet the Komodo would be. They're independent, can feed themselves if necessary and you'd likely never have to worry about picking up the poop since they're lizards and lizards don't leave giant piles of feces behind (scientific fact I hear). And hey, if you let him roam free, he's likely to establish a healthy boundary around your home; protecting you from criminals and house thieves alike.

Well, my Komodo idea was a real longshot but not as crazy as some other folks out there. For instance, my uncle's neighbor possessed a boa constrictor in his basement and a former coworker of mine kept chickens in his house. The chickens didn't lay eggs or anything, he just liked chickens a lot. I'm not going to judge this person or cast stones, but it does make one wonder what the attraction is. I even ran across a family that owned a gecko. You know, the popular lizard from the Geico commercials with the accent. What does one *do* with a gecko, I wonder? Watch it stick to walls all day? I'm at a real loss on that one, but hey, to each his own.

This was where I hit my roadblock. The one thing I had dreaded the most was happening. My efforts were beginning to weigh on me. Finding a decent pet was as taxing as finding a girlfriend. My once short list of criteria (German shepherd, younger, maybe mixed with a retriever) had been stretched to the furthest ends of the animal kingdom and back again. And yet, I was still unsettled. This pet of mine would need to be playful, yet relaxed. Intelligent but willing to forego intellectual confrontations in order to run and play. And most imperative of all, this pet needed to have a loving quality that shined even in the darkest of times. Yes, I wanted a pet that could act as my significant other, minus all the really cool intimate parts (come on, folks. I'm not that desperate!). I just know what I'm looking for in a pet.

Have you ever noticed that pet/owner dynamic where the two resemble one another? I'm not limiting this observation to pure physicality either; personality too. Every apartment complex I've inhabited had at least two or three people with such a pet/owner relationship. One of my favorites had to have been a girl in her mid-20s who walked a large husky at her side regularly. Huskies are a really cool dog if you ever get one, but this one was unique in that it was extremely thin. Not anorexic thin, but slender and short haired. The owner was a mirror of her dog and when they walked, it was as if their steps were in perfect sync. It makes me wonder if the dog eventually adjusts to the owner or if the owner adjusts to the dog? In my experience, it's usually the dog getting the royal tug and reprimand for walking too fast so my bet is on the owner dictating pace. Then again, watch a stout man try to halt his French bulldog and you've got a tug of war game worthy enough to be on primetime television (Wipeout, anyone?).

Concerning cats and their owners, I'm sure you know by now that I don't have much to say that's overly positive. That being said, I'm going to refrain from going down a dark path on the topic of felines. A good friend of mine had a cat for several years and was very content with the arrangement. Whether or not there were plots to assassinate the owner (in the cat's head) is unknown. Fish aren't nearly as cunning as their primary predator, the cat. And they aren't exactly lovable either. You can't hug a tank full of guppies and expect your warm sentiments to be returned in full—that's just crazy. In fact, such behavior could be frowned upon in certain social circles. Just what I hear, of course.

With gerbils, hamsters, parrots and other forms of fauna out of the running, my search was coming to a close. A search that was sunk before it even got out on open water.

I just couldn't resolve to purchase an animal that didn't have my aforementioned criteria. This was depressing, but it made me feel like I should have bought the first dog I saw and been done with it. That's the most effective way to shop, is it not? Quit looking for deals, just get the first one off the conveyor belt so you don't waste time looking around. If only things were that simple in life, we'd all be much happier. I would also have a companion, thus negating the need for this ode to the animals I long to own.

But here we are, months later and I'm still without a furry little friend. My effort to fill the void in my life has gone unfulfilled. No dog, no cat, no fish, not even a filthy guinea pig—all aspirations of being a pet owner have been thrown to the wayside.

At any rate, I am satisfied with not settling for second best. I knew what I wanted when I started and I never deviated. Yes, I did my spelunking and shopping around, but I never allowed myself to get too caught up in the mystique of pet ownership. There's some solace there that I find overly comforting. And if you're not ready to take care of something else, then you're just *not* ready.

For as I'm writing this, I look across my apartment at the singular aloe plant I've had for the past four years and realize that it desperately needs a repotting. My aloe plant is the only living proof that a single guy like me is capable of caring for something other than himself. Trouble is, the little green beauty has begun to wilt, a none too pleasant view if you're a plant enthusiast. I may have been better off with a cactus.

The little vines of my plant are spilling over the side and down the counter like hot wax from a burning candle. Only a single branch remains, sticking straight up like a middle finger salute saying, 'hey, you need to fix this before I die, buddy'. I interpret this as a grim reminder that if you let anything sit for too long, it becomes way too much even for itself, unable to leave space for something else to cohabitate. But hey, you can always trim it up, give it more room to breathe, and start anew. Which is what I intend to do in the near future. And I'll do that right after I fix up my aloe plant. Nobody likes getting flipped off on a daily basis; least of all from a plant.

Downright Good Thought: The single greatest gift I ever received . . .

. . . was a crock pot.

I really wanted to devote a whole section to my crock pot so here it is. You see, my eating habits have always been marginal at best. I'm not obese or super skinny and I can fit into most compact spaces fairly well. If I had to place myself in a category, it would be something like "slenderly fit." At least that's what others have described me as. Over the years my coworkers have said things like "skinny ass"; "thin man"; and the occasional "Malibu Ken" (due to my gelled hair fixation). I suppose the last one doesn't really coincide with the other two, but I thought I'd throw it in there for good measure. Anyway, I can usually eat what I want, when I want, and still have a physique that's similar to one who has a colony of tapeworms inhabiting his intestinal tract. To that point, I've never really worried about eating poorly. If what was going *in* wasn't affecting me on the *outside*, then why change anything?

Well, we can't all live in a fantasy land filled with heightened metabolisms forever. That much is true, but we can start to eat healthier. And hey, let's face it; I was going to need a full-on intervention in order to change my diet. That's when I started doing a little something called "happy hour." And by happy hour, I mean several happy hours a week. For those who don't know (or who skipped the last chapter), the happy hour is a social gathering intended for the consumption of alcohol at an affordable price. The goal is to enjoy one's self while basking in the delight of cheaper, less expensive beer. The process, if repeated often, will leave a growing number of empty carbohydrates festering in one's midsection. This is also known as the 'gut'—an area that I had no experience with my whole life. It was around that time that I made the connection between said happy hour and my expanding torso. Something had to be done about this. To many of you guys out there, my talk of "slenderly fit" fast becoming "slenderly-leaning-towards-not-so-fit" may sound girly or even not masculine, but when you're trying to impress the ladies, you need to bring it strong.

This is about the time I had an intervention. Not the kind where you profess your addiction in a room full of strangers; the kind where you decide that you're going to eat healthier every now and again. Unfortunately for me, I had very few resources. I was a lousy cook for one thing (as you know already); the leftovers I received from third-parties covered only about half the week and my idea of a home-cooked meal usually consisted of scrambled eggs with toast. Sure I could make BBQ chicken but to lather one's chicken with heavy sauce isn't exactly healthy. The better meals took longer than my acceptable time to prepare (which is a window of about 10 minutes honestly) so that was demoralizing to my schedule.

I needed something else. Something that would fulfill my every need without too much maintenance; something altogether amazing, slim, and perhaps even nice to look at; something that understood what I wanted out of life and was willing to engage me in that pursuit—what could it be? This thing that would love me for me and what I was trying to accomplish; what was *it*? The hours of racking my brain led me to the only logical conclusion I could come up with: a crock pot. The one device on Earth capable of transforming four unrelated food items into a singular plate of edible goodness. The crock pot has no equal in my eyes. And seriously, what else is there that can do all those things I mentioned?

Take the pan-cake for example. Not familiar with the pan-cake? Well, let me enlighten your world. When one is living alone, one tends to experiment with certain things around one's home. Aside from tormenting your neighbor's cat or constructing forts out of couch pillows, you can find yourself playing around with food. It's amazing what a little batter, a little bit of strawberry juice and some whipped cream can do in a crock pot. Now, I wouldn't recommend putting the strawberry juice or the whipped cream in right away. Instead try making the pan-cake first and then go from there. It'll feed at least five people if you do it right. And if you do it wrong, you're still left with one big, flappin' pan-cake. Delicious, my friends and easier to construct than those couch forts too.

When the pan-cake ended favorably, I realized you could bake other goods in the crock pot as well. Goods like my kryptonite—brownies. Ladies, if you ever want to know the way to Mr. Faltot's heart, it's brownies. Caramel fudge, peanut butter, heck even lime mint and beer taste good inside of a brownie. There's just something about the moist, chocolatey awesomeness of a thick brownie that makes me feel so good inside. The taste is borderline orgasmic for those who can relate (and if you can't, maybe one day you'll understand). And if you can further relate, I would never suggest reenacting an infamous scene from a '90s movie involving "warm, apple pie." The experience isn't worth the price of a mutilated pie and no, it just isn't the same.

The most important thing the crock pot did for me was to put me on the right path with my diet. I didn't crave greasy French fries or bar food like I had been. No, I wanted to come home to my crock pot meal instead. I actually started looking forward to the experience. When someone asked me about happy hour, I'd respond with a resounding, "I'm sorry, but I've got a meal at home with my name on it and I can't be late."

Yeah, I got some odd looks but the eyes looking at me had to have seen the trimmed waistline I was sporting now. No longer was I a slave to the social hour that turns regular guys into rotund fatties. Nor was I headed down the path of perpetual d-bag, another unfortunate side effect of one too many happy hours in a row. My crock pot was making me a better eater . . . and a better person. Hallelujah, right?

Absolutely.

My intervention was working and I took note of the other perks associated with my newfound love. If you ever need to pick up and move locations, then just pick up and move the darned thing too. All the crock pot consists of is a pot, a lid, a dial and a cord to plug itself in. The crock pot would be considered a failure in the complexity department but I see it as a glorious invention for its simplistic ingenuity. Just don't leave it sitting near anything flammable. This includes, but is not limited to, paper towels, hand towels or even Pop-Tart wrappers. In fact, throw out those Pop-tarts altogether. You're too old to be eating those anyway. Once you've learned where to place your crock pot, you can set a timer in the morning, come back eight hours later, and voila! Your meal is ready to be had. How freakin' nice is that?!

It'd be like having a spouse (man or woman to be politically correct here) at home making you meals before you get home! Minus the nagging; minus the mood swings; and minus the incessant complaining about how you never pull your own weight around the house. But perhaps the biggest minus of all is this: no sex. Ah yes, the great equalizer. In times like that, you could always just whip up some brownies and get yourself close to ecstasy. That's always an alternative. I don't speak for everybody here, but it's routines like that which will help get you through the lonely nights.

Or make you feel even worse.

So before you start looking at that black, cylindrical pot like it's a person, I suggest you get out and start searching for something that can do more than just make you food. The crock pot may love you, but there ain't no way you can love the crock pot back.

Seriously, just stick to the brownies on that one.

Epiphany: One can learn plenty about someone . . .

. . . by joining a bowling league.

I love to bowl. I don't mind if no one else shares in my enthusiasm for the sport; I just want people to know that yes, one can be passionate about the game. I was introduced to bowling when I was young (about 9). I joined a local league with some friends and we bowled every Saturday. I didn't own a ball yet, but I really enjoyed throwing an 8 pound object down a lane in an effort to knock a bunch of stuff down. If Sigmund Freud were alive to see this, he'd argue the sexual side of the game. The rolling of the ball; the thrusting of a round object down a narrow passage trying to score at the other end; and of course, the chance to do this successfully 12 times in a row hence attaining the "perfect" game.

Yeah, you'd enjoy that one, wouldn't you, Sigmund?

Pop culture teaches us that bowling goes as far back as the Paleozoic era. The Flintsones' Fred and Barney were avid bowlers at the local Bedrock lanes all those yesterdays ago. True, their story is a little far-fetched but in reality, bowling has origins in ancient Egypt, Rome, and the middle Americas. There have been several variations but you're probably familiar with the most recent version: a team of four to five guys/gals getting together on a Thursday night to try and beat another group of four to five guys/gals in 10-pin, 10-frame, handicaps-optional, *bowling*. What's not to love?

Not everyone can be talented in certain sports. Star running back Adrian Petersen wasn't born to be a swimmer and bazillion-time gold medal-winning Michael Phelps wasn't born to be a football player. It just wasn't in the cards for these guys. However, each of these gentlemen can at least pick up a 12-16 pound ball and roll it down a 60 foot aisle to knock over some pins. But don't get me wrong, I'm not degrading the sport of bowling whatsoever. There is some serious skill involved if you want to be an elitist on the hardwood. The greats like Norm Duke and Walter Ray Williams, Jr. weren't born with marble balls in their hands (that we know of); no, it took plenty of time and lots of practice to become a superior ball roller. Take it from someone who knows.

And yes, that person is me.

Honestly, I fell out of bowling when I got older. Not literally, but I did so right around my teenage years. This was partially due to my involvement in other sports such as baseball, basketball and track. There just wasn't enough time anymore and when you're in high school your Saturdays are *the* day for doing extracurricular activities. Choose wisely, my teenage friends. What you choose to do on your Saturday will dictate what sport or activity you ultimately become a part of for the next four or five years.

I walked away from the sport but the memories stayed with me. I was a decent bowler back then, to say the least. My average was about 120 as a youngster, which is pretty darn good when you're barely pushing puberty, I figure. So when my buddy Mitch came to me, inquiring about joining a league, I figured it'd be a cake walk. How much can guys improve their bowling games anyway? This offer was even more attractive due to my growing need to curb those lonely Thursday nights. I weighed the options in my head and came to a conclusion: who was I kidding, really—this sounded fun. I could probably use one of the lane-provided balls and not pony up the dough for a new ball too. No problem, right? I'd be back to my 130 and occasional 150 games in no time.

Or, so I thought.

You can probably surmise that my first night at the bowling lanes was not a pleasant one. I blame Mitch entirely for this. For one, he neglected to tell me that if I didn't have the following items: my own shoes, my own bag, and my own ball—I'd be scoffed at and ridiculed. Imagine what it would feel like if you peed your pants in elementary school and that's just about the same feeling I had that night. I was totally exposed and with nowhere to run to. Out of some 80 men at the bowling alley, I was the lone idiot walking up to the main counter asking for a pair of size 11 shoes. And when I got shoes that looked like they were stolen from a traveling circus, I strolled around to find a bowling ball that fit my taste and my fingers.

Some of the balls were too big. Others were too small. Some I just couldn't fit my hand into while others just didn't look right when I picked them up. Some were damaged, some were chipped, and some just looked so lonely that they were pushed to the end of the rack liable never to see the light of day again. If those at the end of the rack had voices, they would be screaming "Lord, just put me out of my misery already. I've had enough."

As fate would have it, I did find a ball that night. And I'll give you one guess as to what it looked like. No, it was not the clear, tulip ball from the movie Kingpin—nay, it was a bright pink cosmic bowling ball that weighed about 12 pounds. I know what you're thinking. *Really, man? Really? Out of all the bowling balls, you chose a pink one?* And my answer for you is this: yes, yes I did. So not only did I sport clown shoes, I was now masquerading as either an overconfident man comfortable in his sexuality or a guy who clearly had an identity crisis as it related to fashion. Either way, I had to make this work, so I walked over to my teammates and made my introduction.

This was my first lesson about myself—my failure to prepare. I've always been good at managing other people, but not always myself. So when it came to this bowling league, I was definitely exposed for who I was inside. If you saw some of the other men at the alley, you'd recognize how many of them had several bowling balls at the ready. They brought large carrying cases that ferried two to three balls at a time while other bowlers had bags with flippin' wheels on them. Wheels? On a bowling bag? Who knew? I certainly didn't, but I did make a mental note to hurry up and buy some shoes ASAP before next week.

The team I was placed on consisted of a wily bunch of characters. Besides myself and Mitch, there were three other members. This included my other college friend, Gary, his father, Gary Sr., and Gary's father-in-law (whom we'll call "Guy"). Each member of my team was outfitted with their own ball and shoes. Even Gary and Mitch sported new bags that looked similar to what you'd see in an Under Armor commercial. And speaking of merchandise, Guy was clearly a hoarder of all things bowling. Not only did he have multiple balls, he also had a towel, tape for his thumb, and a device that I can only describe as a condom for one's pointer finger. Apparently it helps with gripping the outside of a ball, but if you ask me, it's gotta be all mental. This little accessory is probably illegal to use in a few states too. Gary, Sr. had his own ball and shoes but he was the most "old school" of any of the players. Why you ask? Well, his bowling ball told me that story. He referred to the thing as "Old Blacky" and like its name; Old Blacky could very well have been as ancient as a fossil in a museum. If (and when) he retires, Old Blacky should either be donated to the Smithsonian or shoved back into the part of Stonehenge where it originated from. Gary, Sr.'s ball sported chips, cracks, and dings that made it appear like it'd been through hell and back again. And for all intents and purposes, Old Blacky may very well have been.

As I put my pink ball next to Old Blacky on the ball belt, I had my next revelation: every ball at the alley had a very distinct and unique make. Like pets that take on the personalities of their owners, bowling balls may very well project the inner persona of their handlers. No two bowling balls were the same. I've come to believe that if two guys appeared at the bowling alley with the same ball, one of them would go out and get a new one immediately. This is in complete contrast to the guys who are caught wearing the same shirt at a party. Where it's cool to have the same clothes, it's *not* cool to have the same weapon of pin destruction. I was surprised by this at first, but as I surveyed the balls of my teammates (yes, that joke will not get old in this rant), it all made sense.

For example, Mitch is a 6'6" Irish redhead who carries around an off-colored gray ball called "Venom." The venom part is certainly misleading for a guy like Mitch but the color of his ball, gray, is often associated with security and neutrality. Mitch, being the happily married and mellow man that he is, clearly favors security over anything else in his life. And with regards to neutrality, the guy knowingly runs from confrontation (despite his size). I've also known him to avoid cities out of the fear of being mugged by someone (sorry Mitch, I had to put that in there).

Reluctantly we had to replace Mitch after a couple years. His entry into fatherhood pulled him from the bunch, but luckily, we have more than three friends. Another of our compatriots, Isaiah, soon joined our crew. Like a midseason cast change on a popular sitcom, Isaiah swept in as Mitch moved on to other endeavors. Mitch wasn't taking a starring role in a movie. Instead, he was taking an active role in his newly born daughter's life. Admirable and more important than even bowling, I say. We bid Mitch adieu and focused on our new recruit.

It was apparent that Isaiah had not bowled very often, if ever in his life. Like me, he had no ball to call his own and his style was very similar to mine: go up there, throw it hard and hope for the best. "Ike" eventually got his own ball though: a green and blue sphere with finger holes the size of peas. Yes, Ike has thin fingers. And thin fingers represent a meticulous nature and desire for accuracy. If anyone amongst our group thought he knew something, anything in the world, Ike was quick to research the truth and let us know the possible error of our ways.

"Hey, when did Seinfeld first air?"—one of us would ask.

"I think it was 1988,"—one of us would answer.

"No, it was 1989," Ike would retort, quickly looking up the answer on his smartphone.

"Damn you, Ike. That was fast."

"Yes, and *correct*, as well . . . ."

Ike's slow approach and careful release mirrored his own methodical nature. Sometimes his ball went straight and other times, his ball was not so straight, but he carefully attempted to plot out each throw when it came for his turn. And when he threw that ball, we all watched the green and blue swirl hurtle towards the pins in a manner that I can only describe as "precise."

Gary, on the other hand, carried with him a black and red "Black Widow" ball. Now, Gary is also another married man like Mitch (to Guy's daughter no less), so I'm not going to point out the irony of the ball's name. No, that'd be too easy, but the reddish coloration did represent something about Gary—a short temper and even shorter appreciation of his own performance. Nobody is a bigger critic on Gary than Gary himself. His disdain for a poorly thrown ball would tempt Gary to choose between his expensive Black Widow ball and another he kept at the ready—a blue-colored Motiv. The Motiv was the go-to ball for Gary when things weren't going his way, but he didn't just throw this ball like his Black Widow. No, he'd *chuck* it down the lanes with two hands rather than one. This would seem odd to some but surprisingly, he would be effective with this technique. This talent of his revealed an inner resourcefulness for any situation. And if you knew Gary, you'd know that when it comes to being ingenious or mastering the obscure, Gary is your man. My only regret is not pushing Gary to audition for the show "Minute to Win It"; had we been more forceful, my friends and I would all be millionaires.

This leaves us with the two father figures of the group: Guy and Gary, Sr. Guy was the founder of our troop, team Elite and thus, had a way about him that said "yeah, I own the place." I honestly didn't know how to take him at first. I hadn't grown up with him so I had no idea what to expect, but that's what made Guy so enjoyable—not knowing what to expect. I've already mentioned the multiple bowling balls and accessories had had so if I was going to judge him based on this alone, that just wouldn't do him justice. Aside from his bowling prowess, the man was famous (well, infamous) for pulling quotes out of thin air that often baffled or bewildered the rest of the team.

"Hey, you know that one guy? You know, from that TV show?" (No, no one knows?)

"Don't worry—you got your average . . . ." (After someone did absolutely terrible).

"That was a good ball . . . and I don't mind tellin' ya that either." (Immediately following a great throw).

And one of my personal favorites . . .

"Lots of traffic out there. You must have just got here . . . ." (in reference to a player who was struggling for much of the night but finally succeeded in throwing a strike).

Indeed, Guy had several layers to him. As the season progressed, more and more of those layers peeled off, revealing more of the "Guy" within. There was a layer that took great pride in historical references. Guy would make it a point to talk about boxing, another indulgence of his. How we faired at the lanes that evening could be comparable to a fight between Ali and Frazier. Guy also opened my eyes to the concept of "good Christian colleges."

"Yeah, I ran about an 11.4 in the100 while in college," I'd boast. "I didn't do track but I could have maybe made an impact on the team considering my times."

My accomplishments didn't impress Guy whatsoever.

"11.4, eh?" he'd say. "You must have went to one of them 'Christian colleges', didn't you? A time like that would be nothing at a big school."

"What's that supposed to mean?!" I'd shoot back, but Guy would rebuttal with an explanation that started with 'good people go to school to learn', but 'jerks go to school to be professional athletes.'

"You know what?" I'd say back to him. "I never thought of it that way . . . thanks for clearing that one up."

"Hey, that's what I'm here for."

Indeed, Guy, I appreciate your candor. This insight made me wonder how many "jerks" there were in the NFL, the MLB, or the NBA. If Guy's observation holds merit, then every Division I school with a competitive athletic program knowingly prescribes to the mantra of recruiting the self-reliant, not the faithful. An interesting theory, to say the least, but I still find myself disagreeing. However, it is noteworthy to mention how the obsessive pursuit of a goal can block out the desire to find God in one's life, hence Guy's comment. What may have begun as a well-kindled fire, lit in the belly of a young man by God himself, was transposed and morphed into a self-contained self-righteous flame burning only for the self. If that's true, then Guy's correlation between walks of life and athletic prowess is possibly true, but only within that context. Imagine an athlete who harnesses the fire instead. Rather than containing the fire for his own purposes, he spreads the wealth among those around him, igniting and burning the internal doors of others who smothered the flame inside of them. I've been out of competitive collegiate sports for a while, but I do recall many "rally the troop" moments and when the war cry was felt by all, our team was unbeatable.

I guess you could say our bowling team has a long way to go in that regard.

Last but not least, there was Gary, Sr. (who I'll refer to as Senior from here on out). It wouldn't be far from the truth to say that Senior's bowling ball was a physical representation of Senior himself. Old Blacky may have looked like an outdated fossil, but it hit pins like a seasoned soldier crushes the skulls of his enemies. You see, Senior had a habit, albeit an unintentional one, of intimidating the friends of his son, Gary. He had grey hair, a grey mustache, and deep-set eyes that gave you a look as if to say "don't say anything stupid or I'll pop ya one." And trust me; I kept my mouth shut for a good portion of the time to avoid this scenario. My resolve was to be nice enough so as to warm up to him. And as the weeks went by, Senior's gaze turned from "menacing" to "fairly hostile"; a mood that I was far more comfortable with.

The more lighthearted part of this story is how Senior's ball moved like he did. Started off slow but when it needed to pick up speed and put a hurt on the pins, Old Blacky got the job done. I was frustrated by how his slow and steady approach actually worked but I took note at every chance I got. I observed Mitch's big, looping curve and found that the ball performed this way due to his larger-than-life hands with wide grip. This was an advantage that smaller-handed people like me or Ike just couldn't compete with or imitate effectively. Gary was busy altering his approach when something wasn't clicking and Guy would just buy a new ball if the last one didn't suit him anymore. Each bowler handled their ball much in the same fashion as their own lives.

All that being said, we're back to me now. You know—the guy with the pink bowling ball. If we want to get all analytical on my ball of choice, I'll have you know that it was the only one there that fit my hand properly so I couldn't help but choose it. The only alternative was suffering through another that had the chance of falling off my hand every time I brought my hand back to throw it. So let's not analyze that ball too closely and skip to when I actually bought my own, ok?

I didn't go the entire season with that pink generic ball. Oh, hell no. If I had, I probably would have been shunned by my team a good four to five weeks into the season. In order to keep that from happening, I decided to go shopping. Ball shopping, that is. So off to the nearest pro shop I went to claim a mighty round ball for my own. Just like King Arthur needed Excalibur—I required my perfect weapon of destruction. And since I also needed a proper consult, I took Mitch alongside me. His Irish heritage made me feel like William Wallace marching against the enemy.

The maximum weight that any ball can be is 16 pounds. No more than this or you're cheating. Who came up with this rule, I do not know; I just know that you can't get one heavier than 16 pounds (despite your best efforts to attain one on the black market). As you'd guess, I wanted a bruiser. A real killer type ball; the kind that would make the pins scream in silent horror as my 16 pounds of marble death barreled towards them.

That's when I saw her.

She was a green-colored, sparkly round orb of power. This particular brand of bowling ball was called the Storm Spitfire. The name was cool enough, but she was also exactly what I was looking for—a weapon that would intimidate my opponents as well as the pins. Weighing in at 15 and three-quarters, she was just the right size for a guy like me; not too big and not too thin. She seemed to call out to me from behind her glass casing. A perfect sphere if I ever saw one. I knew I wanted her the moment I placed my hands upon her nice, round curves (the ball, you pervs) which then prompted me to ask the shop guy to drill her for me (once again, to make the finger holes, you gutter brains). I had to wait a good week before I could call her mine, but I figured she'd be worth the wait (which is a true statement, by the way. No hidden innuendos in that one). And when the day finally arrived, I left work early to pick her up. Absence had made my heart grow ever so fonder.

"Bob" from the pro shop had done a fine job in the week I'd been away. My new ball was shined up like a spiffy hot rod, her marble coating radiating quite nicely. I placed my fingers deep within the three drill holes and I swear I heard her purr gently. I asked "Bob" if I could take her for a spin and he calmly answered "'yes." It was as if he knew just what I was about to experience and it warmed his heart to be a part of that experience. Then again, he was probably weirded out from my reactions and wanted desperately for me to leave his shop. At least that's what Mitch told me, but whatever.

New ball in hand, Mitch and I walked to the nearest lane to put our names in. I waited eagerly for the pins to drop down, eagerly anticipating the pin-killing at hand. And when those pins dropped, I looked them over as if they were criminals set to be executed by gunfire. Spitfire, that is. When it was my turn, I walked up and took my usual spot about two lines over on the right. If you're an avid Wii bowler, that means I was standing relatively close to the gutter on the right hand side, but not all the way over. If you're not a Wii bowler and never bowled before then I applaud you for making it this far in my little rant. You deserve some props. So if you're still with me, you might as well stick it out to the end. I promise to explain why I moved so far over in the next paragraph.

You see, I had to move that way because I knew my ball would curve down the lane. My pink ball was not made to swerve like the professionals. No, it was merely meant to withstand the likes of birthday parties, bad bowlers, and those who neglected to buy their own ball when they joined a league. On the contrary, my new ball was rumored to have the kinds of curves that would make Sofia Vergara jealous (but in no way ever stack up. I would never speak poorly about your physique whatsoever, Ms. Vergara. Trust me when I say this) so long story short, I had to move over a little bit to contain the power of my new Spitfire.

I strode up to the foul line, pulled my hand back, remembered the countless YouTube videos I watched on Walter Ray, and brought my hand forward to send her rolling for the first time. Everything proceeded exactly as I had imagined. She rolled off my fingers nicely and landed on the hardwood with a firm yet gentle rush. All my steps had fell into line and for a moment, time stood still. She rolled over the second arrow, curved slightly to my left and struck the pocket hard. FYI—the pocket is the ideal space to hit the pins on the first throw if you're trying to get a strike.

I wish I could say what I threw was a strike but sadly, it wasn't. The stars were aligned but apparently I needed more practice. That was fine with me though. I was ready to take on the challenge before me. I could feel the potential for 300 games rumbling within me so I was not afraid to continue forward. The rest of my team breathed a collective sigh of relief when I showed up at the lanes the following week. I was met with more cheers than jeers, but this was mostly due to my newfound ballmate. Those pesky scores of mine needed to change for the better and this was the way to do it. A guy can't survive in a 36-week season if you're only sporting a 130 average.

In due time, my scores did improve, but I certainly took note of my competition. Each team of five had a cast of characters which would make for some great Saturday Night Live skits (and we all know that show needs them nowadays). One team consisted of mostly office workers. Their pleated pants, brown-rimmed glasses and awkward high fives gave that away. Plus, all their bowling balls were a drab brown or black color. Then there was the truck driving crew. These guys were led by a massive 300 pound man with hair down to the small of his back. Though his name will remain anonymous (and for good reason), he's the only bowler, save human being, I can honestly say I've ever feared to merely lock eyes with. His bowling ball even had a black and purple stripe that looked like the spine of some beaten opponent he'd engraved on his ball. I didn't want his next bowling ball to have my teeth in it or anything so I kept to myself every turn around the bend.

Another team was rather culturally diverse. Two white guys, two black guys, and a fifth bowler who seemed to have some Middle Eastern blood in him. In all honesty, he may not have been mid-Eastern at all, but when he stood between the ethnic duos, I think my eyes were tricked into thinking he was an off shade of both colors. That's probably the logical answer there. What wasn't so logical about these guys was the amount of alcohol they would consume. We normally bowled three games on any given Thursday so that makes for a good three hour night if all goes well. In the span of three hours, you may drink one beer a game. That's the standard but these guys didn't play by the usual standards. One game in and they were about four to five beers deep. Once game three came around, the five of them were so tanked that it wasn't unusual to witness a spilled drink or a member bowling out of turn. This behavior was coupled with loud, obnoxious cheering that could be heard 20 to 30 lanes down. Surprisingly (at least to me), these fellas were well-liked. Their attitudes had you either shaking your head in disbelief or laughing at their one-liners and open candor.

Other groups were not as colorful but just as memorable in my eyes. One such group had all senior citizens. The five men on this team had hair as white as snow and the only guy who didn't sport gray hair had a limp in his step and hunch in his back. In between throws, I swear they'd pop pills and trade expressions that screamed "what was that? I don't think I heard what you said." I kid, but I liked playing these guys. They were old school for sure, but their bowling game didn't reflect age-old wisdom. In fact, I believe they were the worst team in the league, but none of that bothered them. Every week they'd show up, brag about their place in the standings, and then throw a few cold ones back to enjoy their one night out. One of their bowlers approached me after an evening of bowling to tell me how he hadn't seen such tough trenches since his days in Vietnam. Granted, any man over the age of 55 could pull that card on a youngster and make him believe it, but there was something about the way he said it that made me think he'd actually *been* there. If he was a vet, then he'd be part of an era that my generation has little to no connection with anymore. Only the history books can tell us what happened there now. I find the living to be far more interesting than the text of a US history book so my only hope is that this guy told his stories to others who would listen besides me.

One other unique band of characters I want to mention was the Handicapped Crew. I mean no disrespect to these gentlemen, but you can't avoid noticing how half their team has some sort of a physical ailment. Their cars even had the handicapped stickers in their windows. One of the guys even rode in on a wheelchair. And yes, he's the one I remember the most. His chair was motorized so he didn't require that someone push him around. And when he got inside the lanes, he stood up, dragged himself to the lane and placed his bowling ball on the rack. At first glance, you'd wonder why he needed the vehicle at all. He was bigger than average but nothing about him screamed "hey, I need a wheelchair." Then one day in spring he wore shorts to the alley and it became all too obvious as to why he had the assisted transportation. Starting at his ankle and running up his leg was a bruise of sorts that looked like damaged tissue. I didn't know what that meant but it looked extraordinarily painful. Every time he walked, his leg jutted out like a wobbly noodle and if he applied too much weight he'd likely fall over from the force. This made his approach very difficult but he suffered through regardless.

The resilience of "Joe" really struck a chord with me. Here was somebody who clearly didn't have the physical capacity to perform at 100%, but even so, he still showed up. An admirable thing when I know plenty of people who'd throw in the towel if they had some form of handicap. It's that kind of "never surrender" attitude that people pick up on. Even the Even those who were considered the party animals showed a level of compassion for Joe.

"Hey man," one of the party guys would say. "Let me grab that ball for you. Stay where you are."

Surprisingly, Joe didn't take many handouts. He never asked for one if he could help it. He'd grumble and groan about the helping hand, but eventually he'd give in if he knew he couldn't make it back to the ball rack without writhing in pain. There was a strange code of honor at the bowling alley that I never thought existed. Shocking to say the least, but present nonetheless. Maybe this guy Joe was a great bowler back in the day? Or maybe he'd been such a regular at the alley that he became a local legend of sorts? Longevity, no matter what you do, can often speak louder than likeability. If you stick around for a lengthy span of time, people will take notice. And that's deserving of some praise apparently. Kind of like being the matriarch or patriarch of your family; there's an unspoken respect you are deserving of. In Joe's case, it was likely his tenure that got him props from the other teams. I say this because it certainly wasn't his jokes; those were painful to get through at times:

"So," said Joe. "There are 3 Mexicans heading into a bar . . ."

"Yeah, Joe?"

"Yeah . . . and they . . . well . . . hold on, let me get back to you. I don't quite remember the rest right now."

"Oh . . . well, alright Joe . . . ."

See what I'm talking about?

At times though, Joe's punch lines were very entertaining, even funny. His good nature and humble attitude made his jokes that much easier to laugh along with. He had a surprisingly infectious persona; one that wasn't too over the top but just enough to capture the attention of all who shared the lanes with him. As such, nearly everyone in the league knew who Joe was and if he didn't, he'd know soon enough. Joe was excellent at spotting newbies on the hardwood and he never hesitated to pull them aside to give some advice. I once saw Joe stay a good half hour after league night was over just to show a group of teenagers how to curve their ball just right. There was no way Joe could show them how to do it himself, but he was evidently good at explaining what needed to be done to get the best result.

Joe's outlook on things was rather remarkable considering his situation. I know plenty of people who can't even get out of bed in the morning because their hair looked weird or a hangnail was just too damn painful (a little extreme but you get the idea). Tiny details such as these don't bother, Joe. He somehow knew that there were bigger things at stake here so to have such a rotten disposition was not going to get him anywhere. To that end, Joe is an inspiration to anyone who has ever said, "I can't." If I ever start telling his jokes though, I'll I've been bowling one too many years.

The mileage these guys had, like Joe, did not slow many of these guys down. But I did make another interesting observation. I noticed a direct correlation between body mass and overall skill as a bowler. The size of my opponent's midsection was often proportionate to the level of talent. In essence—the bigger the belly, the bigger the game. Whether you were young or old, a larger waistline meant you had the makings of a bowling god. At first, I wondered if this were merely a side effect for all the time spent at the alley. One's torso is heavily used when throwing a bowling ball, of course. So if one had a larger midriff, then that would mean one could be a seasoned bowler, right? This seemed to make the most sense in my head.

Since my game had been suffering, I pondered the addition of added girth around my hips and belly. Would a dramatic increase in overall mass equate to a substantial increase in my bowling scores? This was certainly worth a shot. Every time I reached for a beer or ordered my favorite patty melt from the snack bar, I reminded myself that I was headed in the right direction. *Bigger belly, bigger game,* I thought. This was the way to do it. But the week we played a team of construction workers whose best bowler was the size of a toothpick; I concluded that poor eating habits and an even poorer selection of foods at the bowling alley was the more likely culprit. I couldn't make a strong argument for or against my theory so my little experiment ended.

The consumption of beer and patty melts did not end, however. That was something I was not willing to give up just yet. Until the food vendor changed and my world was altered forever. From then on out, it would be pizza. Not my favorite choice of dinner food, but at least it could be shared with my teammates. We could share in a large 12 cut pizza, even if we were terrible that night. Not a bad deal by any means.

When you're engulfing large slices of cheese, you have some opportunity to take in more of the surrounding bowler's styles. For instance, I observed the various approaches of my peers – these are the manner in which bowlers threw their bowling balls. Some walked briskly to the line while others took their time. Some took four steps; others took as many as eight or ten. No two approaches were the same. Confident players watched their ball the whole way till it struck, but the cautious players hung on as if their ball were attached to them as it rolled down the lane. Some guys were impeccably fluid in their motion while others were so rigid, you'd swear they were made of stone.

No two bowlers had identical styles. This just simply did not exist. What worked for one guy most assuredly would not work for another, I figured. And much of that was due to the very nature in which their ball was thrown. One player, in particular, released his ball in such a way that after four years of bowling, I still have no idea how he throws it. All I know is that when he leans over, tilts his head in the opposite direction of the lane while lifting his back leg like he's doing a reverse drop kick, I know that he's going to get a strike. If one were to judge him on his technique alone, you'd say he was a fool. But in the few seconds it takes for his ball to get down the lane, you'd sooner shut your mouth than mock him as the pins he's aimed at will crash and land somewhere out of sight in due time.

If there were a powerful method that I needed to learn, it would have to come from within me. I'm sure this guy's teacher did not instruct the blind reverse drop kick system – this man developed it on his own somewhere along the line. I was in need of doing something similar though. The challenge excited me, but I resolved to never teach myself an approach like his, lest I injure those around me. I'm more than ok with that decision.

When the Thursday night would come to a close and the last pin had been struck, we bowlers dispersed rather quickly. But for those who didn't have anything pressing to attend to, there was the bowling alley's bar area. If you did well that night, you could toast a few cold ones to your credit. And if you performed less than average, you could still pour out your troubles via 16 ounce mug. Just don't drink and drive. Seriously, don't.

But that's not all you could do.

As I've been saying, bowling night is typically a "guy's night" out. You hang with your bros, smash some pins, have a few cold ones, and then go on your merry way. There's not much more to it than that. So what happens when you enter a female into this picture? And an attractive one at that? Well, you have the makings of a modern day social experiment—a bowling alley full of 50-some single men who simultaneously see a pretty girl walk into their establishment. Allow me to break down the order of events:

1) *Shock* and *awe* take hold—the mere notion that a knockout would be frequenting this local joint was unheard of; especially at this hour of the night.
2) Next is *intrigue*—why is she here? What made her choose this place? And most importantly, is she *with* anyone currently at the alley?
3) And finally, there's *execution*—someone has to play the martyr and figure out why this beautiful woman has decided on Louie's Lucky Seven Lanes. It's Thursday night and there are a million other things she could be doing. For the sake of the pack, someone has to go break the ice and uncover the truth.

So let the fireworks commence. I've only had this situation occur a few times in my life as a bowler; but they all ended the same way. Some guy walks over where she's sitting (usually the bar) and takes a seat. Then there's another who comes walking by . . . and soon another . . . and then another . . . and then another. It's like a pack of wolves honing in on a target; like a guppy dropped in a piranha bowl; like vultures circling a wounded prey (ok, you get the picture), these same guys who were once helping good ol' Joe at the lanes were now reverting to behavior similar to that of male monkeys asserting dominance in their troop. Very primitive, but not without understanding. And ladies, I'm here to tell you right now—if you ever, EVER, are feeling low and unwanted, come to a bowling league some Thursday or Friday night. If you sit at the bar, be it by yourself, or with a friend, I guarantee that you will at least get *some* attention that evening. It may not be the kind of attention you really desire (or even wanted), but it may serve as a quick pick-me-up to boost that self confidence. Just don't go home with any of them; I implore you.

I, on the other hand, wasn't necessarily looking to pick up chicks. I was there to kick ass and take names. No washed up, 60something banker or truck driver was going to oust me in a game of bowling. I just couldn't allow it. I mean, could you? I don't care if it's the PBA tour or a backyard game of horseshoes; I want to win. And with my new ball, shiny shoes, and duffel bag, I was ready to rip those lanes a new one. No stopping this guy.

But alas, glamorous accessories do not make a man. Nor does believing you'd immediately turn your game around by simply buying a new ball. No, only a fool would think that . . . so yes, you're listening to a fool. I knew that I needed to learn how to have patience with my new ball and what comes with patience is another endearing trait: mastery. Take this potentially poor analogy if you will. You may fish in the same watering hole for 10 years and never catch a thing, whereas some guy next to you could walk right up, cast his line in the water and snag the biggest catch you'd ever seen. Sure, you're pissed and filled with utter disbelief, but that's just life sometimes. However, what you may be not considering is what background or unknown skill this guy brought to the table before he cast his line. Nobody picks up something immediately and simply masters it. That sort of thing just isn't realistic, nor is it plausible. What *is* true though is that through a series of mishaps, learning experiences and sheer determination, one can eventually uncover a method for achieving the most desired results. In my case, it would be how to consistently knock down pins without cursing up a storm afterwards. The other fisherman may have learned or known something that the other fisherman did not and that's what separates his good fortune from the others.

But hey, I'm no stranger to sheer dumb luck either.

We all can't be masters of bowling though (sorry, young hopefuls). It's just not in the cards for some people. But for those who do, it really shows. There's a certain precision that permeates through the seasoned bowlers that causes newbies like myself to take notice. You can't help but watch and listen. *How does he do that*, you may wonder. *How does he make it look so easy?* I've asked these questions at various points in my life that were not just bowling-related and I'm sure you have too. It's intimidating when you're in the presence of a "master", be it bowling or some other field.

The league I was in had a few masters of its own. Some of these guys were my age and some were far older, but they all had the same quality about them: they had a game plan and they stuck to it. Somewhere along their bowling journey these guys stumbled onto a particular technique that worked. An extra step on the approach, perhaps? Moving one foot to the right instead of the left? Or maybe there was a certain way they released their ball and they never looked back? It's simple, little behaviors like this that quite literally separate the men from the boys. Those who toil in endless insanity by thinking their same tactics will get them different results (sans Einstein) and the others who understand that the only way to kick butt at this simple game is to make an adjustment that not only follows fundamental strategy, but also feels comfortable. Would Cal Ripken's batting stance work for Ken Griffey, Jr.? Probably not, but Mr. Ripken and Mr. Griffey, Jr. were looking for the same result—a hit.

And that's what I needed to figure out. How to not only master my game, but also myself in the process; all the while maintaining a state of relative comfort with my technique. Yeah, it may sound philosophical, but I wasn't willing to get embarrassed anymore. Things needed to change and thus, I practiced. I practiced hard and I practiced long. I even practiced in my sleep. I held my fingers in my bowling ball whilst I slumbered and I even went as far as constructing artificial lanes in my apartment.

Ok, so maybe I didn't do that last one, but I did get a miniature bowling set one Christmas. And yeah, that thing probably had no influence for improving my skill, but it sure looked neat. I mean, who has tiny bowling lanes in their apartment, let alone their house? That's pretty cool if you ask me. Ask someone else and you may get a different answer, but if you're inquiring my opinion on the matter, I like the concept.

All these tiny measures I had been taking were adding up though. I could see my improvement week to week. My average crept up from 150 to 160 and as if God himself had orchestrated the moment, I was sitting on 179 by the last week of the season. If you can imagine a good movie montage, then I suggest you do so right now. Now let's get to the good part.

Before we got to bowling, I busily did the math to see if finishing with a 180 average was possible. By the looks of things, I needed 614 pins to fall in my favor. Any less would plant me firmly at 179. To some, averaging 200 pins a game seems impossible but I'd done it before and who was to say I couldn't again? Besides, I had trained for just this moment. My team was in dead last so all aspirations of 'team' accomplishments were out the window. Yes, team Elite was not exactly living up to the moniker, but hey, as we say in Cleveland—"it's just another rebuilding year."

And so, it began.

We did our best to beat the other team, but we also did our best to end the year on a high note. I was chasing a personal best in average while others were just trying to end the season with dignity. My first game started off strong with a 209, and my second game I planted firmly on 191. Yes, a very ironic situation math-wise, but I was sitting precisely on 400 pins going into the final game of the season. I knew what I needed to do—214 pins or bust.

As I said, I had experienced a few 600 series throughout the year but this was for all the marbles (or bowling balls, I suppose?). Bragging rights were on the table and my team knew what I needed. I needed to step up to the plate, remember my training, and to put it bluntly—not screw this up. And for 9 frames of bowling, I didn't screw up whatsoever. In fact, I was screwing up the pins. I could hear them screaming as my ball hurtled towards them. I had a string of strikes, a few spares and an open frame in there with a few throws to go. I needed nothing less than a spare in the last frame to break 214 and then keep it out of the gutter on my last throw to seal the deal.

No problem, right?

When it came to be my turn, I waltzed up there, took my ball and threw a doozy of a curve right in the sweet spot. This was it. I walked away confidently but as I turned around, I stared in disbelief as one single, solitary pin stood on the far right, mocking me from 60 feet away. It was the dreaded 10 pin. The one pin in all of bowling, besides the 7-10 split that all right handers struggle with. Well, you only struggle if you're a novice bowler, that is. Those who train and hone their skills as a great bowler see no problem with hitting this dreaded loner at the back of the pack. The greats of the game laugh on the inside as they scorch their back-up ball down the lane, crushing the 10-pin with a solid knock. They then walk back to their seat as if nothing spectacular transpired at all. Just for the record (while we're on the topic of showboating), could some of you pro football players take note of that? I mean, come on guys. Act like you've tackled someone before, will you? It's really unnecessary to always celebrate every time you make a catch or a tackle. I'm just saying.

Back to the bowling, rookies to the game may view picking up the 10 pin as something akin to performing open heart surgery with a blindfold on. Yes, it can appear to be that daunting in scope.

I know what you're thinking though; this should have been easy for me, right? I should be able to pick up my ball, move over three spots and whack that pin away. Well, in a perfect world, that'd be just the case. And in that perfect world, I'd rear back and chuck my ball behind my back just for sport, but sadly, this is not that perfect world. I took my ball, moved over slightly and threw it just like I had trained myself to do throughout the year. Only problem is, I missed my intended mark by about a foot and my ball skidded into the gutter a good five feet before it even got close.

Wow, that's it, eh?

I sulked as I walked back to my team. My head was hung in utter disappointment and shame. I stood waiting for the machine to register my final score as graphics from the 1990s showed two animated pins ducking for cover from a poorly drawn bowling ball. The thing is, the animation looked like a pile of dung being rolled toward a pair of Q-tips with eyeballs (why those graphics never get updated is beyond me, but whatever, I sort of felt like a big piece of feces so maybe it was appropriate). When the score appeared, I saw the damage I had done: 213. A 613 series may be great to some, but for me that night, I needed that series to be 614. Talk about some bad luck, eh? Even after all the practicing and all the studying, I still wound up short. I was no master by any stretch of the imagination, but I had come about as close as I could to achieving my goal.

Just then, Guy decided to chime in.

"So, did you get it?" he asked.

"No, I don't think so," I said, sadly.

"Maybe you should check again," he said and so I did. I added my total pins for the year, divided my number of games and slammed the equals sign on my iPhone calculator.

180, exactly.

"Well, how about that?" I said, aloud. "613 gets me *exactly* a 180 average for the year. I can't believe that."

"Well," said Guy. "You *did* get your average, after all."

My teammates laughed at me for my previous math error whilst I enjoyed a silent moment of triumph. I guess sometimes you don't really need to be a master; you just need some dumb luck thrown in there too. You can't control every outcome in life, you just have to *roll* with the punches sometimes and hope you don't *strike* out too often. The materials you carry around don't completely define you as a person and if you can *spare* that extra time to learn more about yourself, then you'll never wind up in the *gutter*, no matter what you do.

Yeah, I had learned plenty about the other guys in my bowling league; that much is certain. But I think I learned a good deal about myself too. Like my work ethic, my own ambitions, and how much I like a good *pin*, uh, I mean pun. Pun, pun, pun. Oh, whatever. After that last paragraph, you had to have seen that one coming.

Theory: Some of your best (and worst) nights . . .

. . . are the ones you can spend completely

by yourself.

Ugh. So here you are. It's a Saturday night, just around 6 pm and you still have no plans for the evening. You're staring at your George Foreman grill and debating whether you should start that bad boy up or just let her sit a while, thinking that maybe one of your friends will be calling you to hang out. Then again, you could *call* one of them rather than wait, but you're probably worn out from always taking the initiative the last couple of weekends. And so, you begin to rationalize your next move.

Yeah, if they want to hang out, they'll call me, you think you to yourself. *Yeah, that's what they'll do.*

And so, you sit.

And wait.

And wait some more.

You look at the clock and it says 6:01 pm.

What?! It's only been a minute! This is asinine!

At about this time, you decide that you should take some kind of action. It doesn't really matter what that action is, you just need to do *something.* The evening is creeping in fast and your stomach starts to howl so you figure that food is the most important item to be satisfied. To the kitchen you go to concoct something right quick.

So what to make? You could be all Betty Crocker and make an elaborate feast, but where's the fun in making a big meal for just you? Not a whole bunch, unfortunately. So you skip over the cookbook and take a page out of the fast food playbook. Hot pockets? Hamburgers? What about spaghetti then? The answer is nay; spaghetti will take too long and what if one of your friends actually *does* try to contact you while you're making that? You'd have to stop boiling and stuff all that linguine in a container for later use. And that's just not cool. That being said, you decide on the most logical thing: a granola bar. Hearty, full of wheat, and goes down easy; it's the perfect pre-dinner snack food to tide you over in case something happens.

I never knew how many grain bars were in existence until I lived on my own. There's Kellogg's, Sunkist, Kashi, heck, even Aldi's has its own brand; each of which just as sugar-filled as the last. I've sampled them all in my quest for a balanced diet and I can't say that I prefer one over the other. This variety of fruit-wrapped bread, mixed with a few preservatives, is ok in my book.

There was a time when I went through an all-organic phase. You know—when you think that buying organic food will make you lead a healthier lifestyle. Since there are no added sugars or preservatives, you're more "natural." I couldn't get past how lame that sounded. Sure, I've seen parts of Super Size Me and have entertained documentaries on eating purely vegetarian food, but I still enjoy a steak or two when I can. Moderation is the key with anything. However, there appears to be a real connection between several long-term diseases and eating certain dairy or meat products. If there's a larger conspiracy afoot then I wouldn't be surprised.

For example, I've discovered that the major food distributors are all in cahoots with each other. That's right; I know what you're up to, Target, Wal-Mart, etc. You may think I don't know that Post acquired Kraft foods a few years ago and you may also think I don't know the retail brands (Giant Eagle, Target, etc) are coming down some of the same zip lines, but I do! Can't pull the wool over this guy's eyes. True, shopping at Aldi's may not offer the big name brands or the most diverse selection, but it's certainly filling and keeps me from emptying my checking account every other week.

I enjoy fuel perks as much as the next person, but I really begin to wonder if I'm truly saving anything.

For example, I once tracked my activities for a month. If all went well and I didn't travel too far, I'd have to fill my tank up after five days. This is all assuming I'm running on a tank that was 14 gallons large. If gas were about three dollars to the gallon, then I'd be spending about $42 each time I filled up. That's well over $100 every month for gas. But if I shopped at Giant Eagle to receive fuel perks each week, I could save $.10 a gallon. If you're still with me, that's $2.90 times 14, which equals just about $40 for filling up. In essence, I'm saving $2 every week. But, if I shopped at Aldi's, I could save more than $2 a week on my food. If you throw out some of the nutritional advantages, then I think you can make up your mind on this issue yourself.

Back to the night at hand, you may settle on a small meal to appease the appetite. Once you're done with that, you may head back to your couch to allow for proper digestion. And as you sit, you check that clock of yours once more.

7:15 pm? Ah, come on! How am I supposed to stay busy when it's only a quarter after seven?!

Well, that may be a disappointment, but you still have options available to you. The first and most obvious is the television set. It's the one source of entertainment as readily accessible as that neighbor who desperately wants you to hang out every weeknight, but you still manage to say 'no' regularly to. So let's say you give in this time and turn on the tube to see if anything is worth watching. You find reruns, comedy specials and the occasional infomercial—basically, there's a lot of crap on television, but we'll get to that later.

At this juncture, it'd be nice to have some sort of a hobby to keep one's self busy. If you're a raving narcissist with a lot to get off your chest, you open up your laptop and start typing up some rant on living by yourself—but since you probably aren't fitting that description, you might dabble with something else. Crochet? Baking? Maybe you like to reenact scenes from popular movies like Indiana Jones or Lord of the Rings? Not to say that I've ever done such things; I've just heard rumors. All I'm saying is that you need to find something to keep your mind active; not necessarily busy. A busy mind keeps you from being focused on the task at hand—and that task is finding something productive to do.

I've done some research as to what some more common hobbies are. I wasn't overly shocked to find that women fancy men who are football enthusiasts, rock climbers and surfers. Men, conversely, like women who take up dancing, cooking or yoga (the last being an obvious appeal if you ask me). The one hobby not listed, which I knew should have been, was to be musically inclined; specifically in the realm of drums or guitar.

My mother had given me a guitar when I moved out. She told me she had received this from her father. In a way, the guitar was something like a family heirloom. Wonderful, right? The last thing I need is a potentially priceless artifact hanging around my apartment. I accepted this gift with full knowledge that I was taking on a heavy burden. I was responsible for something special and I needed to keep it safe. The tension of what to do and what *not* to do made me uneasy. Do I play the guitar? Or do I let it gather dust like a fossil at the Smithsonian? The thoughts of making my air guitar days become reality eventually won out—I wanted to play. I wasn't doing this for the appeal by gosh; I really wanted to learn.

Plus, I knew it couldn't hurt with the ladies either, I'll admit.

I immediately went out and found an instructor. The one I settled on worked for a local studio and from what I could gather, ran a side business to teach lessons outside of the studio. When I first met him, I expected an aged master—like a Yoda—but what I got was a guy who was a little younger than me. This was not the most humbling part of my experience though. No, when I first went for my lessons, I had to sit and wait for the student in front of me to finish. I stood eagerly, guitar strapped over my shoulder, as I waited for the other musical prodigy to exit. To my surprise, a young boy no more than 10 came bounding out of the practice room, small guitar in hand. The teacher then shouted "and remember to practice your chords, Joshua!"

Oh, great, right? This "kid" in front of me was not only a third my age, he also had the same name as me! I stared down at the little Hendrix-in-training and gave him an unintended dirty look. I didn't mean to do that, I just felt a bit disappointed at that moment. Had I waited too long to acquire this trade? Should I be wasting 12 bucks a week to come out here and get schooled by some dude who I could probably give a swirly to? I decided to dismiss the thought as tiny Josh's dad came strolling in. He glanced at me and gave *me* the look of "just what the heck are you doing here?"

I believe he got a dirty scowl in return.

The embarrassing parts out of the way, I made my entrance to one of the practice rooms and sat across from my new teacher. He had Buddy Holly glasses, a thin frame and a shaved head. This might be the first things you'd notice on a person, but something else caught my eye. You see, the most distinguishing trait on him was his shoes. He wrapped his shoelaces around his ankles and then shoved the excess lace underneath the tongue. I thought this was something I had imagined, but with each subsequent visit, I noticed he did this over and over again. After several visits, I knew that this subtle act of shoelace manipulation was not a mistake, but intentional.

You'd think that being the inquisitive person that I am, I'd ask why he did this, but I never did. Not once. Are you disappointed? I hope not. Because what follows next may disappoint you even more. As I said, my teacher was a nice guy, but he was missing the main reason as to why I was there. He wanted me to learn the chords, to become more acquainted with the strings, their locations, and how to read the sheet music in front of me. But let's get one thing straight—I really just wanted to rock out to Free Bird as soon as possible. Simple as that.

Instead, I'd go home, open my sheet music and start strumming Hot Cross Buns to myself. Yeah, that wasn't so appealing to me. It wasn't but two months later that I became fed up with my training and discontinued my newest hobby. This was my fault for doing so, or just another example of my ADD kicking in since I couldn't stick to my guns long enough to learn anything. I walked away feeling like a failure. All things considered though, I had certainly gained some nice experience in the realm of music-playing. That and I'm sure the late nights spent practicing (if you can call it that) kept me out of trouble.

As I took my trip down memory lane, I decided to pick up the old guitar and give her another go. It's funny how the term "like riding a bike" doesn't really apply here. Strumming a guitar again after so long is like trying to build a house out of a deck of cards. It requires a level of patience that I just don't possess. I stumbled over my notes as I tried to recall any past knowledge. The strings were my enemy, it seemed, but I did start to feel better. I may be alone in this apartment, but I'm not completely alone when I have something to sing about. A nice song helps one pass the time. Even if the lyrics are complete trash.

> *Oh, how I sing*
> *A song for me tonight*
> *And as I sing this song*
> *I feel quite . . . alright?*

Songs like that are rather uninspired, but that's what you get when you mix wine with a resurrected hobby that's better off staying dead. Isolation makes us do weird things, but the mere state of isolation can teach us much about ourselves. Such as where our mind goes when it's unoccupied by matters of the day. If you're a single guy in his mid-20s, then your mind will likely drift to that person of utmost interest to you—which, in case you're wondering, is a girl. If you access to her phone number, you consider the text message route. If you don't, you may Facebook her and see what she's up to, but let's assume you have her number already. A phone call is way too personal and you wouldn't want to interrupt her night like some creeper, right? So a text is the safest way to go.

"Hey, what's up?" you may say, but if you're in a hurry or you've been wallowing you sorrows in a beverage, you may type something different. It may be something closer to "Hry, wahs upp?" which is more akin to a three-year old's level of grammar. If your phone has spell check, you may be lucky enough to input something like "Get Thais yo." How my smartphone creates "Get Thais yo" from "Hey what's up" is beyond me, but on more than one occasion I've had a friend or relative ask me why I'm telling them to go get an Asian person on a weeknight. The obvious response to their question is "Not mish you!" which is code once again for "Not much, you?" If this occurs, you may spend the next day explaining how yes, you *do* miss them, and no, you really didn't mean to suggest they find the nearest Thai place. And if you're really, really lucky, you had this conversation with that girl you like. Not that I would know anything about that . . . .

But if the above doesn't satisfy you or if she doesn't respond in due time (which is more likely a blessing), you'll continue to shift through other friends in your contact list. (What are they up to? And why aren't they out with me? Well, there's only one way to find out!) These folks are familiar enough that you could call them, but if the hour is late (say, after midnight) you may incite a problem if you call them out of your own sheer boredom. Chances are they are likely sleeping from a long day of work or relaxing with their spouse/special someone and now here you are interrupting their night. This can make someone feel like a total jackass. We all love to hear from our friends now and again, but not when the rest of the world is trying to sleep. That's just not cool and if you think it is cool, then you'd best get your head checked. Or maybe just consider getting new friends because your current ones may block your number.

Well, once the friendship circles are closed off and any potential mates are exhausted, you circle back to a world you should have never contemplated returning to whatsoever:

63

the *ex*. Never, and I mean never, text or call an ex when it's after 10:18 pm. I will repeat just so this sinks in properly. Do not, under any circumstances, contact that ex after 10:18 pm. Any time before that may be acceptable, depending on your situation, but once it's past 10:18, you've reached the point of no return.

Why? Well, for one simple reason. Your ex is likely doing something they want to be doing and really don't want to be bothered, least of all by you. If you were really interested in seeing them, you would have texted or called them earlier so a late night contact just reeks of desperation and an inability to move on. Plus you will only be reopening a world which you don't want to be a part of anymore. And if you're the conniving type that likes to get even, do you really want your ex to have the satisfaction that you're unable to carry on your life without them? I mean, come on—you're only hurting yourself. But then again, if the fates allow it, you may end up texting them "Get Thais yo" and that's probably better than any message you were thinking of sending in the first place. You may have to explain why you wanted them to get Asian food, but that's an easier clear up than "I can't take it anymore, I'm still in love with you."

As the night wanes on, you'll do more channel-surfing than ever. You understand that your options are limited by this point. Most people are either just going out or retiring for the evening but since you've already decided on a night in, you buckle in for the long haul. And thus, you find yourself in Late Night Television Land.

I don't watch a ton of TV, but for the shows I do watch; I follow with great vigor. My reasoning is that if I'm going to spend time being entertained, then I had best get involved on a level where I actually care if the show is on the air. Over the years, I've become attached to regulars like House, Law and Order (SVU, of course—we miss you, Elliot Stabler!), Chuck, The Big Bang Theory, Whose Line is it Anyway, and Fringe. I was a one-time Sportscenter watcher but that has lessened in my adulthood. I miss the days of TGIF, with shows such as Full House and Family Matters. That kind of television would always put me in a good mood regardless of the type of day I was having. Now that I'm older, it's a rerun of House that keeps me entertained on a Friday night if I'm all by my lonesome.

Once that show is over, I'll look at my clock once more. It'll say 9 pm in big, bold digital numbers more often that not. *Criminey, this just sucks.* At this juncture, I debate whether I should change my clothes. Maybe there's somebody out there still fighting the good fight to go out and be social? I hold on for another hour in the hope that it'll turn around. What should I do to pass the time then?

Well, if you're me, you make one last ditch effort to reach the outside world. A group of mass texts will go out with one purpose: find the poor sap that is as bored as you this evening. But since you only get 1/3 of the responses back (all of which being a 'negative'), you have to find something else to bide your time.

I tend to pull out my laptop and start typing. I'll try to create a few witty passages here and there, but after about 10 minutes, I'm bored with this distraction. Besides, I always block out Sunday afternoons or weeknights as my time to sit and write so this is outside my realm of acceptable habit. It doesn't help either that my want to be social outweighs my want to write so in short time, the battle within is quickly over.

Ok, I need to find out what those other guys are doing.

So you follow up with another text to see if they got the hint. A few seconds later, you see that they did get the hint you wanted to hang out; they just didn't realize how desperate your situation was till the second one came through. Despite your predicament, no one comes a calling and here you are again; alone in your apartment.

When the last rejection letter arrives, that's the time I'll move to my bedroom and change into something a little more comfortable. It's my typical wardrobe for nights in—boxers and shorts with a white t-shirt. Sometimes I wear moccasins but if it's warm enough, those aren't really necessary. And yes, I'm well aware that makes me sound dorky but hey, feet don't always get the best circulation so you need to let them know you still care about them (your feet that is).

I'm usually in denial about my evening so I keep my clothes out anyway. As I walk back to my living room, I do exactly what I normally do when I can't make a decision on what to do next: I pop on my Xbox 360 and play a game of Halo or Street Fighter (If you don't believe me, then please check out my first book, the prequel to this one). The "newb-crushing" and screwy banter only lasts for about 25 minutes though. The novelty of being a 20something who still enjoys defeating teenagers in a virtual world grows old quickly; especially if you have none of your other friends partaking with you. After some good old-fashioned fun, I switch the system off and return to my temple of thought.

What to do next?

I go back to my phone to see if anyone texted me and see that no one has. Since I have an iPhone, I check my Facebook page, my Twitter account, and my email all in one fell swoop to see what's happening out in the "real world." When I don't find anything I like, I put the mobile device down and consider doing something else. But what though? Oh, I know. Let's turn on that television again. That's brain dead enough for me to pass the time, right? So I turn it on and start channel surfing like a true couch potato.

Sometimes I wind up on the E! channel (shocking, right?). This station is the focal point for non-stop news on celebrities, their lives, and all the mistakes they make therein. Hollywood is as much a place as it is an idea in America. On a map, it's merely a place with a marker that says "Hollywood" but overlying that caption is the idea that one can lead an amazing life by living there. That means you can get rich quick and enjoy plenty of attention. And all that attention mixed with nice things is the draw—be it negative or positive.

So here I am, on the E! channel, watching the latest news on America's most wanted and hated public figures. Not surprisingly, I find a celebrity is ranting about a social issue in America as though they are the authority on the subject matter. You know, discussions on whether or not gays should marry or health care reform or increased taxes. The vast majority of these people (celebrities) are disconnected from "commoner" life, so how do they know anything about how the world works? If you want to know how bad or rough it is, talk to a school teacher; or a small business owner; or a nurse. These people can paint a more accurate picture of what life is really like for the masses.

At the end of the day though, everyone's entitled to his own opinion. No matter how distorted or misleading it may be. You, the individual, just have to figure out who or what to believe. Kind of like when someone speaks out on abortion, immigration, or dare I go there again—gay marriage. Former Growing Pains actor, Kirk Cameron, got himself into some trouble with his fellow actors when he spoke out against gay marriage. Mr. Cameron gave an argument that the marriage of gays was unnatural and therefore a difficult thing to condone. Other celebrities lashed out, claiming that Mr. Cameron was "outdated", "hates gays", and is clearly "not up with the times". One other critic even went as far as to say that Mr. Cameron was a "failed actor". The last comment is clearly not very kosher. Isn't it clear that a petty comment against another is simply seen as petty? It distracts from the real issue: arguing whether or not Mr. Cameron is right or wrong; not the status of his place an actor

But this is what happens when people's beliefs are thrown into the fray. We become uncomfortable and detract from the real issue. I give Mr. Cameron much credit for having to courage to speak up on something so controversial, be it right or wrong. His critics did not agree with this, but that's what discomfort does to people. Had someone of less credibility, such as Snooki or Honey Boo Boo's mother said something of the same nature then no one would have cared as much, I figure. Their words would have been dismissed as mere nothings and the rest of us would have gone about our business.

So as I sat there listening to the chatter of the E! channel and reading the reports about Mr. Cameron's debacle, I wondered whose side the media was on. Was he progressive? Was he truly "outdated" in his thinking? It's a hard thing to argue nowadays, but when you're all alone in a room with only your thoughts, you have the opportunity to think a little more clearly. No distractions, just your own insight and intuition. I wonder how progressive the world really is when it demands change but has no idea what that change will do; even look like. I'm speaking towards Mr. Cameron's critics, not Mr. Cameron, per se. When a complex issue is reduced to the most unimportant details, you ponder what's really at work here. Then again, I'm only getting a few angles of the whole story so I'm doing the best I can to discern truth with what I believe myself. I see this applicable to any argument, great and small.

So what's the *right* answer to someone who makes a blatant riff towards other's beliefs? Personally, I would want Mr. Cameron to continue sticking up for what he believes and see if everyone else does the same. Do his critics feel as strongly about gay marriage as Mr. Cameron does? Or are they just raking in an opportunity to get some time with the media? These are other celebrities, mind you. Some may *want* to be in the limelight and will do so by any means possible.

That's the glorious tragedy that is America—you can say what you think, regardless if it's how you feel about a topic, all in the hope that your remarks will pull you into community with others; even if that community has malicious intent. If the other side caves in, then you might walk away with a personal victory, but in the grand scheme of things, you're really just making your beliefs and opinions known. If other people don't like it, then that's their agenda. But if you continue to stand up for what you believe in, then people will eventually respect you for it. Even if these people disagreed with you from the onset. For example, look at the civil rights movement. Guys like Martin Luther King and Malcolm X fought for equal rights in a tough time. They were more than groundbreaking individuals, they were rule breakers. And it takes the type of person who isn't afraid to make changes to be a true rule breaker. Not the kind of rule breaker that smokes dope in the boy's bathroom or drives home drunk—that's just acting a fool. But to act upon truth exposes a belief in our bones; it is more than just an impulse response to something that's controversial in the world and when truth is there, others take notice.

All right, I apologize for the short sidebar there. Where was I?

That's right, the journey into the night. You begin to see commercials that feature celebrities who get press for the wrong reasons. Nearly all of the U.S. heard about Charlie Sheen's physical, emotional, and personal breakdown when it went public. Granted, his show at the time, Two and a Half Men, was the number one comedy in America, so that kind of press warrants attention. However, with all the bad press that Charlie received, he still managed to appear in ads that featured cars, cable networks, and other commercials promoting big name brands. I guess any press really is *good* press, after all.

But should it be that way? Shouldn't you promote somebody who has a cleaner image than Sheen? Don't get me wrong, the guy is funny when he wants to be and I love the show (past and present). But when a person takes a nosedive like he did, shouldn't the right thing be to help him get back on his feet rather than exploit his . . . well, exploits? I suppose the old saying of "any press is good press" may be applicable in this situation. When it comes to advertising, what's trending is the way to go. Regardless if it's "bad" or "good." People need their attention grabbed if they're going to pay any mind to something. There needs to be a dynamic intrigue at work. With so many social media outlets, the most shocking and attention-grabbing is a tornado that's out of control. Think for a moment what's more entertaining to you—video of a train slamming the side of a car or a peaceful plain of grass swaying in the wind? I suppose that's a matter of perspective, but if I really think about it, I'd rather see what happens to that car than those innocent blades of grass. So if I'm presented with a product that's advertised based on the train slamming, I can't help but not look away.

So yes, I am glued to my television, watching Charlie Sheen's goofy commercial and not even paying mind to how I really feel about Charlie's situation. I'd rather be entertained than concerned. A sad realization if I do say so.

As I look over at the clock, I see that I'm past the hour of 10 pm. Regardless of what day in the week it may be, I'm still in the thinking that I can go out. Rather than text my friends, I check to see their Facebook statuses and if they've "checked in" anywhere. From time to time that creepy feature can actually come in handy when you're too lazy to text someone.

When I see that nobody's making any movement, I decide to shift gears once more. I've got a good portion of energy stored up, so I need to expend it somehow. My mind drifts to my laptop for a brief moment as I contemplate a path that will only result in feelings of shame and guilt. The tissue box is far from my grasp (as are any woolen socks) and a tiny voice in my head says "do something else" so I quickly decide to derail my thoughts to something else. Anything can work so long as it's physically stimulating. Then, as if it's screaming my name out loud, the speaker on my mantle grabs hold of my attention and yells "play me." I switch into some workout attire and prep for a nice round of Pilates or weight-lifting. This is actually one of my favorite pastimes when I am faced with nothing better to do.

I love a good instrumental to work out to and that instrumental must be dynamic in its presentation. No Lady Gaga or heavy metal for this guy; I need something epic playing to make me *feel* like I'm doing something epic. And why the heck not? I am actively making my body stronger and that's a grandiose thing that I'll notice, as will anyone I encounter.

Composers such as Hans Zimmer, James Newtown Howard, and John Powell can get my blood boiling with a big ballad symphony. I may not be warding off charging gladiators or flying on the backs of dragons, but a powerful melody made up of tympanis and trumpets can make a person feel like they're really there. Once I've made my selection, I start cranking out some push-ups, sit-ups and other various forms of body-testing work. You'd be surprised what you can do at home, on your own time, with a little music and a little bit of creativity. Just remember to stay away from open windows. You don't want your neighbors thinking you're some kind of weird karate wannabe with all your sporadic movements. I've gotten a few strange looks in my day so just be aware that people can and will attempt to spy on you if they can.

My work out over, it's back to being bored. I'm really sweaty to boot too. Extreme perspiration I can handle; it's the bored part that really sucks. If you're like me, then you may contemplate calling your family. It's incredibly late but there's liable to be someone awake. And how could your parents have plans tonight? That would be inconceivable.

And so you may call them . . . .

Ring 1 . . . .

Ring 2 . . .

Ring 3 . . .

You are about to hang up when the voice of your mother answers.

"Oh hi, son. What are you doing?"

"Nothing much. Just hanging out being bored. What are you doing?"

"Well, your father and I ended up having the Richardsons over. Oh, and the Johnsons are here too. And do you remember the Talbots from church? Well, apparently they know the Johnsons! Small world, right?"

"Yeah, small world . . . ."

I know what you're thinking here—that never happens, but let me assure you, it has. I've had nights with nothing to do and no one to see while my parents enjoyed a night of socializing, fraternizing, and fun. It's ok though. They've earned it and I'm happy they are having a good time. It's just depressing how their night of entertainment just so happens to be on the one night where I'm bored out of my mind.

The appropriate thing to do in this situation is to just say 'ok, have a nice night' and hang up the phone. So let's say you do say that and then return to your lovely night in. *What else is there to do? Well, there is that box of tissues over there* . . . . NO! Cool that notion before things get out of hand (no pun intended) and find something else. That's what you gotta do.

And what I gotta do is head to my laptop (but not for the wrong reasons). Since it's getting late, I feel calm enough to do some writing; it's one of the most therapeutic things I can do. So I write. I crank open my latest entry and start typing from there. But of course, not five minutes into my work, a text message come through that says something to the extent of "Hey, what are you doing?"

Perfect timing, eh? It's one of the friend out enjoying himself at late hours of the night. So I walk over and pick up my phone to see who it is. To my surprise (but probably not yours), it's a girl I used to date or have had relationship discussions with in the past. Liquid courage has essentially taken over and transformed itself through instant messaging and though I know better, I'm bored enough at this point to play along with whatever game is about to unfold.

A few texts later, you must understand a few realities are taking place here. A) this person is mildly intoxicated and b) they want you to be where they are. Pretty big conundrum right? To go or stay? That is the real question of the moment and so, you debate. Is it worth your time? Is it worth their time? And do you really want to get showered, dressed and head out when it's nearly past midnight? If this were me and it were five or six years ago, I'd probably be jumping at the opportunity to leave.

But this isn't that time anymore.

I know I have a church commitment at 9:30 tomorrow so I can't skip that this week. Then, I have a baseball game starting at noon which I have to drive straight from church to get there so there's no time in between to even eat really (unless it's at the BK Lounge). And to top it all off, I was out late the night before and didn't sleep much thinking about how I needed to get groceries so I could work out on Saturday before I ran to help a friend move out while still making it back in time to shut off my crock pot before I ruined the next day's chicken meal. In all that commotion, I couldn't wrangle up anybody to get together this evening and am now paying the price, theoretically speaking.

Yeah, I hate responsibility. It's a real buzzkill to someone who just wants to do what he pleases. You probably hate it too but you send a text back saying how you "can't make it" but make sure you "get home safe" and "text me when you get there, ok?" And when this friend denies your sober reasoning and logic, but ultimately accepts your offers, you say farewell and hope that no situation arises where you'd actually have to go save this person from making a poor decision.

What you really hoped for was a text from someone else, but never got it. Not from one of your close buddies, or your mom, or your brother—nay, it's from that special someone you're *really* interested in. You've obviously had your fair share of opportunities to turn things around and let her know the way you feel, but for whatever the reason, things just haven't worked in your favor. In which case, you retreat to your bedroom to sleep before you're tempted to play video games or actually grab that box of tissues sitting on the counter. You're still a little sweaty, but come on, there's no one else here to impress so a shower can wait till morning.

And as you lie there trying to fall asleep, thinking of what others may be doing on this particular night, you fade off into a light slumber. But before you head into a full blown REM snooze, your phone buzzes just one more time. You don't want to answer but you at least have to look. If somebody's in trouble, you have to put your big boy pants on and come to the rescue. Thankfully this is not the girl from before; it's one of your buddies.

"Dude, where r u? Didn't (insert forgetful friend here) text you back to say what we were doing? We're at (insert local hangout here). Come out!!"

You're kidding me, right? That's the most natural reaction to such a message. But just then a funny thing occurs. Your friend texts you again before you even start typing a response.

"Dude, nevermind. That girl you said you were talking to is here and she's all over some guy! Good choice being wherever you are!"

You can't help but smile when that happens. Irony has a way of teaching us hard lessons, but luckily our inherent wisdom wins out once in a while. Or perhaps it's something else? You know, like a guardian angel looking out for you; keeping you from chasing an unattainable object. And so, a night that began with thoughts of loneliness ends with feelings of divine protection. Go figure, right? Call it what you will, that's something worth sleeping soundly about.

That much is true.

Theory: Spending money lavishly is no way to impress people . . .

. . . because let's face it, you are single.

I went through an awkward, yet taxing time once in my life. It wasn't in junior high or when I grew facial hair for the first time. No, it was when I started spending my newly earned money like a child, a child with no concept of what it meant to budget finances or balance a checkbook. I'll never forget the first paycheck I ever received. I remember feeling very "sink or swim." What to do with this new sum of money in front of me? Do I spend it? Do I invest it? Heck, do I buy some video games with it? My mind was like a bowl of fruit in a blender; basically, I felt erratic. I finally decided to go home before I did something truly irrational like buy a new blender and a whole week's worth of fruit. Hindsight reminds me that this was a good decision.

So there I was; situated in my one and only chair, staring across 750 square feet of apartment at the first of many bi-weekly earnings. I marveled at its splendor from afar, but I eventually crept closer and gripped it tightly with both hands. *So this is what one acquires when one establishes himself,* I thought. *How amazing.* There was a row of numbers on this wonderful slip of paper that represented my wages for the past two weeks. I felt like a million bucks, even if the numbers themselves didn't add up that high (and believe me when I tell you, they certainly did *not*).

So I was back to where I started. Do I spend it on something? I looked around my apartment and began formulating my next big purchase. My entertainment center was falling apart and my TV looked like something from the Calicovision days. You know, the type of television you see on vintage TV shows like The Cosby Show and Step by Step. I think I had ripped off the antenna at some point because it didn't fit properly in the space provided for it. I had no choice, ok? That thing needed to go or else I'd be without my boobtube.

I didn't want to spend money on a television just yet. I vaguely remember depositing the check the next day with no plan in mind as to what to do with it. Instead of going the TV route, I elected to buy a set of silver canisters. My intention was to house certain items like flour or sugar if I ever needed these ingredients. I figured these types of things were a good start if I were to become more domesticated. Before you judge me, try to level with me on this. The cans were cheap and appropriately practical. By foregoing my first desire, I was hoping to set myself up for better buying behavior later. But I found myself completely unsatisfied with this decision as I realized I had no understanding of the need for flour or sugar. I knew you needed these things for baking or adding spice to your tea, but beyond that? I was quite lost. I knew what having a bigger TV meant though. That was something I was certain about.

A few weeks later, I mustered up the courage to step into an electronics depot and look at big screens. I probably looked like a minnow in a shark tank to some of these sales folks. Within five minutes I'd been approached by nearly every employee within the mall. My big, doe eyes must have looked like blood in the water to a seasoned sales rep. I did what I could to hold off the feeding frenzy; it was the only way to get what I came for.

To prepare, I did some research prior to this venture. You see, LCDs and plasmas were at war with one another when I went shopping for the first time. Plasmas had great resolution but the risk of cancer made for a real bummer. On the flip side, LCDs were just as good but without the unhealthy side effects. As I'm sure you deduced, I bought the plasma. A nice big plasma TV; 42 inches of glorified 1080p (whatever that means) with the opportunity to mount the darned thing like a 12 point buck on my wall. It was glorious. I'll admit it; I went home and cried. Another proud moment for me. I decided the best way to celebrate was to make myself a pizza from scratch (thanks to my new silver canisters). The pizza turned out terribly but the TV still gives me high definition to this day. Sure I have to ignore some leakage of plasma every now and again, but that's forgivable every time I watch Avatar or Lord of the Rings in Blu-Ray.

The nights that followed were enlightening for me. I never knew Jerry Seinfeld had a slight swerve in his curls until I got my new television. And I never understood true high definition till I saw Olivia Wilde walk onto the set of House for the first time. She may have been "13" on the show, but she was "number 1" in my heart (that's a lame joke, but I thought it was cute at the time I wrote this). Basically, I had much to be thankful for, but all this TV wonder was conducted without a friend nearby. This saddened me. Sure, I could brag about my enlarged monitor to my friends when we were out and about, but why would anyone want to come see the thing? They all had families or houses of their own, but most importantly, their own big screens. This created a small, but not so subtle, contest among the lot of us who owned one. The competition culminated when my friends and I settled in at a buddy's basement for a night of Halo and lo and behold, my friend Isaac unveiled his new 46-inch monstrosity.

"Whoa, whoa," I said to him, as Isaac lifted the cloth from his new television. "Just what is that?"

Isaac is normally a nice guy, but in this moment, he took great pleasure in digging at me deep.

"Your move . . .," he said, calling me out like a master chess player or a heavyweight boxer defending his crown. My brow furrowed in envy. Well played, sir Isaac. Well played. Indeed, it *was my* move, but would it be a good decision to retaliate? Should I head on out to my retailer and trade in my leaky plasma for an even bigger screen? That question was answered for me when my other buddy, Gary, purchased a projector screen for his basement. The size of his projection screen was a good 60+ inches; enough to make a grown man weep. Once I got wind of his latest purchase, I debated how important this duel was. Do I front the money? Do I sleep on the couch so as to allow for more optimal viewing? No, I resolved to not go down that road. Ah well, I guess. Tail tucked between my legs, I accepted my defeat.

It took me some time to get over that one. I won't lie about it. But since I wasn't going to win any "big TV contests", I turned my attentions to another material possession: my wheels. Since college, my way of getting around was a maroon-colored '95 Chrysler Eagle Vision. Not a bad vehicle if you like any of the following: low to the ground, decent gas mileage, and a length that could rival some tugboats. I wasn't trying to win any beauty contests, mind you. I just needed the most efficient way to get from point A to point B. And that was fine.

For a while.

Then, like a bad storm creeping in, I began to feel a need for a faster, better and to be honest, more stylish vehicle. Call it a quarter-life crisis if you will, I wanted my sports car. Better yet, I *needed* my sports car. I had neglected getting one when I bought my first vehicle and now I was going to make up for it. I knew that if I never got one now, I'd probably never get one again. My friends and co-workers gave me the same logic, but naturally, my parents said otherwise. Well, they were somewhat divided on the issue. My mother knew the dangers of possessing a high performance vehicle in the middle of the snow belt but my dad was on the other side of the fence. He had lived through the muscle car era of the '60s and knew full well what it meant to have that sleek piece of metal sitting in your garage every morning. But when it came to arguing this point with my mother, my father did his best impersonation of Switzerland and threw up the neutral flag. This strategic maneuver left me completely outnumbered and without any hope of attaining what I wanted.

Normally I'd concede when this type of battle took hold, but the visage of me in a nice ride was all ready planted deep in my noggin. And when two of my closest friends bought beamers for themselves, I couldn't take it anymore. I needed to keep up with everybody else. I was not about to be denied. So I woke up one morning, drove down to my dealership, and traded in my car for a brand spanking new 2012 Hyundai Genesis 2.0T. I was so proud of what I had done that I called my parents directly after I signed on the dotted line. I then spent the next half hour trying to convince my mother that this was a good decision and then took another half hour detailing the specs to my excited father. It was a day torn by several emotions, but I got what I wanted—a proverbial chick magnet that would make me smile every morning I walked to my car.

Or so I thought it would be that way.

In reality, sports cars attract two types of people: retired men and other guys who wish they had your car. That's pretty much it. If you were waiting for something like "hot babes" or "soccer moms" then you're gravely mistaken. Movies and television lie, my friends. The media lies like bad dates, people on food stamps with no accountability, and that weird uncle who convinced you as a child that walking outside would cause the grass to turn to lava. Thanks for that one, Uncle Rick. I'm still scarred from your days of babysitting me.

Truth is your car is really all about *you*. The car, like a peacock out to strut, is an extension of yourself and your own personal statement to the world that "yes, I am here." It says how much money you have (or are willing to spend to impress others). It says what type of car you like to drive (or just like to look at). And it also says what time of your life you're in. It's natural for a bachelor to want a nice vehicle. Driving a well-designed car can be likened to having a well-groomed mane in the middle of the African savannah. Female lions, aka lionesses, really dig a lion with a nice mane. This displays a sign of good health and proper breeding; the traits suitable for passing on to the next generation.

But here's a question—do women consciously go out looking for guys who have nice rides? Well, yes and no. For every gold digger I've come across, I've encountered an equally non-materialistic hippie. But it sure doesn't hurt to have some shiny wheels at your disposal. No self-respecting woman is going to enjoy being chauffeured around in a cheesy molester van or a clunky P.O.S. Otherwise she'll find another place to roost.

I will admit that owning a nice and shiny sports car can be both a blessing and a curse. You may attract the wrong types of people, but at least you're attracting something. And that's better than nothing at all for some people. Plus, it's a good conversation starter.

"Hey, nice car, man," says guy 1 to guy 2.

"Hey, thanks man," says guy 2 to guy 1.

"Is that a turbo? Or a V6?" says guy 1 to guy 2.

Guy 2 searches his memory for what the dealer told him. And when he has absolutely no idea what it is, he looks at the back of his hood to see if there's a clue. Alas, he's in luck. A large "2.0T" is plastered on the back. That's gotta mean "turbo."

"Oh, it's a turbo model," says guy 2 to guy 1, confidently.

"Nice . . .," says guy 1 to guy 2.

And there it is. Even if you aren't attracting all the ladies, you'll still be presented with the opportunity to strike up discussions at gas stations with total strangers. Just rest assured that your audience will likely be a war veteran or another guy your age. And if a girl ever asks you if you "like" your car, don't answer by saying you do because it's "on my Facebook" page. That's the wrong answer. Instead you say to her that you do like your car, but it's nothing *special*. Not like her, that is. It just gets you from A to B, if nothing else. That's a much better answer. Take it from a guy who's owned a sports car or two in his day. Some women get so turned off by your answers that they're liable to call you out on your poor choice of words.

"Do you think you'll love your car more than me some day?"

"Is this how you got your last girlfriend?"

"Are you planning on keeping that forever? I can't see you driving around any kids in it."

Yeah, there are all kinds of responses warranted from those statements. Too bad you're on the receiving end most times. And also (before I forget), be on the defensive when your girl (space) friends see that you have a nice car. They may be your friends, but they are also girls. If their perception of you is purely what they see, then their opinions on you will reflect precisely what they see too.

"Wow, that's a nice car. Have you scored yet in that thing? I just can't see it . . . ."

"Have you named it yet? How about Priscilla? Or maybe Patty? No? I'll be sure to let your next girlfriend know it has a name."

"I think you should call it the 'PD'. You know, the 'Panty Dropper'. I think it suits you."

Ok, so aside from that last comment, I think you're seeing the bigger picture here. You'll really just need to roll with the punches and understand that you like what you bought and that's that. Eventually some lucky lady will like you for you and the car won't even matter. Or the expensive dinnerware. Or the overly priced couch. Or the vintage aloe plant sitting atop your counter. So try not to fret over the matter. Then again, pigs could fly tomorrow and the wrong people will finally quit breeding but we all know those won't happen. So be sure to enjoy all your nice things while you can. Because when you get older, the nicer things in life should be more intangible than tangible anyway. That's just the rumor I hear these days. Don't quite know yet if it's true.

Downright Good Thought: The dreams of your youth . . .

. . . tend to die hard in adulthood.

Well, I've talked about my bowling league. And I've talked about my inferior cooking skills. And I've touched on a love for money being the root of all evil when you're a bachelor. Trust me when I tell you: it really *is*. None of these topics are outside the norm of things you'd expect a single guy to think about during his alone time (minus sex, of course. That'll come later).

The one thing (aside from sex) that I haven't mentioned yet, and I'm happy to do so now, are the dreams we have when we're young and what these dreams mean when we're older. Have I ended up where I wanted? Do I feel content with life? And did I ever envision myself as the person I am *now* versus what I promised myself to be *then*? This is not as easy reflection to have with one's self.

My dream was to become a professional baseball player. No, it wasn't to be a writer or a playwright; I kid you not on this aspiration of mine. I wanted to be a pro athlete. To be utterly specific, I wanted to play shortstop for the Chicago Cubs, and if fate were to have it, I would share the field with my all-time favorite player, Andre "the Hawk" Dawson. This was an actual dream of mine.

Unfortunately, that dream never did come true. As did so many others I had when I was a kid, but this one was most meaningful to me. My passion for good sport and competition was expounded through the love I coveted in baseball. When the professional season started, I'd make it a point to memorize player stats as presented in the Sunday morning paper. There was even a time when the only book I'd rent from the library was "Cooperstown", a compilation which catalogued the histories of every player in the Hall of Fame. Each individual's career stats and totals were laid out by the years in which they played. You could view the accumulated accomplishments of a fabled athlete like Babe Ruth on a page or two, reliving the legend that was the Yankee slugger of yesteryear. Like the Sunday morning paper, I made good on memorizing the stats of the game's greats too.

I was obsessed to a degree but my fixation never strayed from baseball lore. I couldn't always remember the complete Pythagorean theorem but I darn well could tell you what year Henry Aaron broke the record for all-time homeruns (it was 1974, by the way and I didn't even Google that one as I typed this). My love for the game went beyond the stats and the pure competitive nature though. I was good at baseball; pretty darn good.

It's easy to love something when you excel at it, but I felt like baseball made me *great*. People respected me for my skill and were quick to congratulate me when I succeeded. I dominated t-ball leagues regularly and as I grew, I became a leader on my all-star teams all the way onto high school. I was the only freshman in my class to start at the varsity level and what's more, I was a shortstop; the one position most coveted by the standouts of every respective school in the area. In the summers when school was over, I played for the best team in the Pennsylvania/Ohio area, the BB Rooners, who in consecutive years won more than 60 games while only playing about 70. And when I got to college, I continued a moderate success that tested me against other athletes at the collegiate level. I earned three letters for my exploits post-high school and though I could no longer play for my traveling squad, the Rooners, I still managed to participate on local teams in the OH area; still playing shortstop, still batting near the top of the order, and still being looked to for leadership on the baseball diamond.

And then, as if I had been crippled by a debilitating injury, I was graduated from college and the journey that was my baseball adventure stopped altogether.

For the first time in my whole life, I endured an entire summer devoid of throwing baseballs, running bases, and enjoying the company of at least eight others who felt the same as I did for the game. This was probably the saddest summer of my newly made adult life. Not because I didn't have a girlfriend or that I was living alone, but for the simple fact that my life was without something that I loved so dearly. What made my situation worse was the promise I didn't hold true to myself. The promise I'd made as a young boy to my adult self: to be a professional athlete. I was 23, living in a city I was unfamiliar with, working at a job I wasn't confident in, praying for a nice woman to meet and yet all those things paled in comparison to the black hole left in my personal universe.

If I could have gone back in time and seen myself at the tender age of seven, back when this dream of being a professional athlete started, I don't know what I would say. Would I tell him that his dream would never come true? Or would I encourage him to keep playing, keep his chin up, and always remember that your journey is just as important as your destination? To be honest, I still don't know what I'd tell myself if I could take that time machine backwards. I know where my mind and heart were at that time in my life so any shred of doubt from my future self would arguably destroy my fragile little hopes. So I wouldn't want to go that route, I figure. No, that just wouldn't be right.

For one, my parents were my biggest supporters and fans throughout those years. I loved how they'd come to every game, regardless of the location, and cheer me on to another great performance. My mother had little to no knowledge of the game, but after years of watching me play, she became as versed in the game as the late Cubs sportscaster Harry Caray. And to be brutally truthful, it took more than a few years for her skills to develop. The difference between quarters and innings was a real hurdle for us, but we managed to get through that one with a little patience and practice. My dad, on the other hand, was a former player himself and loved the game as much as I did. He and I had similar aspirations to play professionally so my father and I connected on this most basic level once he saw that I took an interest in the game. My father and I never really got comfortable with each other until I got older, but that relationship started on the baseball diamond. We'd play catch, he'd show me how to throw harder, and when I was old enough, he built me a personal pitcher's mound so I could practice even when I wasn't at the field. Unlike some other kids, I actually used that pitcher's mound when I was able so for that, I am grateful. Thanks, Dad. It sure didn't go to waste.

Secondly, baseball gave me a sense of belonging. A feeling of purpose and direction which helped define who I was. I said I was good at baseball and when you're good at something, people tend to take notice. They look to you as a credible source for succeeding and enjoy watching you when you're at your best because no one else seems to do it quite like you. My teammates depended on me and in turn, I depended upon them. No man is an island, eh? Whoever I played for, I earned my stripes and was soon a member of the clan having proved my talents.

Thirdly, baseball had brought me respect. I belonged to the teams I played for, but that community extended beyond just the guys in the dugout. It penetrated the lives of others who watched me compete. Even complete strangers would approach me after a game to say, "Hey, you're really good. I love watching you play, man." It may be my pride talking, but a singular gesture of praise is powerful enough to lay the foundation for a tower of positive self-respect and self-esteem.

In my younger days, I had not recognized any of these things at work, at least not consciously, but now that I was older, I could feel all the emotions rushing to the forefront of my mind. I could feel the connection I had with my parents changing; I could feel a lack of community around me; and for a short time, I could feel my worth diminishing for not having a ball, glove, or 32-inch bat in my hands. What an odd time that was for me. When my summer was over, I decided to never go through that again (at least for another short while). I went on the internet and searched for local ball teams that would take a 20something player, willing to pay for a jersey and umpires, which might meet my expectations. Within a few weeks I met a coach (we'll call him Rick) who had such a team. I was surprised to find so many other guys, like me, still playing baseball in the summer. This wasn't t-ball or youth league either; this was wooden bats with umpires and actual baseball fields to play upon. We're humbly referred to as the "weekend jocks", men who have jobs but still long for some competitive sport on the weekends. But not just any sport, we're talking about baseball here. Not softball, not beer-drinker's volleyball . . . *real* baseball (or about as real as one can get at our age).

And yeah, I've been playing with those guys ever since.

Some of them are married, have kids and a mortgage but the spirit is still willing. So every Sunday, for about three to four months, creaky bodies get pulled to the ball field as if it were a scene from Field of Dreams (minus the theatrics). And old knees, rickety arms, and careful eyes come alive again as if we were all kids once more. Granted, not every one of us can make every game, but we manage as well as we humanly can. Ironically, the issue of "Dad can't get a ride to the ballpark" doesn't really hold weight anymore so other excuses abound. "I have a wedding"; "In-laws are in town"; or "I have to be home with my kids. I haven't seen them all week."

The last one I deem to be the most acceptable. People get married every day and in-laws will always be around, but having the opportunity to play with your kids? Yeah, you should probably take advantage of that as much as possible.

I know that I won't be playing forever, but I'll take a few more summers of good, hard-nosed baseball if I can manage. Since I'm a single guy, I certainly have no excuse *not* to make it to a game or two so until a priority shift takes place; I'll be eagerly headed to the ballpark. I'd be lying though if I didn't mention my incredibly awesome habit of showing up 15 minutes before game time. Rolling in just moments after the rest of my team has warmed up has earned me the moniker of "The Franchise"—a name born out of this idea that I do not require adequate preparation. I will admit that I've always been in relatively good health (knock on wood) so to spend 45 minutes of stretching and throwing would only be a waste of time, I figure. That's just not my style anyway. Additionally, I do enjoy a good church service on Sunday morning if I can get there. Baseball is a real passion of mine, but one has to give props to the Big Guy first since he made everything possible after all.

Speaking of which, the ones who made me possible—my parents—will still find time to watch their son play. Some 20 years later and my biggest fans are still plopping their lawn chairs down next to the dugout or bleachers to observe a game. My team had turned out to be a good collection of characters as well; a true rarity with adult sports. Very seldom do you find a decent group to spend your Sunday afternoons with. And so, all this activity was giving me my self-respect back. My hiatus from the game was short-lived; a fact I was more than content to live with. It was this simple act of putting on some cleats and hitting a ball around that brought me back to a time when I was ever optimistic as a youngster.

I remember taking a plastic whiffle ball bat, walking out into our driveway, picking up a few small rocks, and then crushing each and every one of those rocks into the sunset like I was Andre Dawson. I'd call out the score before every hit as I'd scream aloud the situation at hand. Bottom of the ninth, two outs, two runners on and the best pitcher in the pros staring me down from 60 feet and six inches away. And you can't have a big moment like this without a record about to be shattered either. No, that just won't do. A homerun here would assure my spot in the annals of Cooperstown and baseball immortality for sure. So I'd comb the ground for the perfect round rock in order to achieve maximum distance. When I had found one to my liking, I'd take my bat; toss the rock in the air, and smash that little pebble as far as any six-year old could. The imaginary crowd would go wild and I'd take my pretend lap around the pretend bases for my final curtain call.

Life was sure sweet back then and my dreams were even sweeter.

So I guess I wouldn't tell my younger self to do anything differently. Even if I were standing there, face-to-face with the smaller, mini version of myself, I wouldn't want to change a thing. Instead, I'd encourage him to just keep playing, keep dreaming, and keep looking for those rocks on the pavement's edge. They may be small, but with every hit, he'll be better prepared for what life has in store for him later. And that's something his adult self (aka me) will appreciate once he gets there.

A quick list of epiphanies . . .

. . . or the "idiot's guide to living alone."

If it still smells good . . . then you can eat it.

If it doesn't, then please throw it away. My stomach can handle just about anything. Old salami, stale bread, even a box of Cheez-Its that have made it through three relocations (yet were never been opened) . . . you name it, I could probably engulf it with minimal side effects. But I will warn thee—do not, under any circumstances, think that your stomach can handle spoiled milk. Dairy is public enemy #1 of things-to-not-eat-when-past-expiration. So no, no, and no. I'd sooner partake in a cage fight than be force fed spoiled milk. A broken nose or a busted jaw pales in comparison to the backlash of curdled milk consumption. Bruises will heal and bones will mend, but the scars within the lining of one's stomach will last forever.

People who tell you that you need a roommate . . .
clearly have no confidence in you living alone.

This is an unfortunate one, but true all the same. It's the politically correct way to tell someone you care about the errors of their thinking to live on their lonesome. Reasons for this could range from untidiness, foul cleanliness, or just irrational spending. Maybe it's a relative that's watched you grow up and *knows* the dangers that living alone can produce for you. It could be anything but depending on how it's presented, the subliminal message of "find a roomie" gets planted in your head like a newly birthed seed. And that seed will grow into a beanstalk, tearing through your dreams while you sleep as you muddle over the true meaning behind the advice that's been given. And more than likely, you'll be sleeping all by yourself (which isn't a bad thing either).

Take advantage of second floor living . . . you'll get the excess heat in winter from the bottom floors.

This is a great thing I learned while living in my first apartment. You see, there's a scientific marvel that takes place when you live on the second floor of any building. And that marvel is known as *heat*. Heat is an amazing thing in the winter. It just so happens that hot air rises, and as it rises, the hot air does a good job of keeping you warm. All because the guy or gal below you was just trying to keep themselves warm instead. You may never actually meet your bottom floor buddy, but they are your friend nonetheless. And here you didn't even have to bake them brownies. You're just living off their heat like a leech sucking blood out of its host. Ah, what a great feeling. Relish in it, my second floor friends. Relish.

When moving locations, the amount of "free" food you provide . . . is proportionate to the amount of "free" help you get.

It's no secret that I've relocated plenty of times. Each move became a more arduous task than the last. The first one entailed the use of my parents' vehicles; the second involved a friend's truck; and by the time I got to the latest move, I needed a conversion van, three cars, and a loading dock. You tend to accumulate a ton of crap when you live alone (which still boggles my mind) but since you can't move everything on your own, you need some "hired help". The only problem is, nobody works for free these days so you have to come up with ways to acquire certain aid.

In my experience, I've discovered that a large cheese pizza with pop is equal to 2.5 college students. This equation changes if you add a six pack of beer though. In which case, the result is now equal to three adult males. Add the pizza and you have the makings of a basketball team (with one really tall guy to cover the extra .5).

I will caution on one thing though: don't always think that three adult males are greater than 2.5 college students. In fact, college students will work for less, do not bark back when given orders, and there's a good chance their endurance levels are higher. You're probably better off trying to get college students in that case. They're beyond critical thinking, semi-efficient when given proper direction, and easily bought with a few pizzas; the future of America at its finest.

Always try to get a place that has a pool . . . for these are better hangouts to meet people than any other (sorta).

This one is obvious. If you're trying to meet new people, why not just try the most readily accessible place of commerce? The complex you live in, of course. It's the perfect scenario. You're both wet, nearly half naked, so what do you have to hide? Nothing, really. It'd be no different if you were sitting around in your pajamas or underwear if you think about it. So strike up a conversation and see where it leads you. You'd be surprised what you find out about the people you live near (for good or for bad).

HOWEVER (warning, spoiler alert! coming), I will forewarn that the public pool can also be quite the opposite of what I described. I've been out catching that all important summer tan when the underbelly of American society rears its ugly head. True, these people may be "pool crashers" but more than likely, they live close to where you live. And it's worse if they bring children because let's be real here—the fact that they're breeding is even more disturbing.

And if you can . . . try to get a place with a fireplace too.

The fireplace is a highly underrated bonus at any apartment. It sits idly year round, waiting for that moment where you decide to open'er up and strike a match. I'm not a pyro by any means, but I love a good fire. There's a certain something about making a fire that gets my blood boiling. Plus it's a fun thing to do when you're bored. Just don't be breaking out the bear or leopard-skin rugs. Nothing says "I love living alone" like an overly done fireplace. Keep it simple, my single friends. Just keep it simple.

Showers are always optional . . . but only if you intend to spend the night alone.

I'm a clean person by nature. I don't appreciate feeling like there's a layer of filth on my skin thick enough to repel bee stings. I like to shower daily and if you're a human being, then you should really be doing the same if at all possible. But there are those times when you're single; when you're not doing much; when you're probably going to huff it alone, that showering before bed can become optional. Even if you've spent the evening bobbing for apples in beer, playing mud volleyball, or painting "Strangers Always Welcome" on your friend's new front door (which is fun), you can still roll into bed without any accountability for your overall hygiene. Nice.

Matching furniture is not required . . . but dinnerware is.

I bought the majority of my furniture at garage sales. I wasn't looking around Target, Wal-Mart, or even Levin Furniture when I got my first set of items to sit my rump upon. In fact, the first love seat I ever owned came from a buddy of mine who just wanted to get rid of the darned thing. Then I acquired a coffee table before it was punished by a wood chipper. I even transformed Rubbermaid storage cabinets into dresser drawers. Each of these items made their way into my living room at least once and for that, I'm not super proud. But when you live alone or are single, it's not that big a deal. You're only shopping for your own comfort, not for the collective agreement of two persons. However, it's very important—and I stress this—to have matching dinner plates. Guys, ladies like a guy who has his act together in the kitchen. You don't have to be some stellar cook from World's Top Chef, but you should at least have the know-how to get blue dinner plates along with blue cereal bowls. Not that hard is it? That way you can show you are color coordinated and you're also not color blind. That's good enough for a point or two in her book.

What's in a name . . . if you've heard it twice.

This one may be out of left field, but let me explain. What I'm referring to are the names of those you date. Rita, Virginia, Stella—these are the names of people you dated (and hopefully did so as righteously as possible). You liked her, she liked you; you worked together; you bumped into her while you were out and about; whatever your reason, you thought it would be nice to start dating. So what's the worst part after you break up? Well, running into another Rita, Virginia or heaven forbid, Stella. Dating women back-to-back with the same first name is like downing 2 dozen wings, turning around, and trying to do it again. Personally, I'd try to eat the second plate of wings, but I am fully aware that not all people share in my wing fixation. So here's some truth: you liked that food the first time, but when you look at that second plate, you're painfully reminded of how you felt nauseous once you were done eating. So why go through that again? And so soon. Instead, give yourself a break in between, reload, and then head back for round two. Hopefully by then "Stella" will no longer hold the same stigma she once had and you'll be more than ready to give Stella 2.0 a real shot.

If you tell your married friends you have too much going on . . . they know you're lying.

This one's a given. When you're single, the only time you're busy is when you're working or you're actively dating someone new. Those are the only times you're not doing much. Yeah, you may be volunteering time in town or hanging with some friends, but if you wanted to, you could leave at a moment's notice. The reason being that you're single and you have no one else to answer to but yourself. That's why when a family member calls and asks for you to stop by in a couple hours, the excuse of "I'm busy" just doesn't really fly. So why not be stand up and just say "I don't want to come over today." That's not impossible, is it? To some people it may be but you'd be surprised the type of respect you get from others for your honesty. Sure, there's probability for a lack of invites in the future, but hey, you have to take the good with the bad, people.

Learning a second language in your spare time . . . doesn't make you cooler.

When I was in high school, I took four years of German. My heritage is Anglo-Saxon, Eastern European and my grandmother grew up *and* lived in Germany. You might say I have some strong roots to the people of Deutschland. I've always wanted to visit there and I've always wanted to learn the language. That way, when the time arrived for me to visit, I could carry on conversations as though I were from the area. The only trouble with this is finding the time to learn said language. Being single will give you the time you desire. Rather than work or some other extracurricular, you have a chance to make time for this venture. And with audiobooks all the rage these days, you can pop one in during a drive in the car and before you know it, you're learning how to say "I hate my job" in the language of your choosing. Sounds easy and simple, but the reality is that it takes tons of time, commitment and a wallet willing to be emptied on countless Rosetta stone tapes to make it happen. Ultimately, who needs to be versed in German these days? Even the Germans are learning how to speak other languages. But hey, if you want to sit around with your friends speaking in foreign tongues, then be my guest. With the way things are going, Mandarin would probably be a better choice anyhow, but I'll leave you with this—habe ich nur sie suchen was dies be deutete, nicht?

People that tell you to travel . . . don't travel enough themselves.

This one is a no-brainer. The ones who tell you to travel are most often the ones who wished they had the time to do so. What these non-vacationers don't realize is that they can travel whenever they want, but instead, they come up with a plethora of reasons as to why they cannot. Finances, kids are home, we just took a vacation a year ago, etc . . . . the list goes on. Therefore, they want YOU to take these vacations for them. You're single, you're not "tied down" and you obviously have money to blow on a vacation.

. . . by yourself . . .

Yeah, that's the crazy part. These people who tell you that you need a vacation are the same folks who want you to adventure on your own. Go to Africa, be in Europe, traverse the wild outback of Montana (a scary thought); these people say you ought to do these things because it's "that time in your life." Apparently once you're married or with someone special, you can't travel anymore. Well, I'm here to tell you that's a load of bull. Travel when you want; travel when you have the money; and travel even if you don't have the money (for a while) because if the heart is willing and you desire the trip, then go for it. Then once you return from your said vacation, you can tell all of your stay-at-home friends that you had such a terrible time and they should just save their money. Yes, a little reverse psychology may get them moving and out of the house and stop their need to live vicariously through you.

Theory: Chicks dig the jerks . . .

. . . and I finally know why.

I couldn't wait to write about this. I really couldn't. It's a topic that has been boiling up inside of me like a bomb about to explode and now, I've finally reached critical mass. The debate is as old as time itself. Ever since Eve first tempted Adam in the Garden, men (and women) have always wondered why girls prefer the "bad boy" over the "good boy"; and in some instances, why "nice guys" prefer "bad girls." Since I'm one of those nice guys, I have often found myself in the dreaded place known only as the Friend Zone. It's a familiar moniker that has run rampant through popular dating magazines and silently crept into real-life application. And in all fairness, the Friend Zone does exist. But why does it exist? And why do women prefer a self-centered douche bag over a good man? Well, walk with me a while.

First off, the Friend Zone is a terrifying and alienating place for any love struck guy. It's the one arena no man wants to be in when he's making a move on a woman he cares about, but because he's such a "nice" guy, he rarely ever acts like he should. And by acts like he should, I mean he never truly *acts* the part. You know what I'm speaking about; the qualities that women find attractive in men. Confident, ambitious, witty, and most of all, packing a little cash in the pocket . . . but wait a minute, aren't these the qualities of the "nice guy"? And aren't all those dillholes out there the complete *opposite* of what I just described? Yes, they are, but for whatever the reason (and I promise it's coming soon), women gravitate towards the only asshole in the room that talks. Well, ladies and gents, I will wait no longer. Here is the cold, hard truth as to why so many decent girls just can't get enough of the pricks, jerks, and downright douchers that exist out there.

To help me explain, I'll lead in with a scenario. Pretend you are out with friends and that one special lady shows up (gals, just play along or pretend you're the female in this example). You want to impress her somehow so when she arrives you, the nice guy, will approach her and start a conversation. You'll think of something witty, something charming, to get her attention. Ok, got it. Maybe get her a drink? If you're not at a bar, then maybe some orange juice will do. Chicks dig orange juice. Trust me. But if the drink/juice trick doesn't work, then it's off to the races on just trying to break the ice. You don't want to come off being desperate, but you don't want to be too hard-to-get either. You really just want her attention and somehow keep that attention for as long as you can so she knows you're interested. Not exactly an easy task, if I do say so. And because of that task, you may get your panties in a wad (and a tight one too) so don't screw this up. This is your moment to make an impression.

So now the moment has finally come and you go to make your move. You stick to saying something witty first. You know, something like "Did you see that grass out there? Talk about green, eh?" . . . . ok, no. Scratch that comment. That's just lame and not witty. Maybe a cheesy pick up line then? "How much does a polar bear weigh?" Oh God, no. That may work in some circumstances but not right away. What about something overly sexual then? Something like "Hey, I think you're hot." No, that's probably not a great opener unless you're really drunk. Or she is really drunk. And at that point, you probably aren't trying to make a lasting impression anyway . . . .

So all things considered, you walk over and decide that the best thing to say is ultimately, "Hi." And guys, that's all it should be really. Otherwise you put yourself at risk for being known as the "bad polar bear joke guy." And let's face it, that's just as bad as being in the Friend Zone.

Nevertheless, you go for the kill. You walk over, you state your mind, and THEN, out of nowhere, in swoops Johnny Jackass. Johnny's the one guy that nobody wanted to invite because he's such a tool. And by tool, I mean a complete jerk. He's always loud, obnoxious, and thinks that he's the center of the universe. He likely sports a fake tan and believes that it's always sunny in his world so he wears sunglasses in the dead of winter. He's also fond of sharing his bowel movements with the rest of the crowd. "Hey, I just took the biggest dump! I've been having the squirts since lunch. Don't know what I ate, but damn!"

Yeah, I suppose he's what you'd call oh, I don't know, a *douche*? But anyway, here he comes. He sweeps by, steals the conversation, gets the laugh that *you* wanted from her, and then he's off to the next group of people to perform a similar douche drive-by. Major buzzkill if you're that "nice guy" that was waiting around for the opportune time to speak.

But there you have it. The girl you wanted to talk to; the one that you have such strong feelings for and have been waiting to make this moment happen with has suddenly shifted her gaze to Johnny Jackass. Despite the fact that he called you a name, pushed two people out of the way to get to her, and yelled some obnoxious obscenity in another person's direction, he's still being sought after by your girl. So wait, back up. How in the world did this happen? And better yet, how does this continually happen? You're left speechless for one and you'll likely spend the next few hours analyzing Johnny Jackass' movements to find out what his secret is.

Here's some knowledge for you though: there's no secret to Johnny's success. He's just being an immature donkey turd. And that's far easier to be than a nice person, or even a gentleman for that matter. I've tried to be the Johnny Jackass myself. I really did give that identity a try (ask some of my exes . . . but on second thought, *don't*). This role never suited me though, but I tried anyway. I'd be overtly loud, talk a big game, and wear designer apparel that sported skulls and weirdly-shaped crosses. After about a week, I stopped doing this. In the end, I resolved to try another tactic: I figured that in order to conquer my foes in the dating market, I had to get inside these guys' heads. See how all those Johnny's operated, you know? See how they moved; mimic their behavior; and ultimately see what drove their apparent success.

To be honest, the answer came quicker than I imagined: these smooth talkers and ignorant fools got away with their antics because they were *physically attractive.*

Yeah, that's all. Isn't that sad? Our perception is to first judge the exterior without any consideration of the interior. We, as human beings, tend to act more nicely to those we deem to be 'good-looking.' We also accept the opinions and views of attractive people as the standard for what's right and what's wrong. How else do you explain the influence of Hollywood's biggest stars? An apparently normal person can be transformed into a Johnny if he has above average looks. You must hear me on this—it is the truth. For example:

If I know deep down in my gut that the person across from me thinks I'm good-looking, then I *know* I can bypass certain niceties to get what I want. That translates as "not having to be nice", "not having to wait my turn", and finally, "not being receptive to other's needs or wants". *I'm* the good-looking one here so people should respect me for that. That's the thinking of a Johnny Jackass. The same can be said for women, too (Bitchy Betty's, if you will). And if a Johnny or a Betty can pick up the scent of an admirer in their midst, then they already know that they have the upper hand in that relationship. Even if both parties don't recognize it consciously, this phenomenon will still come to fruition if the relationship takes hold.

See how that works?

Would it be correct to state then that we are most impressed with those who are beautiful *and* act beautifully too? Yeah, you may have good genes but do you do anything that's worth being excited about other than your *looks*? With plastic surgery being as advanced as it is (just ask our friends in Hollywood), anybody can get new cheek bones, fuller lips, and a nicer rump. Those attributes can be acquired quickly but a persona that exudes good nature and positive strength is not so easily come by. That's a major turn on for this guy. An indomitable character is both precious and rare. Ladies, you are all gems—carefully molded, carefully shaped, and carefully formed; you are not artificial creations.

But that's not all, my friends. There's another big reason for Johnny's chosen lifestyle.

In addition to having a potentially physical advantage, there is another not-so-apparent tool that Johnny employs. But first, do me a favor and don't listen to all those foolish MSN, Yahoo, or Google beat writers who think they know something about dating. I've been in the trenches and can tell you how it truly is. And how it is, is this: women like jerks because a jerk makes her feel special and she feels special because that's what our culture tells her is *special* and if that weren't enough, all you 'nice guys' just don't have the fortitude to market yourselves properly. You see, nice guys are nice to *everyone*. They don't sell themselves as the cream of the crop; nor do they exude what it means to be a *great* man. No singular male stands out to be different than the others—he's merely just *there*. Good guys should be sounding their horns from the mountaintops; not cowering in the shadows. The shade that's cast by one immature guy is not enough to cover a decent guy in a crowd—it takes the combined efforts of many to hide away those worth finding, but this is the great debacle. Why are these good guys hiding at all?

One of the problems is that nice guys may be 'nice', but they have no idea how to treat a woman if they dated one. These guys understand certain truths like opening doors, respecting space, and refraining from drama, but what else? There are certainly a number of qualities that these girls are looking for—so what to do? Possessing head knowledge is only one piece of the pie; eventually you need to have experience on the matter, don't you? So rather than putting themselves out there for someone they care about, they sit back and watch the more "experienced" guys have a go at dating. This, of course, is foolish and I blame any decent guy for sitting on the sidelines too long.

Can you imagine what it would be like if every young man—about to hit the dating scene—were equipped with the skills necessary to really woo a lady? And I don't mean "woo", as in getting her into bed—I mean knocking her socks off like a real man should. Being supportive, having direction, possessing authority yet is being tender—what if the halfway decent guys out there suddenly hit the market aggressively with these character goals in mind? That concept probably sounds a little outrageous; especially to someone whose been wronged so many times (male or female) or who views a relationship as purely recreational. It'd be chaotic, would it not? Could the female population even handle it? What would become of the Johnny's out there? Natural selection tells us they would either die out or have to adapt to their environment, thereby becoming more like their competition.

The core issues are environmentally driven. When in groups, we tend to see things through a different lens than if we were one-on-one. Cockiness is misinterpreted as confidence. Being overly abrasive is displaced with taking action and the entire courtship process is seen as a clever cat and mouse game where the cat always walks away unscathed; the mouse wondering what just happened. This can go both ways, I'm aware of that, but I'd prefer to call out my fellow brothers-in-arms on this one. We want to be manly men, don't we? So why not play the part?

You see, every woman wants to feel special to you (the 'you' being men). Inside her heart is a beauty she wishes to unveil to a worthy candidate. So when you (the man) talk to your friends, you rave about how amazing she is. She's not a trophy or even your property, but she is still *yours* to show off and be excited about. But hey, if you rant and rave too much, your once cutesy compliments become relatively unattractive. How does that happen? There is a balance here, my fellow men. Be sure to make note of that. She longs to be your equal, not the idol you ogle over like some trophy on the wall. And at the end of the day, she wants someone who is going to make her feel *secure*. Do not confuse this with overbearing behavior. That's just as bad as misguided worship. Instead, use the assurance of good words to make her feel at ease—communication is vital. A man's tongue is best used when giving good wishes so use it for those reasons. That's for ladies too. Then you can use that tongue of yours in other manners you see fit (and yes, that was meant to be not so subtle).

So this is all well and good but what about some real-life situations? What if you're in a room full of other "nice" guys, trying to impress a lady and yet, she chooses the one who has the most destructive behavior? Is it because you're nice to every other woman? Would she rather have a man that isn't likely to be "nice" to other ladies, thus giving them the impression that you're overly desirable? I've stayed up speaking with guys and gals alike on who is the more jealous of the two genders.

In truth, both sexes have their moments. If you ask a female, she'll tell you that women are more jealous. They're catty, full of gossip, and enjoy the reactions they receive from a man they are trying to work over for a response. If you ask a male, he may tell you that men are the more jealous creatures. They'll buy things for a potential mate, want to physically fight another guy just to prove a point, and even stalk a girl until she finally succumbs to his courtship. Yeah, it's all about the chase and the challenge, for both sexes. But if you're a jerk, and you're not a regularly nice person to everyone else, do the chances of being with somebody suddenly *increase* because you treat one person more nicely than the others?

Funny world we live in, eh?

Let's take a moment to digest all of this. When you take a step back, doesn't it make sense? I mean, every girl I've ever known (who complained about that one "jerk") had some of the same underlying things to say about him. For example:

"He is such a dick. I can't believe what he did."
"Why can't he grow up? We were always fighting."
Or . . . .
"I don't know what I saw in him. He broke all his *promises*."

The last quote sums up everything, I feel. You see, guys (all guys included), there's something you need to know about the above scenario. There are some crucial parts being left that you must fill in the blanks for. You see, the one-time Prince Charming did something he shouldn't have—break a *promise*. I have found that women need reassurance verbally as much as they do physically, perhaps even more so. And if someone is to make a promise to her, then they'd best keep that promise. Otherwise it's hell on Earth as we know it. Who wants that anyway? Certainly not this guy, that's for sure. The trouble is that guys will make these promises and never intend to keep them and thus, they are transformed into this jerk above all other jerks.

Judge a man by his actions, not his words, ladies. Nice guys tend to shy away from talking a big game. They may view big promises as being insurmountable so they keep their mouths shut. Meanwhile, the guy with the most to take and the least to give is hastily making his moves on the ladies. The horrible thing is that these good guys *should* be making big expectations. They *should* be ready to walk over to the girl of their choosing and say, "Hey, I think you're really special and I can make you happy" but no, they don't. They'd rather sit in a corner, hiding away as though somebody will eventually come and approach them. I know because I've employed this tactic myself and it's probably the dumbest thing a guy can do when he's attempting to date.

Well, aside from being a complete asshole, of course.

But all this talk still boils down to one simple fact: nice guys are just too darn, stinkin' nice. And that's just not cool in a girl's eyes. Men are supposed to be aggressive, dominant, and ready to take charge. Not submissive, needy, and indecisive. Primitive and pretty basic, but it's the absolute, damnable truth.

So here's the eternal conundrum—if we are judging people based on their interactions with others, shouldn't we perceive nice guys as the best in the bunch? The cream of the crop; the bee's knees; and so on and so forth. I mean, these guys aren't less confident or less attractive necessarily; they are just more adept at keeping their lives in relative order without the need for disruption. So once again, shouldn't that be a really attractive quality? I mean, come on ladies. If what you want is to feel secure in a relationship, then isn't the predictability of a good guy something worth being happy about? Ok, here's the dose of reality of again: it's not; and I could scream till I'm blue in the face to make that point but the number of attentive ears this knowledge would fall on is very little. Girls aren't looking for that comfortable stability necessarily. They're looking for safety and strength—so the insensitive one is the obvious choice.

Go figure, right?

But alas, there is a silver lining to this story. Time passes and eventually the immature Johnny Jackass begins to show his true colors. His lack of commitment, couth, and in many cases, values, begins to show and weighs on the woman greatly. She begins to wonder what it was that brought them together in the first place. She wonders why everyone else is telling her to move on and find somebody else. And most of all, though she may not totally realize it, she wonders why Nicely McNicerton is still talking to her despite the fact that she's with the other guy. It's an all-too familiar story and one that repeats itself over and over again.

I suppose the fact of the matter is this: people like what they like and the heart wants what the heart wants. You can't change someone for that simple fact. I've said before that it's much easier to change a person's mind, but it's an entirely different matter to change their heart, and this definitely holds true to just that. The more mature decision would be to desire a man's stable, responsible and reliable nature. These would be seen as datable qualities. When you're young though, it's more about the adventure and the challenge than actual settling. You've often been told to what is good for you, but a stubborn heart will chase the unattainable in a hope that the prize is greater than what was all ready promised.

And that leads us into the next part of this rant. I believe in the theory that nice-guys-are-nice-to-everyone, but there are some other key issues that come into play too. For one, girls like a challenge. She wants to be that girl that changes you from boy to man. However, if she can essentially walk all over you, then this is a sign to her that you don't have a lot of backbone and probably won't stick up for her in a pinch. McNicerton would rather employ a diplomatic solution. Women like guys with *power*. Power over others; power over groups; power over direction in life—are you getting the tingles, yet? That's where true confidence shines; not the fake imitations who parade around as though the world owes them something. I'm speaking of the I-wear-shirts-far-too-small-for-me and the I-gel-my-hair-so-often-that-it's-likely-to-fall-out-if-I'm-not-careful and who can forget the I'm-extremely-loud-and-obnoxious-because-I was-either-ignored-as-a-child-or-I just-love-to-be-the-center-of-attention guy. Yeah, those dudes are a real treat and easy to spot among the masses. However, they're not so easily discerned if you aren't aware as to what's happening around you.

When it comes to impressing the ladies, there's an element of fear that comes into play. The "nice guy" moniker is also mixed with a "fearful guy" mentality. A nice guy is less likely to put himself out there to someone for *fear* of rejection or *fear* of ruining the balance. Why you ask? Well, because the nice guy understands what it means to be nice to someone and actually care about what the other person thinks/feels. This downplays confidence and replaces it with fear and even some lighter forms of rationale. Women pick up on this, even without knowing it, and decide within a matter of seconds how much fear (or macho gusto) you're packing.

The same goes for either sex, really. Popular research points to the time frame being about seven seconds, but it's probably more like four to five. Seven is just far too generous in my eyes. In a matter of moments one sizes up the other physically and then depending on what you say next will eventually formulate a first impression. To quote an infamous and popular newscaster from Saturday Night Live—"It's science."

So does this make anyone feel better? I'm guessing probably not, but at least you have more knowledge on this never ending debate. People can say what they will, dating sites will tell you what's what, but take it from someone who has actually *lived* it. Experience speaks more volumes than speculation ever will; however, experience can also make us vulnerable to the harshest of circumstances. If you can accumulate some wisdom along the road of life, then you're ten times ahead of the guy next to you who is constantly asking himself, "What if I did that? And would that *really* happen to me?"

The answer is: yes, it *will* and guess what—it's going to be a bad experience.

I want to close this out by saying there is hope for all you "nice guys" out there. No, not that you will eventually get the girl you want; that's not in the cards for everyone. What we *want* and what we *need* don't necessarily coincide with one another. No, I leave you with the intellectual capital to combat these situations. Be honest with yourself, if a girl is continuously interested in "that guy she always complains about", then you're better off walking away entirely. The same can be applied to any person you're trying to gain favor with. If she's busy complaining about him to you, then she'll probably turn around and do the same about you someday. No attention-loving, games-playing, silver-spoon-fed, spoiled Jersey Shore brat is worth a good guy's time. Unless she's super hot, of course. Then you might be able to make an exception. Just for a little while though; then I suggest getting out of there as fast as you possibly can. In fact, forget what I said about her just needing to be really hot. Do yourself a service and walk away entirely.

I'm sure I'll experience more douch drive-by's before it's all said and done, but that's not a problem I can't manage.

Remember what I said: be sure to assert yourself when the time arises. Market yourself, but do it in the *right* way. It's a sign of strength that will eventually grow into a newfound respect for both you and that lovely lady you're trying to impress. And be sure to use big words too. Johnny's aren't particularly good with big words. Like a well-documented essay on complex social struggles for stereotypically unassertive men, big words will make those guys wonder what just hit them.

Downright Good Thought: Dating . . .

. . . I'd rather have a mating season (sorta, but not really).

Well, here we are. The dating chapter of this book; I am fully aware that you have probably been waiting anxiously for this section. What secrets do I have? What terrible stories do I possess? Well, to be honest, my intent here is not to spread incriminating tales about people I've dated or encountered. That just wouldn't be right. However, I do recognize the need to reference certain turning points in a person's life that can be used as wisdom for others. To paraphrase, I would hope that you don't make some of the same mistakes I did, but that you would also find encouragement in areas where I recognized opportunities for personal growth.

With that, I wanted to start off with a nice quote I stumbled upon:

"A comfortable old age is the reward of a well-spent youth. Instead of it bringing sad and melancholy prospects of decay, it would give us hopes of eternal youth in a better world."—Maurice Chevalier

Have you ever committed an act or participated in an activity that later gave you the feeling that your very life had been sucked out of you? If you have, then you are already a witness to what it feels like to be in a poor romantic relationship. When I went searching for a good quote to help describe this chapter, I wanted a quote that revolved around a prize. I chose reward because this is what we believe will happen for us if we embark on a romantic undertaking: we are setting ourselves up to receive something of great value. What the nature of that reward is may be indescribable to the one who is seeking, but we seek nonetheless.

Ms. Chevalier's quote rings that if we are wise in our youth, then we will have an enjoyable retirement. In other words, if we don't make a ton of mistakes then we can reflect on a life that was filled with joy rather than heartache.

So what does that mean to the person who continuously finds himself in bad relationships? More specifically, those of the dating realm? This can be a matter of perspective depending on the person. Did I learn from first-time offenses? Or did I keep heading down the same path despite all the warning signs? It's imperative to ask these questions of yourself. Otherwise you may begin to wish there were such thing as a mating season for human beings.

Why do we pursue if we have no semblance of what the pursuit will ultimately result in? I feel this is how the dating scene presents itself to the wayward traveler. There is a golden nugget, dangling at the end of a rope, positioned somewhere off in the distance. We see the nugget and we crave to touch it. Our eyes become so fixated on retrieving the prize that we neglect our surroundings in the process. We forget that the trail ahead may be littered with thorn bushes, hidden dirt holes, or big, steaming piles of crap that if trudged through, will leave us dirtied and disgusted by the time we make it to that golden treasure (if we ever do).

I never wanted that person to be me; that person who followed the golden nugget but refused to remove the blinders. I stayed away from dating for as long as I could. I tore up notes that got passed to me in elementary school; I rejected offers to attend junior high dances; I avoided parties with girls who I knew liked me; I even pretended to be asexual once just so a girl would stop calling me at home.

All right, so that last one isn't true but I did some rather desperate things in my youth. And it was done with the intent to not hurt my heart for as long as I possibly could. Like any other person who fills their head with delusions of grandeur, I tripped up along the way. I made mistakes with the opposite sex and I paid the price; a price that isn't counted in mere dollars or cents, but is tallied by the intangible scars of poorly chosen partners and misguided infatuations. The only person responsible for these miscues and mistakes was *me*. Yes, I had my fair share of moments where someone openly wronged me, but by making myself vulnerable, I left myself unguarded to all the letdowns associated with bad breakups. What I had only heard about, soon became what I actually experienced.

So let's flash forward to the present day, aka adulthood. My past has some baggage now, there's a laundry list of bad choices, and a few poorly imagined expectations here and there. I'm not broken to the point of complete disinterest in dating. I'm just . . . how do I say this . . . *disappointed*. Disappointed that I'd let myself get to that extreme. I never wanted to be that sap that put his heart out there for anyone to just come by and snatch me up. However, this wasn't quite how it all turned out. The mating season sounded like a better alternative. If I were a logical procreator, then I'd be solely looking for a woman to bear me strong offspring. I'd assess every female according to her birthing hips, genetically diverse background, and relative intelligence level. That sounds pretty good, does it not? The catch with that type of thinking is that it ignores the most fundamental of human conditions: *love*.

I understand that this revelation may come off as sounding sentimental or even strange, but the quest for unconditional love is a powerful force embedded in the very fabric of every human being. If it were not for love, we'd probably have a mating season. We'd meet as a group, probably every couple weeks, maybe more; then we'd duke it out till we had our fill of mating. To some, that may sound enjoyable. Why mess around with feelings anyway? These emotions only get in the way of our true purpose in life—making more of us. But imagine being the odd person out at the mating sanctuary. What would that be like? Wouldn't you feel *alone*? And there you have it; you're on the lookout for something more in your life. You desire something greater than just physical contact—you want someone that digs at you under the surface, who surprises you with challenges you could never foresee, but enjoy and who gives you companionship beyond the realm of a handshake or hug. For me, that something else is a supermodel with a master's degree in volunteer work that has no prior boyfriends which presently stalk her. I know you're out there, my dear; I'm sure you are.

Ok, yes, that sounds really unrealistic and I don't want to sound bitter or anything. We all have certain expectations as it applies to dating. We set standards for ourselves; whether they are conscious or unconscious, and we do our best to meet those requirements with each potential candidate. This is all in an effort to be loved by someone.

The pursuit itself can seem rigorous and demanding. You just can't go out with one more has-been or coulda/woulda for fear that your heart may explode. So, if you're like me, you may decide to take a break from dating because hey, you deserve one. And even if you aren't taking a break, you're definitely telling other people you are. Kind of like this:

"Yeah, I'm giving up on women (or men) for now. I just need to focus on *myself.*"

I believe that's just code for Gee-I'm-so-tired-of-trying-so-hard-I-think-I-may-cry-myself-to-sleep-tonight. It's ok though; most of us have been there. Not me, of course (totally kidding . . . .). So this is your plan? You're going to re-focus on *yourself.* Isn't that what you were doing before anyway? Last I checked, if you are single, you have no responsibilities other than you so isn't it all about *you* to begin with? Yeah, I thought so. I have also thought this but I find we do this because we don't want anyone else to see our weak times exposed. We'd rather run and hide behind the usual cop outs.

111

"I'm just too busy with work."
"I can't get into anything serious right now."
"I don't have the time to be in a relationship with anyone."
"I'm just not looking for anything right now."

These explanations are all well and good, but each one masks an obvious truth: that if someone came along that could really "rock your socks", you'd give up your days of being single in a heartbeat. Case in point—a friend of mine (Larry we'll call him) was a real chronic dater when I first met him. He bragged about his sexual conquests frequently and reveled in the reactions he received from those who heard his tales. Typically, I'm not a huge fan of the "hey-I'm-just-looking-to-get-laid-this-evening" type of guy. They're about as cookie cutter as they come. Take me to any bar in town and my D-Bag Radar will blip quite regularly without fail. Therefore, I don't really make it a point to keep this kind of company, but Larry's stories had an underlying message: he was *lost*; much like me.

Larry was completely open about his personal life. He didn't hide anything than wasn't worth telling. He was totally honest about his shortcomings in relationships (and there were many) but this didn't seem to bother him. He did what he wanted and didn't let anyone tell him otherwise. I suppose that's respectable, right? Well, not exactly, but I had officially found the antithesis of who I thought I was at the time. And whenever two opposite people meet, they tend to hang out together rather than repel. Why? I've pondered on this conundrum, but I think it's a combination of many things.

The first of which was this: I saw him and I saw myself. Here were two guys who had everything and nothing figured out as it pertained to the opposite sex. We didn't know how to sustain a healthy relationship. What we *thought* we wanted was not the same as what we got and that was a major problem.

The second reason was this: I saw him and I wanted to help him. And oddly enough, he wanted to do the same for me. I wanted to see him actually discover a real relationship or even find out that he's capable of loving another person. And let's be honest here, my other goal was to keep him as far away from any credible women who could potentially make an extreme moral error by dating him. I was really hopeful that I could help him get back on track, so to speak. On the flip side, he saw me as someone he could bring into *his* world. Here, he'd found someone that was nothing like him when it came to making decisions and in a roundabout way, he was looking for someone to both share in his experiences and even keep him in line. I know that last part may be hard to believe, but it's true. I've always believed that people inherently want to do what's right, but it's certainly not *natural* to be unselfish. Larry wanted to see if I were like him and I wanted to see if he could be less like him.

The third and final reason was this: we were both slightly envious of the other's circumstances. For instance, I could never just wake up next to another woman, in a strange bed, no clothes on, and then filter through my mind about what happened the night before. That's just never been me and never will be. However, I've often wondered what that would be like. Would I hate myself afterward? Would it be *fun* to break some moral standards once in a while? I've resolved myself to understand that a one-night stand is not about life fulfillment—it's life entrapment. The highs associated with this "adventure" can become a cruel addiction that you are liable to become a slave to. I haven't always been a shining example of chivalry, but I have heard enough wisdom to know the dangers of these types of decisions. In Larry's world though, these decisions were a possible weekly occurrence. Not to say that he's getting a hit every time he swings, it's just that what he's looking for is loads different than what I'm looking for.

This arrangement of ours somehow forged a strange friendship. There I was, trying to "help" Larry, and there was Larry, trying to "help" me (which I didn't want necessarily, but was compelled to be active in his life somehow). We didn't hang out a ton; just enough that people around us got wind that we were at least on the level of "pals." And hey, he'd still be considered my pal today.

I soon discovered that by hanging out with these types of guys (not just Larry), there were many things happening. For one, the people close to me now considered me to be the same as *him*; it was not the other way around. You are (and always will be) defined by those you associate with. My personal life stays relatively quiet to everyone around me, but Larry was outwardly spoken about his so that was the difference maker. Guilty by association, right? Why yes, of course.

What I also took note of was the specific types of women Larry preyed upon. Just out of a relationship? Check. How about newly-divorced and distraught? Sure thing. Well, what about a relationship knowingly in a bad place? Bring it on, eh? Larry had it covered. He could sniff out a tormented soul like a dog sniffs out a stray piece of meat at the table. The worst part is, that's just the right kind of analogy to describe his behavior a dog looking for what it presumes to be meat for the taking.

No, it was never the girl that could actually be worth going after; just the ones that will be easily swayed by a cool hand, a nice car, and a quick pick-me-up to get from point A to point B. And during this pseudo courtship, Larry had a jolly good time thinking up new ways to tell his story of conquest. Is that such a shocking thing to hear, ladies? I hope it isn't, but hey, I've been wrong before. Don't think you're getting a free pass on this one either, ladies. You're just as guilty, ya know.

In the midst of all these revelations I was having, I decided to take a step back from dating and get a fresh look at things. Larry claimed to be having conquests, but they weren't really *conquests* at all. If you look up conquest in the dictionary, you'll find that this word is used to describe the various aspects of battle; as such you'll hear it used frequently in history books and war movies. Many times though, its usage creeps into the world of dating. As such, I found an applicable definition online that describes the word in full (and I'll paraphrase):

Somebody who is won over or has been won via some form of strength through character, seduction, and/or against the other person's will.

If you look at that definition closely, you get a better understanding of what a sexual conquest *really* entails. The 'conqueror', as it were, wins the other party through his character and strength. But what kind of strength is that if you're knowingly preying upon those who are weakened? Doesn't that seem a little cowardly? Maybe this dog, um guy, is just smarter to utilize this kind of tactic. I'd use the analogy of a lion pouncing upon the wounded gazelle but that'd be incorrect in this context. Instead, I choose to look at this as an example relating directly to the innate inability to direct one's self towards something greater. As men, shouldn't we be doing that daily? The world asks this of us, so why hide behind a false veil, further crippling our female counterparts?

The last portion of that definition is what really grabs me though: "against the other's will." Is that always the case? No, perhaps not, but through enough coercion and smooth-talking, one can easily get what he wants from another so long as that other person is hoping to find some comfort in the arms of another human being. That's not necessarily against the other's will, but it certainly presents the illusion of security. How many times have you, or a friend, been ticked off because someone promised you something and then didn't deliver? Or worse yet, the other person took something but never gave anything back? I sympathize if that has ever happened to you.

When I was in high school, I took my romantic relationships very lightly. Why get stressed out over something when you have all the time in the world to find somebody you're looking for? There's no rush, right? I mean, your chances of marrying someone straight out of high school are very slim so you wait. And wait. And wait some more. But what happens when you grow tired of waiting? Well, an unwelcome visitor called *experience* comes to visit you—and he does so in the worst ways imaginable. You lose that innocent edge you possessed so long ago. You're no longer like a deer in headlights that knowingly avoids the path of an incoming semi; instead you become plastered on the grill of that semi, struggling to scrape yourself off.

I don't necessarily like this term, but the word *jaded* comes to mind when I think of bad decisions. And the older you get, the more jaded you can become if you're not careful to protect yourself. If you don't think it's true, then let me lay some knowledge down on you. Let's say you have a first love and that love goes awry. From that point on, you may define your love life by that first experience. It's an interesting concept called the primacy effect and is popular among psychology circles. In a nutshell, ask anybody about the events of their lives and they will often recall the first time over the fifth, the tenth, twentieth, or even the most recent. My father is guiltier of this than anyone I know. Whenever I ask him about the cars he owned, he proclaims a few details about his very first one—none of the others even come to mind. Sure, he'll bring up the later models that he came to own, but it was his *first* that had the biggest effect on his life. And what a first ride it was—a 1966 Impala Super Sport. He would later cling to a '77 silver Corvette (which by the way is a vehicle I have never driven but have longed to), but it was the Impala that aided his desire for muscle cars.

Funny thing about this "first experience" jargon is that it's really true. My first kiss in high school was to a long-haired brunette with a tall frame and lightly colored eyes. Do I prefer brunettes more so than blondes? If you look at my dating history, then yes. Does that mean I only desire those types? Of course not, but my first experience was memorable enough for me to look for similar traits in future dates. If you're a Freudian scholar, then you may argue that I'm looking to date my mother; who coincidentally has brown hair and a tall, slender frame. She has brown eyes though so at least it's not entirely creepy. One could also counter-argue that I just prefer brunettes over blondes. That's fine enough too, but that doesn't make one hair color better than the other (despite all the banter you may read about blondes having more fun, etc.). Both hair colors can still cause the same emotional damage, I've found.

My story of dating failure is a familiar one: infatuation leads to reality which then leads to disillusionment and then onto shattered expectations and hopes. That may sound vague, but it's a familiar process to anyone who has been down that road romantically. There's attraction, disillusionment and then an acceptance. You're sparked by this person at the onset, but you inevitably come to be let down by them. They're not this individual that you thought they were (in your head) and so you contemplate just how they'll fit into your life. Do I continue seeing them? Or do I step away in pursuit of someone who fits my expectations? There is no dilly-dallying in this phase; you must make a choice and then move on rather quickly.

What happens when your disillusionment phase continues to be a horrific experience? Well, you may begin to question or become bitter about things you may have not before. Maybe you lost a significant other to that "OSBF" (the opposite-sex-best-friend) so from now on; you cross off people who have a majority of close friends which aren't of the same gender. I've dated girls who have left me for their close guy friends and one even ended up marrying this good friend of hers. Should I be upset? Yeah, at the time I was very hurt, but if I carry a grudge the rest of my life, I'm only hurting myself. People will continue on their lives without you; holding in the pain of a grudge doesn't make them feel any worse, it only cripples you further.

Perhaps you met someone through work and that didn't exactly fair well? I've known several people who have met their husband/wife at work but I've also seen the exact opposite occur; a quick marriage followed by an equally quick divorce. Tread lightly in this arena, my friends. I have heard that one should not pee in his own bed, lest he enjoy the warmth of his own urine.

If you've written off potential work partners, then is there hope within your friends of friends, right? These are great hook-ups because of the convenience factor but if the relationship goes awry, somebody will have to take sides. And nobody likes it when the friendship circle is disrupted by a relationship gone astray. That's when things can get awkward. There are always three sides to every story. His, hers, and what really happened. Your mistakes repeated; your outlook on romantic partners begins to diminish and thereby brings the bar you held so high down to the ground. How good can anybody be out there if all I ever run into is drama and pain? This is the unfortunate side effect of becoming disillusioned over and over again without a proper resolve.

There are some ways out of this dilemma. One is to understand that each and every relationship experience was a failure. That each time I was foolish about who I was trying to date and had no impression of direction or what my heart truly wanted. However, I could also attest to the fact that it was all a learning experience. However, by simply saying it's nothing but a learning experience, I'm just politely and tamely admitting to messing up often. Yes, I *did* screw up from time to time but until I could realize what I was doing, I was only going to continue making the same mistakes. You can either learn fast from the wrongs you've committed or the wrongs will come to define you.

I've come to find that the continual crushing of the mind, body, and soul leaves a person utterly confused. If you're the type of person that needs a visual, then here's a good one. Imagine a glass of water filled all the way to the top. Everybody, including you, starts off with a full glass. You have all your dreams, aspirations, expectations and goodwill poured into this big old glass. Now as life continues to take hold of you, you begin to pour yourself out. The more you pour, the less there is of *you*, theoretically. The less of you there is to go around then the less there is of you to really offer anything to someone else. Because let's be real, in order for you to really "fall in love" with someone, you have to love yourself and be able to give all of yourself to that person. And if they give you all of themselves, then your glass can be filled again. See how that works? One's glass will become smeared and cracked if it's never filled up so before long, it'll be discarded for its misuse and mistreatment.

So who fills the glass back up if it's not you? We can't always rely on other people to be our crutches. People will break and shatter under the smallest of questionable circumstances. I find that a reconnection with one's own self will certainly aid in the refilling process, but that will only get you part of the way. The other portions must be filled with values, strength and support. Only then does the cup find itself willing and able to provide life to anyone who comes to drink.

Sounds like a good theory, but where's the practical application, right? Well, if you've become so tainted by the continuous need to put yourself out there, you will eventually grow bitter and angry. And that's not a fun place to be. What I find is that even though I may walk around with a huge chip on my shoulder from all the hurt, I still want to leave a little bit of space for something that may actually work out. Thus, I may enter into another phase of dating—the CHUG (Covering up Huge Unwanted Garbage). CHUGging, as I've called it, is the pouring out of one's self in huge doses, trying to ignore the fact that one's glass is getting painfully low. And when that happens, things can only get worse. Case in point:

During a late night of just hanging out, another friend of mine, "Bob", confessed to me about his first love and how she hurt him so badly. She bruised him to the point that he vowed to never let another girl break his heart and to that end, he'd make it his duty to make others feel the misery he once did. In a way, Bob sounded like a supervillain in the world of peaceful relationships. Bob, I was willing to sympathize with you, but your resolve towards all other females isn't exactly the best way to go about healing yourself. In fact, healing was never something he seemed to want at all. Rather than correct his situation, he selfishly wanted to bring others to where he was so he couldn't be *alone*. That's where a failed promise takes us: to a place of loneliness. Rather than emerge from our solitary cell, we want others to commiserate in our forlorn prisons; just next door though, not inside the cell. That way, when we look outside, we can see that everyone else is just as messed up as we are.

Bob's first bad experience with dating was so profound that it turned him into a raging man whore. He was the product of one bad incident, it seemed. I suppose for every action there's an equal and opposite reaction, but this appeared to be extreme. We pressed on through the conversation and I was further engaged by Bob's affirmation towards dating. He spoke of how he hated the complexities of relationships and that he wanted things to be simple again. Gone were the days of passing notes in art class or having friend Ricky talk to friend Emily about how you like Gina (although I will admit this still *does* happen in your adulthood; just in a different capacity). Bob was all grown up physically, but on an emotional (and spiritual) level, he was as lost as ship at sea without a compass. He further professed how his lack of empathy made him view himself as a number and that all whom he had dated, were numbers to him as well.

This leads me to the most difficult part of dating: dealing with past relationship baggage. This could also be referred to as the "numbers" conversation. Honestly, I never thought I'd have this type of discussion with someone—I really didn't. If you're unfamiliar with what I'm referring to, I'll elaborate. It's the one conversation where you and your new favorite squeeze talk about the dreaded exes of your past. This may come up casually or it may be forced upon the both of you by a friend's story or through merely running into the ex one day. Anyone who has been hugged, kissed, and unfortunately had familiar relations with (that's sex for all you youngsters) may come to the forefront. I've discovered along my travels of the single world that there are two roads to take on this subject. You either talk about it or you just *never* talk about it. However, when the moment arises, and you feel yourself giving in to primal urges, you can't help but wonder what this person was like with others who came before you. Am I going to be special to this person? Should that even matter now? These are hard questions to come to peace with, but if you aren't pulling a ton of baggage behind you, then you have nothing to fear. However, if you're like me and you messed up somewhere along the way, you have to accept your mistakes, forgive yourself, and move forward. I wish I could give some canned advice and say "get over it", but that's not helping anyone. There's so much more at work here than simply "getting over it."

My advice to you would be to pray about it and if you're not the praying type, then I suggest you talk to somebody close to you. Preferably the person you are currently with. I've said that I'm no saint when it comes to being intimate with someone, but at least I can say my track record isn't overly crowded. For other people though, I've discovered that their party can be rather full. It's a disappointing thing to hear; especially if you've already created your own expectations about this person you're interested in (recalling the disillusionment phase). I've had mentors in my life who have urged me to look beyond this and focus on the here and now. Easier said than done, but if your relationship is to survive, you need to do just that. Be transparent; nobody's perfect and we all have things we're not proud of.

I understand that we're all curious creatures so I'm trying to be as real as possible on these deeper issues in a relationship. Curiosity is a human condition which can get the better of you (or worst) if you're not aware of its power. My own curiosity compounds when it comes to relationships. I'm sure you know by now, I like to do my research on all matters and that also applies to the people I date. I don't always follow my head, but I don't always follow my gut instincts when I need to either. Caution gets thrown to the wayside when we're seeking after something so blindly and it's often difficult to discern *when* it's the wrong something. What I have followed are the objects between my legs, which have almost always steered me in that wrong direction.

121

So what do you listen to when you're looking for someone?

Well, you first look for *your* values to be mirrored in a possible partner. So in essence, ask yourself the hard questions—What do you value? What's important to you? What do you believe you want in a relationship? Does a person who plays games have you in their best interest? No, probably not. And does this person circulate conversation around what they want rather than what the *two* of you can do? Do yourself a favor and look for these signs. Chances are that if you give yourself to this person wholly, you're liable to never receive as much as you've put in. And yes, I'm talking about sex again too.

If a person's physical walls drop faster than a dive bomber jet, then that's a problem. The same can be said for emotional walls. Men may want to get down and dirty early on because they view sex as recreational; a pursuit of a grand adventure. Women may let their guard drop because they think it'll make the guy like them more or vice versa. Neither scenario generates a positive outcome as one party will always get hurt in the process. That's a cold truth that you have to listen to me on.

This is why the "numbers" conversation may rear its ugly head eventually; with or without your consent. In the beginning of my dating life, I was floored when girls wanted to ask *me* that question at all. And when I found out what they had done, it made my mind go crazy. Should people be discussing this stuff? Who do I talk to about this? Why are these conversations messing with my head? Once you have some knowledge about that person, you begin to formulate your option about them. And this opinion becomes a judgment that may forever haunt a person if they're not careful. But when and if the conversation comes about, you must be honest. In my case (and knowing what I'm bringing to the table), I can only pray to God that the girl's answer is somewhere between zero and three. Unfortunately, it's not always what I want to hear. For example:

"Well, it's something like 20. Oh wait, it's 19. I know it's 19.
But that was just one or two times on the last one."
Or . . .
"I think you would be 16. Yeah, pretty sure you'd be 16 if we
did anything."
Or . . .
"Um, I'm not really sure to be honest . . . Wait, let me think
about it . . . ."
Or the most frequent one . . .
"Why are you asking me this? It's not like it matters *now*."

I'm always at odds with myself on the last response. If we always forgot about what we'd done, good or bad, then we aren't holding ourselves accountable for our actions. We're just moving ahead without any sense of reconciliation. Why do you suppose we keep track of our romantic endeavors at all? Is it because our culture has placed enough emphasis on the act to do so? Or is it because the pursuit of a relationship really *is* that important and we want to hold onto that memory? I feel as though it's a little of both. For me, it's about not about just keeping my numbers low. It's about protection; protection from the heartache one experiences and protection from disease. Both are capable of severe long-term harm if you're not careful.

Thankfully, I've been able to avoid the latter my whole life; the former not always.

Personally, I find it difficult to latch onto someone who has a complex and complicated sexual history. Aside from feeling like a future notch in the bedpost, I may develop other insecurities as our relationship progresses. What if I run into their ex while we're out and about? Don't my chances of seeing their previous partners *increase* due to the nature of their past choices? Well, of course they do. And who wants that really? I have been known to be a jealous person at times and I won't deny that, but I am also someone who believes in protecting one's self from the harsh baggage one can accumulate by "dating around." I've been faced with many situations where I could have bedded a woman and then walked away from her, but I always wondered how I'd explain my behavior to my future wife. Why carry that with you into your marriage? Wouldn't she be concerned about not feeling *special* to me? And would she be worried that I'd be tempted to return to this partner should I run into them again? I know these questions may sound weird or ridiculous to someone who doesn't feel the same as me, but even if you don't, I would encourage you to consider the feelings of your future (or even current) spouse. How much anxiety and angst will you cause them by complicating your personal life with multiple, multiple sexual endeavors? True, they may never know anything if you never speak about it, but is honesty an integral part of your relationship? If your answer is 'yes', then you need to evaluate that earlier question in greater detail.

Confession is not the answer either; at least not to the other person. Prideful as I am, I look for a confessional if I find a person making the same mistakes over and over again. Confessing is just part of a larger process. You must also forgive *and* heal in order to be whole for the next person. And you don't do that by simply apologizing to the next person you date. If you really feel like you've healed and moved on, then the other person *feels* that aura emanating from you. Can you relate to that?

Yes, it's a good idea to shop around for the best product in a store, but you don't have to consistently sample everything to get an idea as to what you really want. And yet, this seems to be the mindset of so many singles I encounter. They talk about quality over quantity yet brag about the number of dates they've embarked on over the course of a few weeks. Why though? Being happier does not require competition among my peers, right? So why not practice what you preach instead of acting just as others *want* you to.

I understand that some people will paint themselves as victims of some tragic accident. I've known plenty of men and women who claim to have been coerced by a smooth talker who was later revealed to be a total jerk and that just really sucks. The experience leaves them angry and confused, but more angry than anything because they knowingly gave their bodies and expected something greater in return. No one forced them into bed with these people; they did so of their own accord so I would encourage others to not pass blame. If men continue to believe that it's 'okay' to try and get laid every time they meet someone new and women persist with giving themselves freely then where does the cycle end? If everyone's always upset with the outcomes then why shouldn't we change something?

Which gender needs to help put the brakes on? The answer is *both*.

The culture we live in is a sexually vicious one if you think about it. I, for one, can't (under)stand it. We place so much significance on the act of sex and yet, we treat it like a commodity. Magazines encourage single people to have "vivacious sexual encounters" and thus present "real-life stories" of extreme promiscuity like it's some kind of game to be played. And if we're not playing the game, then we're missing out on something. What that something is, no magazine will tell you, but what they (the magazine) will tell you is that it's something you can't keep missing. Since I've been through enough to know, I can tell you exactly what you're missing—a whole lot of crap and unwanted baggage.

Now, doesn't that like sound fun and something you just don't wanna miss?!

Have you ever considered apologizing to the person you know you did wrong by? Not just from a sexual standpoint, but from a relational one too. I'd say the vast majority of us would never dream of doing such a thing. We'd sooner stick our head in a vice and crank it than admit we'd done wrong by someone. We know we can deal with our own troubles, but what about the other person? Yeah, we often have no idea how this person will handle our apology so we cower and hide in the hopes that the feelings will subside. If we do that for too long, then our conscience shuts the door on us completely. Does that sound like a good thing? No, I would hope not.

Call me naïve, but I never figured that so many people were having sex so early, and as much, with so many different people. When I was 15 and single, I was still thinking of ways to hold hands or maybe get a kiss from the girl I shared study hall with. Meanwhile, and unbeknownst to me, the guys and gals who skipped study hall were sneaking out to their cars or even back home to experiment with one another. You may laugh, but this was a severe mind-melt for me as an adult. Here, I had been hoping that other people were guarding themselves like I was, but the majority was not. Sure, I had friends who kept themselves hidden and safe, but they were few and far between. We all knew that we wanted what these other people were having, but somehow we knew we just weren't *ready* for it yet. We were too young to understand the depth of a sexual encounter and what it might do to us later on.

When I started dating, my stomach dropped with every mention of a past relationship that included sexual intercourse. Girls would tell me it was "not a big deal" to lessen the blow, but all that did was make me angrier. *It was a big deal wasn't it*, I would think. *So why cheapen the act by saying that?* The worst of it was when I'd be out with my date and we'd bump into one of her past flings.

If you've been there, then you know it's not a good feeling. To know that the person standing before you has shared the most intimate of moments with your new girlfriend (or boyfriend) can leave you feeling cheap and undesirable. My first reaction is to beat him to a pulp and leave him bloodied and bruised, but what I usually say is just, "Hi". I find this to be the most agreeable of lines to deliver upon a first greeting. Granted, you can't control these scenarios, but what happens when that occurs over and over? You can't help but wonder just how much this person values themselves. And if they *don't* value themselves, then there's a good chance they may not value you too. Ever been to the amusement park as a child? Let me give you an example of what I'm referring to.

Let's say you wanted to be first to ride the new Tornado, a brand-spanking new coaster with awesome turns and vivacious curves just waiting to be broken in (are you following the subliminal messages here?). This new attraction has been touted as one of the finest ever made, but the only way you get to ride it is if you win the coveted Park Patience Award. You are instructed to show up at the exact time the park opens and that way you'll be first in line and the only one who gets to ride it. So you do just as you are instructed to and when the day arrives, you show up to ride this new coaster. Only trouble is, when you get there, you discover that the park didn't keep to its schedule and opened up a little early. You're miffed because instead of being the first and only rider, you find yourself last in line, forced to watch as the smiling faces of previous riders pass you by as you wait your turn.

Pause for dramatic effect.

Now, am I trying to say that every virgin woman is a roller coaster just waiting to be ridden? No, that's not the point of this rant. And am I saying that all guys are just a bunch of eager riders sitting outside the amusement park of the female world? No, not exactly either (although in some cases, that's not far from the truth). What I *am* attempting to convey is the *feeling* behind the realization that hey, your new partner hasn't held onto a promise that you, yourself, were. And when promises are broken or hope is destroyed, the initial shock one feels can be one of the worst experiences one can have; man or woman. Hope is an emotion tied directly to our own heart and therefore serves as the platform for any/all promises that are made to us. Imagine what that means then in the context of a broken sexual relationship.

Yeah, that's a major 'yikes', isn't it? People get pissed, emotions run higher than normal, and eventually someone ends up spreading crazy rumors that are best left in the swearing jar at your nana's house.

If you live in a small town, then your chances of running into one of these "numbers" (i.e. Tornado riders) greatly increases. A 2011 poll stated that the average number of sexual partners a man will have in his lifetime is seven while a woman will have four. I find both of these statistics to be rather conservative when I think of the numbers I've heard from either sex. Some guys I know have confided in me that they've been with 70 women, perhaps even more. I've overheard women tell me they've only been with one person while others have confessed to not even *knowing* their number. Ignorance can be bliss, but it certainly can make someone long for the days when life was much simpler. When life wasn't about how many people you slept with, but the number of innocent flirtations you could accumulate at recess.

Ok, let's take a step back. I feel as though I'm lecturing far too much here. If you're someone who is reading this and you identify with everything I've been writing, then I don't want you feel like a failure for being overly promiscuous or not waiting for the right person. We're human, aren't we? We make mistakes, we mess up, and we have some major lapses in judgment from time to time. Like wearing socks to the beach or eating outdated cheese, we do some dumb stuff. I, for one, have tried to rectify the past but as you can guess, this got me nowhere. I wanted to correct, even change, the events somehow of past failures through a new partner or significant other. That sounds like crazy talk, does it not? But that's actually what got me upset more than anything. My own disillusionment was not being able to accept people for who they were and where they came from. It's impossible to change what's already happened, but you can at least move forward in the comfort of being better.

Yes, that's easy to preach and hard to practice but how else will you bring back that feeling of being first in line and the only rider of the new Tornado? Only through your own self discovery and forgiveness; not by hiding away and assuming that the other person has done the same. Doing the latter will only result in a noisy machine, worn down by an inattentive operator (the operator being you) whose neglect has made the once glossy roller coaster appear busted and devoid of a marketable glow willing to attract the proper rider.

So hey, if that's you I'm talking about, stir your operator back into action. If that's not you above, then keep protecting yourself as you are able. And if you're too young or too old to really relate to this, then I just want to say thanks for reading this far. I appreciate you.

In all fairness, I want to give the likely retort for all this number talk and healing the past:

"Dude, you should never talk about 'numbers' with anyone. What happened then doesn't matter anymore. Why focus on the past at all?"

Well, I can understand that kind of rebuttal so I have some responses in mind. The first of which is this—sex matters. Obviously it does or I wouldn't have spent so much time on the subject. Is that not one of the primary driving factors in bringing two souls together?

At one time I believed that people kept track of who they'd been with so they could stay away from those of similar qualities later on. This seemed logical enough. If I could recall a bad "type" of person, then I'd be better at recognizing another bad seed later on. This thinking was folly, of course. People can't help but keep record because the act is so densely implanted in our memories. Having sex with someone is like putting a thumbprint on the other person. It's like a mark, or tattoo, that we've left on others which they have, in turn, left upon us.

From a guy's perspective, the first thing you want to do is rip the gonads off of any previous romantic partner your girlfriend may have had. And if you happen to see that person in public, it'll take the power of God almighty to keep you from punching him in the face. I've wrestled with this in most any relationship I've had and I'm fairly certain plenty of other guys have too. We want to be *first*. We want to be the only guy who's had the pleasure of, ahem, *pleasuring* our lady. In keeping with our roller coaster analogy, we want to be the first and only passenger along our lady's ride. So when the knowledge strikes us that some other prick got there first, we get agitated. We get annoyed. And we definitely start wondering the very things we shouldn't be.

How'd he get to her already?
Did she enjoy being with him more so than she will with me?
Was this jerk any good to her? How can I be better than him?

It can be agonizing to no end if you're not consciously aware of what's happening. We commonly refer to this emotion as pure jealousy. You're jealous over the fact that your girl had a sexual relationship with someone else instead of you. But what starts out as jealousy can actually transform into another equally debilitating emotion: *pride*. In order to protect the woman you care for, you must ensure that she feels safe with you, both physically and emotionally. If she has been hurt previously on either of those levels, then the pride of her next suitor also gets damaged. He may feel like he should have been there to guard her. And if he had been there, he would have done right by her instead.

Yes, pride is a powerful emotion that can work against you, gentlemen. I know it's been my downfall on several occasions. The reality is that you can't protect every woman you encounter; you can only build her up from where she is now. The same can be said for women too. If you're in a relationship, ladies, do your best to stroke your man's manhood; not just the physical kind. He may be stoic to you or even emotionless at times, but gosh darn it; he will appreciate it when you assure him that "he's the man". I understand that's a hard thing to do, but hey, aren't we talking about pride here? And if he doesn't appreciate your good tidings, then he obviously isn't the proper one to work your roller coaster (yes, I'm still running with this analogy).

The lingering questions, doubts, and selfish ambitions can cause anxiety on both sides of the relationship. I've been there, trust me, and it's not fun at all. This new person in your life may have turned over a new leaf in their personal life, but what of their time spent all those yesterday's ago? You may not know their whole story and quite frankly, you will never know it, but what you can do is try to trust what's going on *now*. A person's true character has a way of revealing itself eventually so patience is a virtue you must have.

Timing, as it always has been, is everything.

And time is a unique thing I never grow tired of marveling in. If you had met this person some few years prior, you may have had no interest at all. Maybe they were partying too much? Maybe their view of relationships was not like yours? Perhaps clinging to people who weren't necessarily good for them was their ideal scenario. We tend to seek out the people we feel are right for us, but may not be right whatsoever. So here's another reality check for you: we often look for what we feel we deserve. If you feel like you deserve something that looks nice, then you'll go after something that looks nice. This something may be lacking the moral standards and values that you covet, but unless you've made that a priority in your criteria, all you'll get is that surface-level, nice-looking piece of meat.

Such is the learning curve in dating.

If you can decide for yourself that you deserve someone that treats you well, then you're on the right path. This is not to say that you should always be looking for something better, it's more about self-awareness and understanding a bad situation before it gets worse. I guarantee that you'll have happier times ahead of you. No doubt in my mind whatsoever. I know because (once again), I've been there myself.

Ok, so there was plenty of heavy stuff in there so let's take a breather. Dating can be like running a marathon. You may not be able to go full force for the entire race, but at least you can jog when you want. Nobody's counting on you to finish first; just finishing is an accomplishment in its own right. And if you tripped somewhere along that track, then it's nobody's business to tell you that you can't get right back up and keep on trucking.

Personally, I'd get a bike or something because I hate running long distances, but that's just me. You running nuts can keep your fancy running shoes and short shorts.

I know some people may read this and say, "Hey, I've been with plenty of people and I'm just fine." Well, you're missing out on some really awesome stuff here. I've gone after women with the intention of sexual recreation too and it's never ended well. Can you agree with me on that? If not outwardly, at least somewhere on the inside of your own head you can, can't you? I've sought out situations that had 'bad idea' written all over them and still I barreled through like a steamroller which could not be stopped. And for what? A pat on the back from some guy who thinks I'm 'awesome' because I slept with someone? I used to think that was cool; I really did. I mean, that's what every movie or lousy mentor has ever told me so why wouldn't I think it's a good idea? Then, once my conquest was over and I'd gotten that pat on the back from the person I thought I needed approval from, I found that I didn't feel any better about myself. No, I actually felt *worse*. Why did I need acceptance from this person? Why was it so important for me to fit in? How incredibly stupid was I to have believed that. I had promised to live my life as a rule-breaker who would deviate from the norm and yet here I was, staring myself down as the statistic I hated to read about. Copulating with a woman sexually may give a man some temporary high, but it's not a goal any man should have outside of a marriage. Yes, I said *marriage.* Not a *really, really committed relationship where two people are dating a really long time and will likely get married.* Otherwise the casual behavior will only create a perpetual cycle of wanting that'll leave you unfulfilled.

And ladies, this goes for you too. I may have choice words for my fellow males out there, but I'm speaking to your half as well. Why dread having that said conversation with a future boyfriend you actually *do* care about? And yes, I know it's easier said than done, but I wouldn't say it if it didn't need to be said. That's the reason for why we have these encouragements in the first place—to build up people who need it; not tear them down with delusions that giving one's self away is merely just for fun and sport. Sex matters but you, as a person, matter a whole lot too.

You could potentially find yourself in a situation otherwise known as a *flingship* (it's the merging of a fling and a relationship). Flingships are a bit more intense than a friend with benefits. If you want to know where the line is drawn, then start talking about having an actual relationship with the other person and see where it goes. A friend with benefits will think it's weird to be boyfriend/girlfriend or something more, but a person involved in a flingship may actually *want* to take it to the next level. So instead of staying on the fence, leap over and see what happens. And when I say "leap", I don't mean into their pants.

Never be afraid of the consequences you may face for being open with someone. Yes, you could potentially scare someone away, but if that person isn't willing to be open with you, then why bother? Now, I'm not saying to do this on the first date. Or the second. Or the third (see a pattern here?), but I am telling you to at least be honest with yourself. I've had moments where I sat across from the person I was dating and straight up lied about how I felt. I usually did this because I was afraid of hurting the other person or was too scared of what their reaction may be. Yeah, pretty freaking stupid, right? Granted, I wasn't lying about having illegitimate children or that I was seeing other people, but I haven't always been honest about my feelings with another person. You certainly owe it to yourself and that other person to be as mindful of your feelings as you can be. That matters a great deal. It'll matter even more if and when you get married.

All right, so I know what you're saying, "Hey man, you're still single. How would you know anything about intimacy in marriage?"

Well, I don't have plenty of experience in the matter, but considering how long I've toiled in being single, I can attest to how destructive sex can be to people outside of marriage. I've found that a person's "number" is a good indicator of how a person views themselves. If you have a high number (guy or girl), then you may be somewhat deadened to intimacy; you're more paranoid or disillusioned than excited over the thought of being close to your significant other. I'm not trying to hurt feelings here; it's just what I've seen. That's why I see people who have higher numbers as being less in tune with their emotions. The once perfect melody that was their emotional self has been rocked unsteadily by the poor harmony of bad partners. How is that so? And how is that possible? Well, here's a short story as we rewind the clock on my dating life.

During one of the many late nights in my apartment, I was mulling over my latest break up with a girl I had dated. We'd been seeing each other for a month or so but things just weren't feeling right. The relationship essentially ended because she was semi-apathetic towards intimacy. We weren't having sex, but every interaction was met with a stiff arm or a cold shoulder. There was literally no holding of hands, gentle nudges or even a combing of the hair. She gave me the impression that any physical contact would cause her to contract some terrible disease (or vice versa). I tried to figure out what the deal was so I inquired if she'd ever been beaten by somebody. This was a bold move, yes, but I was really concerned about her. What followed was a conversation I was not anticipating: she came out and told me her all of her past experiences. I literally gasped when she unloaded all her information on me. Past partners, cheaters, forced situations, the whole nine yards; it was a story full of misery and distraught. I didn't know what to say so I said nothing. This was not a comforting move on my, but I was so new to dating so my gullible nature showed through.

Her story made me become conscious of a few things. The first was that I wish like crazy I would have met my significant other when I was about five years old. If I had met her then, I would have clung onto her, never letting go until we were old enough to be married. There are just too many unjustified trials of dating that we force ourselves through just so that we can return to that child-like state of being fulfilled. This was a miserable realization but I hope that my wife will someday appreciate that I wanted to know her as soon as I could. (I'm on my way, sweetie!)

Secondly, I wanted to find out why she was so guarded. Obviously she had been through several troubled relationships where she had been taken advantage of sexually. I felt sorry for her, even if I judged her at first. The choices she had made did not make sense to me so I had difficulty really hearing her on what had happened. One message was clear though: the hurt she had experienced had clearly affected her views on sex and the opposite sex, too. She didn't speak of men; she called them 'boys' and that almost all boys were 'jerks just looking to get laid'. How terrible, right? She explained to me how emotional intimacy was not a possibility for her, but if we hung around each other long enough, she'd eventually let her physical walls come down. It was as if she'd arrived at the conclusion that her sexual nature was merely just a 'job' and through this dutiful acceptance, she'd eventually snag some jerk that was a little less jerky than the rest. I was really devastated on her behalf. It was a sad day and made me become conscious to the fact that I just couldn't be with her.

I didn't let the conversation disappear in my head though. This seemed like a serious issue, one worthy of a closer look. Like a curious young mind, I did some Googling to see the effects of faulty relationships on a young person. Yes, Google is a lifesaver but only if you look in the right places.

This is when I stumbled on some articles about the hormone oxytocin. Rather than trust what Wikipedia had to say, I checked link after link until I had gotten a consensus about what this chemical was meant for. From what I could gather, oxytocin is known as the "love hormone." It's released after people have sex and can be likened to a "pair bonding" gene. Oxytocin can also be triggered through other forms of touch like hand-holding and hugging thus enforcing the need and want to be in physical contact with that person again. When applied to sex with the same person, your brain releases this hormone more often and associates the experience with this person. Thus, if you have the same partner, then the bond becomes stronger and stronger.

Hmmm, interesting, I thought. I decided to read further.

The other side of this coin is having *multiple* partners. Once you've had multiple partners, your ability to "pair bond" apparently begins to decrease. With too many shared experiences, the pleasure receptors have greater difficulty discerning which is best. *Crazy*, I thought. Since I had a limited number of partners, I imagined what it must be like to have so many different people, experiences, and images living inside one's heart. How does someone handle that? The space must have been so crowded that it was damn near impossible for anybody new to inhabit her heart. I was deeply saddened by this, but also angry. I became angry at this woman's past partners and hated that none of them protected her (even if she should have been protecting herself too). People of faith believe that we give our souls to another person when we have sex so I suppose oxytocin is the scientific connection between these two concepts. *Hmm. Very interesting,* I thought. I tend to get a little giddy when I find science and faith playing nice together rather than standing in strict opposition to one another.

There was no difference in the genders either, both men and women had this hormone. I figured that God, in his infinite wisdom, somehow knew to implant a chemical meant purely for binding us together through sexual activity. This made sense to me. I was happy to have come to a scientific conclusion for something I had only a hunch about. My mixed feelings of grief and joy were erased from my mind as I had another dark epiphany: If I really wanted to *be* with someone special, then I was going to have to wait until I found someone truly worth bedding whilst *I* waited to bedded too (remember the roller coaster theory?).

Bam!—I was overwhelmed. Our culture is so damned sexual that my new resolution seemed next to impossible. The pressure affiliated with waiting made my 20something male body want to burst. Sex is one of the main topics, if not *the* topic, at the forefront of a young man's life. His gyroscope of needs and wants do not revolve around practical things; there's sex and there's more sex. Every stinking sitcom I watch tells me I should try to get laid every Friday and Saturday night. My peers were telling me the same thing too. These other folks seemed to be having the time of their lives (or were they?). What was I to do? I had an expectation about who I wanted to be and their world didn't seem to sync with mine. I needed to stay the course, but my thoughts of never getting there were demoralizing and thus, I strayed. Even after hearing testimony that rocked my world, I still strayed.

First of all, I thought how do you control yourself or find somebody special when everyone else is out there de-oxytoci-fying themselves? This was the first lie I told myself; that *everyone* was doing it. A lie such as this will cripple your very framework. I'd sit in my chair at night, thinking about how doomed I was. There's no way I was going to find someone, mid-20s, that I was crazy over, who wasn't wanting to have sex for at least long enough for both of us to know how we really wanted each other. That is seriously what I thought; and I persisted in this thinking until it became my way of life. Pretty depressing, right? Considering the women I was accustomed to meeting or going out with, maybe my logic was correct? Maybe everyone *was* doing this to themselves and I just needed to jump on board?

Oh, the lies we make ourselves believe just so we can belong.

Even the nice girls, whom I was friends or just acquaintances with, believed the lies associated with dating. They clung onto boyfriends who had little to no gumption; a complete lack of ambition and who felt it necessary to pour their energies into selfish goals like other sexual adventures. They spent little while taking much. They had girlfriends who acted more like their mothers than their partner; taking care of and even supporting them on a financial level. Ladies, please hear me out on this one: do what you can to help this guy but don't become his mother. He had a mother at some point in his life so he shouldn't need you to fill this role for him now. I didn't know why these girls were so attached to these guys, but I had my theories.

I observed that women who dated these types of guys appeared to struggle with their own self-esteem. They dated "beneath" them because in some strange way, it probably made them feel better about themselves. It's not that dating one of these guys was easier or better, it just meant that their own view of themselves was not very high. They were after what they thought they *deserved,* but they also wanted to be on a pedestal. They wanted their boyfriends to see them as unattainable and precious, even if they didn't believe it themselves and when these guys did something wrong, it was easier to look "better".

So where would the turning point be? What would it take for these girls and guys to think better of themselves and move forward?

If you shoot for someone that you feel is "too good" for you and you fail miserably, you may never feel like you're good enough again. Emotional damage like that can last a lifetime and dictate every future relationship you find yourself in. Here's the cool part though: you don't have to think that way forever. In fact, if you are thinking that way, then I urge you to think better of yourself. If some boy or some girl told you that you weren't good enough at one point or another—then forget them. Their words mean nothing in the eyes of the next person you choose to date. Believe me on that one.

So I resolved that I would be on the lookout for a girl who thought well of herself. That seemed like a plausible goal, right? Well, don't mistake confidence and self-respect for something else, my friends. That same characteristic can be twisted into a falsehood where the individual associates confidence with sexual prowess. Just because someone can sleep with plenty of people doesn't make them a prime person to date. This person is just being irresponsible and may end up with a disease or two before it's all over. And the last thing you need is a disease of your own.

I say these things because every woman's magazine I encounter promotes a feminist movement towards greater sexual freedom. Sure, women work nowadays and still find time to rear families, but that shouldn't change our views on sex. And before you ladies start screaming things like, "you chauvinist pig!" I'm speaking to the men of my generation too. Guys, our sexual freedom has always been part of a failed double standard which should never have existed. You know what I'm referring to—the concept that a guy who beds many women is "the Man." This man who actively spreads his precious little seed is maximizing his chances for reproduction, so we're told. Women, conversely, who bed many men are endangering the integrity of their offspring while leaving themselves open to more diseases, etc. So why on Earth should women feel like they have to compete with that?

I've been a single guy for a long time and there's no written rule that says guys need to bed plenty of chicks in order to be happy and there's no written rule that women should enjoy several partners in order to be loved either. There *are* written rules against that behavior, however, and let me tell you, those rules are some of the best to live by. I've been in plenty of situations where I could have taken advantage of the consensus' thinking, but I didn't. Boy, I'm glad for that. If I regret anything, it's having second thoughts against what I knew was right. And what was right was the hardest thing to do. This lie that I had been telling myself needed to cease. I knew this more than anything.

When I was younger, I created this idea that I would wait for the One. Ironically, when I grew up, all I ever did was date as much as possible. And the people I found were not the best for me, nor was I good for them. They were much the opposite of what I promised myself. So what happened? Did I just forget what I was after? I inundated myself with these questions but in due course, I figured some things out.

I noticed how what I *wanted* and what I was *seeking* after were two completely different things. A-ha! How's that for an epiphany?! I figured that I needed to change *how* and *where* I was looking for women. And I needed to change my own marketing too. All of this would be done in an effort to achieve what my heart wanted; not my head.

As a kid, I always wanted a pet Komodo dragon. I would have killed for one of those big lizards (figuratively speaking), but let's be honest, the thing might have eaten me before I was a teenager. When I grew up, I recognized how foolish and unrealistic that was. So I resolved that the first step in this journey was to come to terms with what I wanted out of a relationship (minus the crazy aspirations and unrealistic parts). That was something I had to be at peace with. The reality was this though: I always knew what I wanted out of a relationship. I was just too damn jaded to see what that was anymore. A major bummer, but exciting at the same time, if you follow me. Once you've looked inward long enough, you're undoubtedly going to find what you're looking for: yourself. And oh, living alone for a good portion of that time tends to help that process along nicely. You get loads more opportunity to doddle in your own thoughts; for good and for bad.

I decided to make a pact with myself (again). I would create a list of criteria to fully represent what I would be looking for in a relationship; for me and for the other person. Care to guess what was at the very top? Yeah, you guessed it: hot. She had to be *hot*. Come on, don't be angry. I'm a nice guy, but I've got to at least be sexually attracted to my girlfriend in order for this to go anywhere. My definition of *hot* applies to an overall attractiveness; not the scantily clad or overly sexual. To me, a *hot* woman is one I look at and go "wow". She could be in a full bodysuit with three layers of padding and I'd still go "wowzers, she's hot."

Once I had a good definition of "hot", I worked my way down the list. She had to have strong morals, similar values, hot, preferably of the same ethnicity but not really a preference, loyal, hot, trustworthy, dependable, hot . . . . I got tired of typing so I stopped. I then surveyed my ideal standards for dating a woman. The conclusion left me feeling a little distraught. How could anybody fit into all those categories? I'd be better off trying to grow a girlfriend out of a test tube. The chances of finding someone who had these traits made me feel like I was searching for a giraffe in a pet store.

But honestly, I was upset over something else. Yes, I was completely unrealistic in my desired mate, but I realized I had missed one very crucial detail—where was the belief in *God*?

Shouldn't that have been just as important as being hot? Or even more important? (that last one took some real convincing, I assure you) Here's some more knowledge for you singlers out there: know thy core beliefs when dating. And just because someone tells you they believe something, doesn't always mean they do. Judge a person by what they do more so than what they say. Unless this person is a pregnant woman; if there were a license to be legally insane for any period of time, pregnant women could own that. I've been around a few to know.

A person's beliefs are not something to tip-toe around with. You have to communicate about that stuff because believe me; it'll come up when and if you have kids someday. Unless of course you're just some idiot trying to have children out of wedlock constantly. Then it's no holds barred, eh? Well good for you. The world does not need more like you though; there are plenty enough already, just in case you were wondering about being special. And that goes for both sexes. I am not biased to either sex as you know by now. If you're a fool, then you're a fool. No gender requirements necessary.

I happened to read a really great quote once that I believe sums up the dating scheme nicely; specifically if you feel you have no sense of direction.

"What you are looking for, is what is looking."—St. Francis of Assisi

St. Francis may have hailed from a place that I'd dare not say aloud in public, but this smart guy was certainly on to something. If you're looking for just about anything, well, you'll find just about *anything* too.

Through all the dating scenarios we place ourselves in, we inevitably end up finding exactly what we were looking for: just another date. The chase becomes the most important aspect of dating and thus, becomes one of its greatest pitfalls. My aforementioned friend, Larry, had become so infatuated with the chase that it had grown to define him. And no matter what he, or I, could say about it, the only people that were going to stop this conduct would be us. In a roundabout way, we were no different from one another (save about 100 sexual encounters, but who's counting . . .). True, we both had baggage, but we were also behaving in the same fashion. There was a formidable shield up and we were dealing with it in our own way. He was trudging through constant hook ups to make himself feel better whilst I ditched my dates early on before I got too close emotionally.

Over time, you begin to wonder just what it is that drives you to this state. I mean, aren't I making this too complicated? Do I really need to make lists to find out what I want? Do I really need to obsess over certain little details about somebody and cross off the ones I don't like in order to decide if I want to be with them? No, I shouldn't have to do that whatsoever. I should just *know* what I'm looking for and not question myself constantly. More often than not, we *do* already know what makes us happy; we just need to uncover it once more.

I, for one, have been at the mercy of those who cannot communicate what they want. And trust me; if you've ever been in that scenario, it just sucks. Relationships are made and broken on communication. It's as simple and uncomplicated as that. Both persons should be on the same page when it comes to expectations, scheduling, and needs/ desires. Sound like a relatively good package to have from someone who completes all of the following, but it's easier in theory than actual practice. We get bogged down, we become victims of events beyond our control and we soon forget that every moment of every day with someone special is not always fun-filled and made of daisies; it is a duty.

Does that sound weird to call relationships a "duty"? I suppose it can when you consider the perception we are presented regularly. My generation has a habit of expecting every moment to be easy or without error, and when we are faced with strife; we turn and run as though we're being chased by a horde of killer bees. Are we cowards for not allowing our relationships to grow and face hardships? Or are we just too cowardly to accept that certain difficulties *should* exist while others should not. True cowardice, I find, is to turn away when the reward is greatest. Dating is no different in this arena. Our reward should be a challenging, fulfilling relationship with another human being; not a fairy tale that refuses to accept reality and change. Sure, some relationships start out like fairy tales, but they will not endure that way forever.

I'm a judgmental person by nature (go figure, right?) but I do give people the benefit of the doubt until I'm proven otherwise. For example, if I am actively pursuing a woman and she continues to neglect me as part of her day, then that's a good sign to me to move on. Time is the one resource you'll never get back in life. Once it's gone, it ain't coming back. So if a person is not willing to give you their time, then you need look elsewhere because it'll just be a waste of time to continue on that path. I am fully aware that sounds harsh, but you have to be brutally honest on this subject. I've seen many a friends and acquaintances continuously pursue that which they will never seize. I'm no stranger to this myself, but I've often required a third party to say, "Hey man, she doesn't like you. Give it up."

To you, my friends out there, I thank you for your unending support and open critique of my failed dating ventures.

If you're chasing after some great prize, you will almost always find yourself still chasing as your prize runs off into the sunset. I Despite what those ridiculous MSN and

Yahoo! articles may say, online dating is still a confusing mess just as much as the "real world" counterpart it markets against. Though the concept may be more socially acceptable these days, you will still find the same gamut of potential weirdos, creeps, and people just looking for love in all the wrong places. In the year I gave the online sensation a whirl, I probably went on about a dozen dates. That's just the number of girls I had actually "met" in person, not counting others who I contacted or had contacted me. I don't consider myself to be a Don Juan or a Cassanova, but the amount of dates one can accumulate through online dating is staggering.

Was it easier than real life? Yes, to a degree. Was it more frightening than real life? Yes, to a degree as well.

Dozens, and I mean dozens, of dating sites are out there. Match, eHarmony, Chemistry, Plenty of Fish . . . you get the picture. Online dating sites have to be making an absolute killing; and I mean that. Not literally of course, that's frightening; I'm talking metaphorically from a financial perspective. The number of sites available, coupled with the number of relationship-seekers has made me better understand the dynamic of people requiring intimacy; we all have this apparent craving and therefore, we try our hardest to satisfy that craving. The fact that commercials are saying it's 'ok' to date online makes the thirst even harder to ignore.

Experiences associated with online dating tend to be just as ridiculous as those you'll have in the real world. Yeah, everything is on a computer and you don't even have to meet the person, but there's no shortage of strange meetings or awkward moments within the virtual landscape. I initially thought that this would be a passing phase for me and I wouldn't devote much time after the first day or so. But, as I have been in the past, I was very, very wrong. You see, the influx of messages one receives when they are "new" to online dating is rather overwhelming. If you are ever feeling down and want to feel better about yourself, then I suggest making up a profile on an online dating site. Make sure you flash a nice smile, say that you're "fun", "happy" and "lively" and let the chips fall where they may. I promise you that you won't be disappointed by your results.

Well, I will admit that the results will be half true. You'll likely attract a good number of folks potentially twice your age, probably some who are too young for you and a large group of people not within your criteria for dating. However, you will receive a ton of fan mail, many of whom will want to meet you ASAP. And if that's not enough, they may even Facebook stalk you to the point where they find your profile and suddenly want to be "friends." How people are able to find someone when you a) never put your full name in your profile and b) don't disclose anything personal other than where you went to school, I don't know (nor do I want to). I'm willing to bet it has to do with mentioning what school you went to. That will stay with you forever. Word to the wise on that last one though—*don't* become Facebook friends with someone you met on an online dating site; just not at first. You need to at least go out with this person one time before you can let them into your world like that. Once again, I'm a guy who knows from experience.

Let's say you get past that initial bombardment of emails, messages, and one of my all-time favorites—the "wink", "nudge", or "poke" (a feature on some sites which is supposed to tell someone you're 'interested' in them but don't want to send a message quite yet). This is one of the lamer features I've ever seen, but it's no different than winking at someone from across a room full of strangers, I suppose. If you don't like winks or pokes, you'll probably sift through what you consider to be garbage as you try to find someone worthwhile. After you've done that, you may settle on a few profiles that you feel are worthy to be returned with a message from you. To even the playing field, you decide to send an ice-breaker to strike up a conversation.

This is where the real fun begins.

What do you say? Do you use a witty opening line? Something like "hey, fancy meeting you here" or something more mundane like "saw your profile; thought you were hot;

wanna chat?" (Ok, I've never used that last one, but I'm sure it's been utilized by my male counterparts considering how I've seen it sent to me). Ultimately, you may just end up with a casual, "Hello, how was your day?" which is just what you might have said to that person had you met them in person anyway. You could also choose to point out all the similarities you share with that person based on their profile. You like dogs? I like dogs. You like traveling? I like traveling. You like to pop the tires off of bicyclers who ferry around their pets in little baskets? Hey, me too! Ok, that behavior is a little disturbing and even wrong but I enjoy it from time to time.

These tactics for beginning conversation are simple yet effective.

The downsides of this experience are the rejections. The non-replies, the total blow-offs, etc.; the simple yet effective "no thank you" is defeating no matter what form it comes in. Online dating just makes that denial a costly one: about $30 a month if you're so lucky. So now you have an empty heart *and* an emptier bank account.

You would think that the money investment with online dating would make you more cautious, but I've discovered the experience to be just as mistake-prone as the living world. For example, when you begin to recognize the profiles of other people you know personally. Coworkers, friends, you name it—the next meeting you have with this person is a dizzying display of paranoia as you try to surmise if that person has seen your profile as well. In the end, you should probably just admit that it wasn't you, only an evil twin or friend of yours who "made you do it." Trust me, that cop out works every time.

I've also had the pleasure of assisting friends with their own dating profiles. A good friend of mine, "Ned", has a slight disability where he is unable to type items correctly. It's like dyslexia but not the same. Basically, he wanted to join a site but was afraid his emails might say more obscene things than positive. So what's a guy to do? Well, you turn to those who can help you. I personally began reading *and* typing Ned's emails for him. This was fun for a while, but when I recognized certain girls responding to him that wouldn't respond to me, I got a little testy. It definitely crossed my mind to put something less than kosher in one of his emails, but I can walk away saying I'm a good friend who did not indulge in making him look silly.

He did that on his own by posting a picture of his pet cat.

If you are having difficulty making the jump to online dating, then I suggest not taking the venture so seriously. You can amuse yourself by sending out mass messages; all in an effort to get some feedback for your inbox. This may be fun at first but when you realize that the pictures of one girl include the pictures of another girl you are trying to contact, you'll probably put two and two together to discover that not only are they friends—they're also sisters.

Awkward . . . .

It'd be the same as walking up to one girl, saying 'hi' and then turning around to say the same thing to her little sister. What's even more disturbing is when that *same* exact thing happens while you're out with friends. There's no hiding anywhere when that occurs. In my defense (on both accounts), how was I supposed to know they were related? If anything, I've proven that I'm attracted to a particular look, face structure—even body type. That's a good indicator that I'm at least being true to myself, am I right?

Lastly, it's highly advisable to not venture beyond your comfort zone when meeting new people online. If you feel like this person is someone you definitely would say 'no' to anyway, then you should say the same to their online advances too. A genius once pointed out that if you continue to do something the same but expect different results, then you are likely an insane person. The same applies to online dating. Just because you haven't met that great person yet, doesn't mean you need to drop all manner of morals, values, or likes just to try something new. It's a waste of your time and a waste of the other person's as well.

But if you're into trying new things, then I assure you there is no shortage of dating sites to fit your preference. And there's likely a tagline to fit each site's description (of which I'll paraphrase for you).

There are sites that are religiously affiliated . . .

Find the match that God wants for you. (Ok, really? And by the way, I doubt God would approve of a woman wearing next-to-nothing in her profile pictures as she bends over in a seductive manner. Am I right or am I right?)

There are sites that promote strength by surveys . . .

Our statistics show that 1 in every 4 matches are good for the other and have high success rates! (Ok, what about the other 3 out of 4? Last I checked, in order for a hitter to be good in baseball, he has to be good at least 1/3 of the time, not 1/4).

And there are sites that are just, well, wrong . . . .

Are you a cougar looking for a cub?

To each his own, eh? I urge you not to get caught up in returning to said sites just because you're bored. Dating sites are eager to make some quick dollars off of your sudden need for potential happiness. Luckily, I didn't linger in this world of online dating for very long. I merely put my legs in, waded around a while, and then got out of the pool. Yeah, I cast my reel and brought in a couple that bit the end of my line (figuratively speaking), but nothing that I liked enough to pull back to the boat, show off, and mount back at home (once again, figuratively speaking for the most part). I just wasn't having any luck so I decided to turn away from the whole concept.

But I also turned away for another reason; one that actually trumped the former. You see, I just couldn't look my kids in the eye someday and tell them that daddy met mommy on SingleAndDesperate.com. I just couldn't bring myself to do that. Yes, I'm fully aware that's a prideful thing and I'm just giving my opinion on the matter, but dammit, it's my opinion and I'm entitled to it. I shouldn't rule out the option though; I just have a hard time dealing with that possible reality.

With me, it's all about having a good story. My father met my mother one day at a bar (sounds cliché' but let me finish) while he was out with some friends while she was doing the same. To hear my dad's side of the story is one thing and to hear my mom's side is another. From my dad's perspective, he walked over to a group of six women, all of whom were smoking, save one (my mom) and decided that she was the one he wanted to talk to. The fact that she wasn't smoking was a plus, but she shone like a ray of light amongst her peers. And when my dad brought the charm down with a simple "Hi, my name's George", my mom was love struck and began asking him if he was in the armed forces due to his 'manly physique'. Yeah, he sure sounds like a stud muffin, right?

Until you hear my mother's side of the story, that is.

According to her, my dad came over with the intention of hitting on each of the ladies with her. He was hopeful that someone, ANYONE, would say 'yes' before he was through. When he finally got to my mother, he gave an opening line that was something akin to "Hi, I'm George." This is the one and only consistency I find in either of their stories. My mother was not overly impressed but considering the less-than-threatening opener, this approach seemed to work.

And I'm sure glad it did.

Turns out my mother actually did believe my dad worked out too. She commented that he was "put together nicely" so that was a major draw. The way my dad tells it, you'd think he'd walked over there looking like Mr. Universe. Funny? Yes. Timeless and awesome to hear over and over again? Absolutely, yes.

I admire my dad's courage first and foremost. For a guy who was married by 18, a father by 19, and divorced by 23, he had some serious mojo to make a move on a woman who likely had no baggage to bring to the table like he did. And that's saying something more than 30 years later. I've never been shy about asking my dad for dating advice, even if I knew what I was getting was complete crap. You see, his words of wisdom weren't always the best a man could get.

"Son, you just have to feel it. That's what I did."

I never appreciated that response, but after so many years of thinking things through, I guess he may be right. You can't force a situation as it relates to our feelings; feelings are tied to the heart and the heart is tied to the very essence of who you are—your expectations, your hopes, and your desires for not just yourself, but for another person to share these significant traits with. This is the single, biggest mistake anyone ever makes in dating. They *force* issues of the relationship rather than being good stewards to each other. Relationships are fragile objects that don't respond well to constant push or pull. A relationship will break under too much strain and very rarely returns to its original state. Plain and simple. With the right kind of push and pull, a foundation is formed; like two bricklayers working on a wall, building in tandem as they construct the fortress for each other. If one worker is spoiled or selfish, then he will refuse to build and the firm foundation will crumble and fall. This is not the relationship you deserve so do not seek out a bad partner to build with. You will eventually crumple as they do. These builders need not be heavily experienced or brand new to the world; they need be only ready and willing to handle the task at hand.

All that being said, there is definitely a call to healing if you've been hurt like I have. How does one do this? Well, the answer is reconnecting with yourself and trusting in God. I won't sugarcoat that whatsoever. In all my dating years, I have only now come to know God and what God wants from you in a relationship (man or woman). Does it sound weird or kooky to say that the "ways of the world" are wrong? Yes, I'm sure it does, but it's *true*. You need only look at the pain others experience, without God's intervention, and you begin to understand the connection that needs to happen. That's what I have learned from my dating more so than anything else. It's not about needing to be "the Man"; it's about being *a* man first (or lady), and all the responsibility and strength that goes along with that. Then you find that what you promised yourself has a way of finding you too.

Does that mean I'm not single anymore? At the time of this book, no, it doesn't—but at least I know what I'm looking for now. I was not anticipating talking about sex so much, but when you consider the nature of any dating relationship, sex is one of its most key components. Sex is often treated as the absolute first priority in a new romantic endeavor and because of that, the two parties will wrestle with its importance. What does it mean? How often? When is it 'ok'? Tough questions to ask if you're not asking yourself or the person you're with. Just thinking about it can cause someone to feel drained. I know it because I've been there.

So all that being said, I'm finally okay with waiting on that promise I made for myself so many years ago. There's a powerful quality in moving forward once you've had your personal boundaries broken down, but you still found the strength to renew yourself. The hope is to keep you from tripping up again, and to protect yourself as best as possible. If I can do that, then I'm sure I'll be in good shape – as would anyone else. And thankfully, that type of a promise has nothing to do with human mating seasons whatsoever..

Downright Good Thought: Always eliminate any stuff from an ex . . .

. . . the trails we leave are impossible to cover nowadays.

This may seem like a no-brainer to extinguish all remnants of an ex, but it's not always so easily carried out . . . or remembered. Case in point, the time that we live in. Unless you've been living under a rock for the last 10 years, you are probably well aware of the dozens upon dozens of social networking sites that one can be a part of. There's Facebook, there's Twitter, there's MyLife, there's Match.com, there's YouTube, and there are still the MySpace faithful kicking it old school.

Essentially you can't escape social media and its ability to track your history.

When you're dating, it's insurmountable, nay impossible, for you to discard and eradicate all traces of the dreaded ex unless you are extremely, extremely thorough. I've seen enough of the show Tough Love on VH1 to know that this is so. I find that show to be rather funny so before you judge me, I suggest you give it a try. The host (a male) "coaches" women on why they are single and how they can change this fact. It sounds like lunacy to me but any guy that can stand up to adult women, tell them that they suck at relationships, and not be afraid of the repercussions has either got the biggest gonads of any man who has walked God's green Earth or he's a borderline idiot/genius. Watch the show and you decide for yourself.

But back to my point, loads and loads of social networking sites means you'll have what I call "breadcrumbs." Like the story of Hansel and Gretel, we leave little breadcrumbs all over the internet that lead straight back to ourselves. Do you have old Facebook pics of yourself and that certain someone you used to date? Well, best get rid of those before you jump into a new relationship. Women are crazy about your old photo albums, even on Facebook. Sure it was fun in high school or college, but when you're an adult working for the man, you need to cut your baggage in half. And start with your Facebook account if you do nothing else.

I heard a stat that about 175 million people use Facebook every day. That's just insane. That means that if you do the math, roughly 55% of that population is female. Then consider that about 50% of that population is potentially single. Then another 15-20% of that population is about your age and let's estimate that 1% is a group you'd be at least semi-interested in. So what's the final number? I'm getting 72,188 if you're following along at home. That's a huge chunk of potential partners out there; but don't forget that not all of these ladies are in your zip code, let alone the same country. But if you happen to land one of those lucky ladies, keep in mind she'll have the same kind of access to your internet history. And just like the last girl that decided to date you, she'll want to post pictures of you two all over the blessed internet. So when the relationship goes sour (God forbid), and you two dump each other, make sure you dump the pictures too.

Trust me on this one, you've been forewarned.

Don't just stop with the Facebook accounts either. There are other risky social sites besides Facebook. I haven't even covered such internet mishaps as old dating profiles, past Tweets or MySpace profiles from the olden days. If you've ever posted something silly or stupid like "I'll never love again" or some ridiculous lyric from a popular love song, then you'd best delete that ticking time bomb before he/she discovers it. An even better move would be to eradicate that profile entirely. You never know when that creepy ex will sneak back into your life again.

I suppose the other alternative is to just be up front and straight about the situation. When faced with questions such as, "Why do you still have photos of you and your ex on the internet?"—You may feel vulnerable or on the defensive. Don't freak out though. I suggest the following answers to these inquiries:

1) I don't talk to her anymore, what's the big deal?
2) We're not even Facebook friends, I was unaware I was still tagged in those photos.
3) I don't have the time to go around deleting my name from every photo I'm in on the internet.
4) (Or my favorite)—I'll go ahead and delete those pictures, but would you please do *me* a favor and delete yours as well? (FYI—this could incite a fight so just be careful here.)

Yeah, those are all semi-acceptable in my book. Depending on the level of crazy your current sweetheart is at, you may want to consider which approach to take. Answers like "I don't even talk to her anymore" are not permissible when you live in the same zip code as the ex and "we're not even Facebook friends" can be like saying "I don't creep on her Facebook anymore so what's the big deal?" Women try to read through a guy's dialogue like they're about to uncover some hidden message; like what he's saying isn't *actually* what he's saying. So do yourself a service, gentlemen and just be as direct as possible. Less is more while more is less than great.

And ladies, if I can offer any advice to you (that is, if you'll even accept it), try to do us guys a favor and be discreet about those old photos of you. Yeah, I can live with a few photos of you sharing the same frame as your ex, but if you're still holding onto half-nude beach pictures and face-sucking exhibits, then yeah, we have a problem here. No, I don't care if you're Facebook friends with him; that crap just isn't that important to me, but if you do so enjoy keeping those pictures of you and him around for safe keeping, then guess what—that may be an issue. How does checking his page everyday for updates help *us* too? What the mind is permitted to do will eventually permit the body to do also.

If none of that is changing though and you insist on us staying together, then I guarantee you that I'll find some nice picture frames for me and *my* exes. I'll then proceed to place them around the house for all to see. Fair is fair, is it not?

It's about as fair as finding that old t-shirt that says "Grover High Eagles" when we both know you never attended any Grover High. Whose is this then? Don't tell me you won that shirt at a volunteer convention or bought it from American Eagle; that's just lame. Instead, let's be big boys and girls and just say where it came from in the first place. That way, I can throw the thing out when you're not around. I don't care if it's your lucky shirt. I find it to be very *unlucky* towards our continuing relationship . . . .

The one thing material possessions can do is to establish a physical bridge between you and another person; the manifestation of a memory you may have had. Now, do we go all Total Recall and erase all our memories of that person? No, absolutely not, but please be mindful of what you covet from an ex. Otherwise you'll find your ex constantly texting you to get their stuff back. And what if your new flame finds that out? Well, the gears in their head will begin to turn as to why you're holding onto some ancient artifact from the past. And if you're not the one whose holding onto things, but your new squeeze is, then you may be witness to awkward run-ins and late night phone calls from *their* ex who is desperately clinging to that old relationship.

Wow, that just sounds awesome, doesn't it?

The same goes for inadvertent text messages. If you're dating someone new and a text comes through on their phone which says "hey, what's up? I wonder how you've been" then don't worry too much, that's not a problem. This situation is a problem if that number shows up as blocked or as 10 digits without a name. That person may tell you "I don't know who that is" and true, they may really not know who it is, but take note: this person may have trouble telling someone, "Yo, it's over. Now move on." There's a fine line between being nice and telling someone to get lost in a politically correct fashion. I'm here to tell you that there isn't a surefire method of success; just understand that the contact needs to end so figure out how and just do it.

In relationships, there's always one party that fears what the other person will say about them once the relationship is over. Here's a word of advice on that: get over it. And get over being a "nice" person in the break up. Who cares if someone says bad things about you when the relationship is over? You've made a decision to move on so do it. If it means deleting that number or burning a pair of shorts (sure, that's extreme), then hey, do what's necessary. Just be prepared to answer why your former admirers won't stay lost if you're caught in that situation. Women may have it harder since men are more apt to stalk past prey, but if you're firm about moving on, then the other party will do the same (hopefully).

You can always get restraining orders too. I hear those are all the rage these days.

Another malpractice is to send "Happy Birthday" greetings to an ex via Facebook or some other social medium. No, you're not being "nice" by way of sending your ex a tiding of great joy; what you're really doing is saying how much you wish you didn't screw up their life (or yours) by being in their life. Let's just get that out in the open now. I've been on the receiving end of birthday messages as well as the one who is sending them out. And there has been one consistent truth with all of them: it didn't make me or the other party feel better. If you receive one, the other person is saying, "Hey, I'm still single so I'd like to keep dragging you back into *my* world even though we parted ways." Conversely, if you send one out, then you are probably still single yourself and therefore are sending the same hidden message to your ex.

See how that works?

Do yourself a favor and don't send one is all I'm saying. You protect yourself from further harm and you protect the other person in the process. It's not about telling you what *not* to do; it's about what helps you move on the best. And besides, who wants their current squeeze to discover old Facebook messages of you sending off good wishes anyway? If you're a giant drama queen, then the answer is likely a 'yes', but if you're not, then try asking yourself just what the heck you are trying to accomplish.

Anyway, am I getting through on this yet? I want to make sure I am. If I'm not then take this example: in the wilds of Africa, male lions compete over prides of females (that's a pack or herd) in order to assert their dominance. If one male lion usurps another male for control and takes over the pride, then the new king quickly sets out to assert his new dominion. Can you guess what he does first? Yes, he kills any and all of the cubs that were sired by the prior male lion.

Pretty gruesome, isn't it?

It's just nature's way and we can't dispute it. Am I saying you should slaughter and destroy the belongings of your girlfriend's ex? No, I'm not telling you to do that whatsoever. Should you expect her to ditch most of his crap though? Absolutely. As I said before, fair is fair. If you're hastily throwing out old shirts, scrapbooks you made for some anniversary, or drowning that goldfish you won at the fair that's named after your ex, then you should expect the same from your new girlfriend. It's a mutual respect you should both be sensitive to. And if this person shows neglect in parting with old things, then be wary for yourself. Lingering items are physical representations of lingering emotions.

So just ditch the old stuff, people. It'll pay off in the long run.

Ok, so we've tackled the dating chapters . . .

. . . but wait, there's more.

I spent a good deal of time on that dating chapter and for good reason. It's the number one topic associated with being a single person. If you're single, then you're obviously available to date. That's a given, is it not? Much of what I talked about may have been hard to swallow, but I feel it necessary to share. Most notably, that last bit on Komodo dragons. Yeah, I thought so. Well, I'm not here to talk about those big lizards in this next relatively short portion on dating. I merely want to discuss some other strange, albeit, awkward situations you may find yourself in.

And let's be honest here: you want to know what to do in those peculiar situations. What is life advice without real-life application? So let's do this thing.

The first is the best-friend-that's-the-opposite-sex dilemma. You, yourself, may be in this debacle right this very moment and trust me, it's one of the most common; hence why I'm tackling this one first. So you like this girl (or guy) and you want to get to know them better and as you try to court them for a date, you discover they have one friend who is especially close. The only downside is that this good friend just so happens to be the same sex as *you*. The most primitive instincts within your body raise red flags as you sense the subtle competition you may have. That's when you should ask how these two became such good friends in the first place. Maybe they've grown up together, went to the same elementary school or maybe their parents were friends way before they were even thought of. No matter what the scenario, there's a shared history which has formed a powerful foundation for them both to stand upon. You, being the outsider, are completely new to this arrangement and may be wondering what all lies within this pillar of experiences.

Did they ever date?

Does one secretly like the other?

Do they rely on each other for advice and support?

Is it really just a platonic relationship? (that means there's no sexual tension).

The questions will swirl in your head initially, thus igniting a short period of paranoia where you may doubt the chances of really getting close to this person. And interestingly enough, there is some truth in your gut reaction. If someone has all ready chosen a certain someone to hear their every choice and critical decision, then the chances are very likely they will continue this behavior.

So how might this make you feel? Do you say something about this opposite sex friend? Or do you just let it slide until you actually feel threatened? It's a slippery slope you tread on for this type of circumstance. There really isn't a win-win you can achieve here either. On one hand, you could become the best friend and eventual lover that the other person is looking for but on the other hand, you may stir the once dormant feelings of the opposite sex friend and thus, turn the opposite sex friend into a tizzy of hormonal imbalance. I've experienced both sides of this phenomena and neither is very satisfying. Someone almost always, inevitably, gets his feelings hurt by another party. That's just the reality of the situation.

Can boys and girls play nice enough that you'll never have to worry about personal boundaries being crossed? Well, I'm not so certain. One time I used to believe that men and women could cohabitate with each other upon the precipice that neither party would advance upon the other. Thereby you wouldn't have to worry about leaving your girlfriend to go out with her boy (space) friend on a Friday night while you go and hang out with your guy friends. One would hope that this is perfectly normal and acceptable.

Unfortunately, things are not always so simple. The opposite sex friend will eventually, always, state their presence as their "best friend" begins to leave them. What's the biggest reason? Well, it's the emotional connection that the friend feels for the other. Two people may never have physical contact with one another but if they communicate on a deeply emotional level, then this can be just as damaging if one party decides to split from the other. Don't think so? Well, let's think of the pillars I mentioned earlier.

Once that rock solid base is chipped away by another person, what do you think happens to that other friend? Yeah, they fall hard. So in order to keep from drowning, that opposite sex friend makes one last desperate attempt to win back their friend. Depending how your date feels with your new relationship, everything could go back to normal. Obviously there's a tradeoff here. If the opposite sex friend is placed back in the picture, then you may find yourself trying to woo another potential mate simply because you see the writing on the wall. This person you've been trying to date clearly has greater ties to a friend than to you and hey, that's a big problem.

I feel like I've always been exceptionally proficient at reading body language. The things we don't say with our mouths can be the loudest messages in a room, and guys are notoriously bad at this. I can tell if another guy likes the girl I'm sitting with. I can sense when a dude is checking out another woman from across the way. That's a powerful ability if you're on the "prowl" as a single guy, but it can also work against you. Do not confuse this talent with foolish jealousy. The best way to push someone away (figuratively) is to act like a jealous psychopath. True, you may have some honorable intentions to "protect" the person you're with, but mere protection can be mistaken for flat out territorialism. And yeah, females lean towards not liking that type of Neanderthal behavior.

So if the opposite sex friend continues to make advances that you're wise to, it's often best to see how your date is reacting. If you feel like a wilted banana in a banana patch (man, I love analogies), then you might want to reevaluate what you're doing. And please . . . and I mean, *please*, make sure you address any insecurities you have with your date, not the opposite sex friend. For as much as that jerk is causing you grief, you're only letting that person "win" if you don't take it up with your date. He/she needs to handle their friend, not you.

Ok, so number two on this list: the Stalker Ex. Notice how I didn't say the Ex-Stalker. They aren't former stalkers, they are current stalkers and they are actively stalking you into your next relationship. It's the classic I-can't-believe-you've-already-moved-on mentality. Men and women are both guilty of such a crime. Since I'm a guy, I've marginally had to deal with that creepy ex-boyfriend that continues to call, text, email, even just show up at events that they know their ex is planning to be at.

Yeah, that's really lame, man. *Really lame.*

Perhaps what's most lame is when you break up with somebody and then realize that *you* are doing the exact same, freakin' thing! You understand that you've hit rock bottom when you're standing in line at Dick's Sporting Goods with a pair of binoculars in your hand. You aren't buying those to site see, you're buying those spyglasses with the worst kind of intentions in mind. So yes, go back to the rack and place them on the shelf. You don't need to follow this ex around; you really just need to focus up and move on with your life.

Some people don't get this clue right away though. They prefer to live in a fantasy land where it's permissible to send evil messages and angry letters to their exes, all in hopes that they'll make this person feel as horrible as they do. It's all about karma really. They were made to feel sick, so they are going to return the favor. This action is remarkably childish and if you ever find yourself doing this, you may as well go purchase a bib or a high chair. You've put those binoculars back on the shelf, but before you go home for the night to wallow in sadness, head on over to Babies 'R Us and buy yourself a rattle. You may not see what the other person is up to, but you can shake the plastic toy to your heart's content.

But here's another scenario—what do you do when you run into the other person's stalker ex? What if they suddenly appear, say at the store, or the restaurant, or at their apartment? Well, depending on the circumstance, you prepare to rumble. Then, after things appear to be 'ok', you start to wonder about the dating habits of your new girlfriend/boyfriend. What you need to do is just play it *cool*. Nobody ever won points with their current squeeze for beating up the former play toy in public. If anything, you'll prove that you've got a fuse shorter than a pygmy in a pro basketball game and that's just not the type of impression you want to leave. Emotions will always run high after a break up so your best play is to . . . just . . . be . . . *cool.*

You can always decide later if this person is worth the hassle of a stalker ex or not. But that's really up to you. I'm a territorial man by nature and since I know a guy will creep around the outside of the village long after he's been excommunicated, I keep an eye out. It's amazing how predictable people can be when their emotions get the better of them. Rational, calculative thought is thrown to the wayside as the more primitive, less intelligent parts of our brain takes over. For this reason, I feel blessed to have a slight edge against my competitors. Not because I'm any better than them, just that I can recognize my shortcomings a little more readily.

Finding a suitable partner is no cake walk so one must be at the top of his game. I have found this subtle yet effective method to work best—the Ring Sweep Glance. This ancient maneuver has likely gone by other names but it's still a clever and modern tactic for identifying who is available and who is not. Some guys do it without even knowing it, but others aren't always so discreet. Women do it too. It's the act of committing a quick glance, aka a "sweep" of the eyes, over the left hand of a person you may be interested in. If he or she is sporting a diamond or some form of jewelry, then you know the hunt is off. No ring? Well, go for it. Just be prepared to deal with a jealous significant other if you go that route.

I've employed the Ring Sweep many, many times myself. It's saved me from certain embarrassment on several occasions, but has also worked against me. For instance, doing the Sweep blatantly can incur the look of "Are you some sort of creep?" when a woman notices you gawking at her hand. And if her hands are positioned somewhere near her chest or hips at the moment of sweeping, then you're pretty well sunk at that point. Thankfully a lot of women enjoy showing off their bling to an audience so you don't have to go searching. There's no mistaking relationship status when a rock the size of a walnut sits atop the ring finger of a lady in question. So if she's flaunting it, then let her flaunt away. Keep your distance and focus on the fingers without a glossy ring around them.

This brings me to an even larger issue at hand: how to deal with Cheaters (and yourself if you ever happen to cheat). Ah yes, *cheating*: the one word that no one wants to hear when they're dating someone. You *cheated* on me. I *cheated* on you. Or a combination such as I *cheated* because I knew you *cheated* (in which case, you better be darn sure you knew they were cheating in the first place). To be labeled a cheater is like wearing a bathing suit to a funeral; or bearing a birthmark shaped like the state of Rhode Island on your face. It's the scarlet letter—the open statement that you have wronged another via some insecurity about yourself.

If you look up "cheat" in the dictionary, it's described with other words such as "deceive", "swindle" and "elude". All of which collectively mean to avoid or manipulate a particular situation. The descriptor that stands out the most for me is the following: "to deprive of something expected". This is the worst offender in the bunch. By placing "cheating" in the realm of denying the expected, you open up the concept to something truly terrible. Not only is this person acting selfishly by straying to another for emotional and oftentimes physical satisfaction (thereby hurting the other party involved), the cheater is also *denying* their partner the same type of fervor, energy, and joy that they are now giving the third person in this equation.

Doesn't that just sound really *horrible*?

I'm sure that many cheaters, and non-cheaters alike, have rarely thought of cheating in such a way. And there are hosts of reasons for why these cheaters commit the act in the first place. Each reason steadily more ludicrous than the last, but consider for a moment that you're actively denying the other person love or care because you've moved on to another person? It's essentially the same as stealing a life away. Where this person was once promised a strong and healthy foundation, that foundation has been stripped away beyond their control.

Cheating as a means to get "even" is something I'll never really understand. A person may anger you over their apparent apathy or poor choice of words but does that warrant a vengeful act of cheating? No, I would hope not. And if the person you're dating views relationships as some sort of battlefield to be won or loss daily, then you need to retreat as quickly as you can. Better yet, call for an air lift to fly you the heck up out of there. There are no victories to be won if you think you're in love with someone, otherwise that's not love at all. Love is the true prize of any solid relationship.

There are a handful of clichés meant to define this these kinds of scenarios. Ones such as "once a cheater, always a cheater", for example. It's a common phrase to define the scarlet red lettered folks who apparently can't be monogamous in their relationship endeavors. And for good reason too. Though everyone is entitled to be forgiven for past trespasses, the act of cheating on a current partner is one that is not so easily forgivable. Nor is it something you should take lightly. Honestly, in my personal opinion, if you've been cheated on once by your significant other, there's a very high probability they will do it again. Why? Well, they know they can get away with it and you'll take them back. It's as simple as that. However, if you leave this person and they find someone new, they may take the ramifications of their past mistakes into account with their new relationship.

And hopefully (I say hopefully) they won't make the same mistake twice. You, on the other hand, can find out who they are dating and text them all the nasty things they did to you in an effort to ruin their next relationship.

Right?

Right?

Ok, maybe not . . . but you were thinking that, weren't you?

I've only been cheated on a few times in my life (that I was aware of) and every time it happened, I always asked myself what *I* did wrong to deserve such manipulation. I've had the awkward walk-in on two people conversing about how they need to let me go, been told ambiguous messages such as "out with a friend" only to discover later they were out with a "friend" of mine; and lastly, I've been the witness to the ill-timed text message that said something to extent of "Is he still there?" Yes, none of those experiences were ones I'd like to relive anytime soon. And within each of those trials, I found out the more unattractive pieces of my personality. Like what you ask? How about jealousy? Envy? Irrational anger?

Yes, each a little worse than the last.

None of those ladies were right for me (or me for them), but I needed a wakeup call to get the facts straight in my head.

Here's a tip for you though: don't' treat yourself like you did something really wrong to be cheated on. I won't gloss this over with some cliché like "you deserve better" or crap like that. No, that's just not my style. What I will say is this: know when to walk away. If you really want to get that other person back for what he or she did, then move on. And that doesn't mean to go date somebody right after you get out of a relationship. Instead, hit the ignore button on your phone when that person calls. Don't give the other party your time or energy. I've had an ex or two that kept emailing me nasty grams with the intent to make feel like a horrible person. True, we had broken up on some rough terms, but to go out of your way to continuously rip me apart? Yeah, that's not very cool. And I'm not going to respond to any of that nonsense either. Instead, I'll file those hate letters away in the event I need some sort of restraining order. That's a far more likely thing to happen so take note: sharks will only bite the line of an angler if you keep throwing bait on the hook. If you pull that line out of the water, then you don't have to fear it being bitten.

Lastly, we have the Nega Self. It's the darker, sinister, more negative side of your persona. The Nega Self acts in a manner that is the opposite of what you would consider to be rational, honest, or even righteous. The Nega Self is only concerned with one thing: getting even. Whatever that means and however means necessary to accomplish this task. When the heart is broken and hope in someone has been destroyed, the Nega Self takes center stage.

The unfortunate part of any relationship is that you may inevitably see the Nega Self reveal itself. A stressful situation may expose inner demons you never thought you possessed. It doesn't even have to be a breakup. The Nega Self can come out at the most unexpected times and when it does, you'd best be aware of it. Need some examples?

Your ex is seen talking with another person by two of your friends. You decide to Facebook-stalk or send nasty text messages asking why he/she is so interested in this new person. Why do you do this?

Nega Self.

Your significant other wants to go to an event (say a play) but you'd rather shove rusted nails through your forehead. Instead of catering to their wish, you make up an excuse to not go and thus force them to stay in with you. This cuts them out of enjoying some social time with their own friends. Why do you do this?

Nega Self.

How about you haven't been out with anyone for a while and you suddenly think it's a good idea to chat up your ex or another person you're clearly not interested in but wouldn't mind making out with? Sure, there could be some emotional damage for your efforts but this is about you getting what *you* want. So who cares what happens, right? Why do you do this?

Nega Self.

For as much as I've warned others about the Stalker Ex, the Opposite Sex Best Friend, or the Cheater, I've actually profess that I've been one of those at one point or another. The only one I can't claim is the Cheater, but only on a physical level. Yes, there are more types of cheating than kissing (among other things). Severing the ties of an emotional bond can be just as destructive as any physical infidelity. Most marriages that end after 20plus years will do so because the physical surge is gone. Without an emotional connection, you're pretty well sunk.

Am I proud of such crimes? No, absolutely not, but it was my Nega Self acting in place of me. Everybody's got a Nega Self ready to cut loose at the most inopportune of times. Be warned out there. Don't think that just because you had a bad experience in a relationship it means you are destined for more craptastic moments. That's some vague advice, I know, but it's silly to think that way in the first place. Why else would you want to wallow in sadness? Is that what you want from life? Unless you're 13 and just found out your celebrity crush will never know you as a person, there's really no place for an emotional breakdown.

However, if you ever find yourself hanging outside houses to catch a glimpse of your ex with another person, then you know you've tripped off the deep end, my friend. So if that's you, I have only this to say: come back to us. You may get a restraining order against you otherwise. That, or the guy who is *in* the house, will come *out* of the house and beat the living tar out of you. Nobody wants that to end their day. That's just what I hear.

Epiphany: Hanging out at coffee shops . . .

. . . makes for some great eavesdropping.

Wow, so how do we follow up the dating chapters? I'm rather confident that the dating portion was what you wanted to read in this book. So if that's all you were after, then I guess you can stop while you're ahead. However, if you're interested in more of the exciting adventures I've embarked upon while being single then by all means, please sit and stay a while; preferably in a bar or coffee shop since that's what this next chapter is about.

I've established that I don't like spending too much time in my apartment. The confined space can likened to a prison cell. But instead of hanging out in bars every night, I've found another outlet in the local coffee shop. And not just the Starbucks's of the world. I'm talking the establishments that you can only find by living in a particular zip code. That's where you can find the true locals of any place you reside in. And when you do just that, you can discover a lot more than what you bargained for.

For starters, I only started the coffee shop thing after I started working full-time. That and the bar scene just wasn't happening. I'd spent some time hanging with my buddies at local bars, much like the good ol' days of college. That was the first and logical choice when you're young, single, and looking for a "hangout" to call your own. Problem is (among many) that once the night closes in, alcoholic aphrodisiac switches people into a here's-my-life-story mode. I have always been a target for these people, who somehow think that my confused look somehow translates to, "Yes, I want to hear all about your life's mistakes, despite how you are stumbling over your words and can barely stand." If I had to grin and bear one more tale about sales man Rick and his struggle with selling hand sanitizers to China, I may have slit my wrists right there at the bar. Nope, just couldn't do it anymore. There's a time and a place to give your life's story to a total stranger. And that time is not when I've had too few drinks to tolerate you.

The ladies I didn't mind as much. But there's always that one girl. You know, that one girl who is also sipping on liquid courage as she makes her way over to talk to you. Easily spotted by any male, these women stand out in a crowd as they are either a) the least dressed or b) the one who can't walk properly in 12 inch heels. It's times like these where I call upon my training. The training I've honed to handle these kinds of situations. First of all, I'd like to think myself a somewhat chivalrous man. I open doors for my dates, pay for meals when I can, and I address my date as lady at all times appropriate. That and I prefer to make the first move. If a lady has been there a while, isn't falling over herself and seems to have it together, then I wouldn't mind having a conversation. But if you're stumbling on your way over to talk to me, that's another story. And when you get there, what exactly is your plan? Why did the thought of suggesting we do a shot together seem like a good idea? Come on now, that's just silly. I hate doing shots. I'd rather be force fed raw dog meat that have to take shots for "fun."

Come to think of it though, that's kind of extreme. I'll pass on the raw dog meat so if you can think of something equally disgusting, we'll go with that instead.

Anyway, the bar scene wasn't really working as the springboard I needed to meet new people. As such, I kept a constant vigil on the Starbucks just a block away from my apartment. With my other eye, I fixed what attention I had left on the new Indian deli just an earshot away. I say Indian because the ownership was clearly of this descent. Appeared to be a relatively nice establishment but I will say this: how more stereotypical can one get? A small shop; opening for the first time; and here it's owned by a group of individuals who are clearly immigrants. Local folks may complain about these so-called foreigners but the same types of entrepreneurs were doing the same thing years ago and they were white, black, and Asian too. So no laughing please, however, if that place ever adopts a name like the "Quick-E Mart" I will probably have to intervene and let them know that it's not a good choice for a name.

The days went on as I weighed the option of Starbucks. Historically I didn't frequent coffee shops because I hated coffee. Why go to a Mexican restaurant if all you want is sushi? That's what I figured, anyway. I've never had a very long attention span for most things unless I'm in the "Mode" (a powerful frame of mind unique to us Faltots that fixates us on one objective until it is completed), so coffee doesn't exactly help someone who is already hyperactive. Plus I've seen friends who suffer from caffeine withdrawal. It ain't pretty. I've seen coffee addicts get the same shakes alcoholics get when they don't have their daily Jack Daniels. Are there support groups for such an addiction? Yes, there are actually. They're called every-other-office-worker-in-America support groups. If you feel the urge to talk to someone about your predicament, then look no further than the cubicle next to you for a fellow addict and shoulder to cry on.

To this day, I still don't understand the need for coffee. I've just have never acquired a taste for the stuff. There was a time when I would drink it out of boredom but that turned out to be a disaster as one should never, ever drink a stimulant when one is bored. That's like swatting at a bee too many times without actually hitting the darned thing; the result just won't end well for you and you'll find yourself sitting in a sweat with clammy hands and blurred vision. I hope that you can understand my hesitance now in this situation. Rather than write the whole thing off, I decided to observe from afar before I actually entered.

Upon further investigation, I found that this specific location might as well have been a nightclub. The sheer number of people filtering in and out was crazy. That's when an idea hit me. If I ever needed extra cash, I'd interview to be a bouncer at a coffee shop. Come on, you *know* they need bouncers. One too many times I've seen folks get salty about their non-fat, mocha-sprinkled, pumpkin latte. With a name like that, I guess I'd be pissed too if the order was wrong. That's a real mouthful to remember when you head up to the cashier so why wouldn't you get all prissy if the barista screws it up? Makes total sense, right? Sure, it does, but if you get too ornery over a bad drink order, then the Coffee Cop (aka bouncer) needs to step in.

Anyway, I finally mustered the courage to investigate and see what the buzz was about. I could at least take my laptop and do some work while I was there, so what the heck? More specifically, I had looked into getting my teaching certificate part-time so this would be the ample time to make that happen (old dreams die hard, eh?). And while I'm at it, I may be able to run into some new people while I'm there. And chances are they'll be sober enough to carry on a conversation too. Just so long as they don't have those coffee shakes I was mentioning earlier. In which case, I'll have to tell them to please leave me alone.

I don't remember what day it was, I just remember I got there. I walked in, ordered an Early Grey tea, and sat down near one of the windows. Ok, so first contact had been made. So here we go.

Open up your things, I told myself, *and get to work.* When I looked around the room, I noticed that there were mostly people about my age. People in their twenties and thirties, I figured. *Not too bad*, I thought. There was a healthy dose of soothing music playing on the loud speakers too. A nice touch to help put any tension on the backburner, I thought. With my laptop out, I got down to business.

My first few sessions weren't very productive as I was often visited by some friends I had made in the area. No, not at the coffee shop, these were people I had met through other friends and at various social events. A good group of people to say the least and am pleased to say I'm still a part of their lives to this day. However, I could have easily ruined these relationships when one of us decided to play a game (albeit a stupid one) where we each had to describe one other with one word and one word only.

Hmm, great idea, right? The guys took their critiques of each other in stride, but the ladies? Well, not exactly. As we went around the group, I depicted three of the young gals as the following: jovial, flush, and fiery. The first was semi-happy with my assumption, but believed *jovial* was too close to being like Santa; the second couldn't understand the meaning of "flush" for a personality trait (come on, of course you can!) and the third was somewhat pleased as this made her sound tough. However, it was lucky lady number four that got the best I had to offer. When it came to her, I used the term "calculating" and all hell broke loose.

Guys, if I can ever imbue proper wisdom upon you, I sincerely hope I make it known that words such as jovial, flush, fiery, and especially calculating are not acceptable when describing a female friend. They just aren't very kosher; no matter what your innocent yet misguided intention may have been. You're better off sticking to the basics like nice, kind, giving, and organized. Ok, maybe not "organized", but at least it's better than calculating.

So as my newfound friends came to the coffee shop less (ironic, right?) I could finally get back to my work at hand. Rather than hit the ground running, I was beginning to succumb to a common human condition. The environment reinforced the apparent need to eavesdrop on every conversation within a 20 foot radius. If a person was especially loud, then I could probably pick out the most intimate of details from even farther away.

A coffee shop is a hot spot for socializing. It grants someone the same type of privacy you'd experience via the sharing of bunk beds. You don't want to hear anything or be bothered by the person above you, but no matter what you do, you can still feel and hear that person move in their bed. The same can be said for sharing close quarters in these places. And don't let the headphones and earpieces fool you. These people *are* listening in to what *you* are saying too. And

I don't say that just because I have been guilty of this. I've seen it happen, but I didn't realize it till I started doing it too.

My awareness of this fact first occurred when I overheard some ladies talking about their marriages. One sounded pissed off that her husband was always traveling while the other sat and shook her head like she couldn't care less to hear about the situation. Once woman one was done rambling, woman two would chime in with "Well, my husband is usually home by four, makes dinner, and gets the kids to bed."

Wow, what a jerk, I thought. Here, this other woman is pouring out her problems to you and all you can do is shove your own fortunes in her face? That's not exactly being a good friend in my opinion. But isn't that the norm? Don't we always try to relate to each other through similar experiences? Pretty narcissistic, if you ask me. Shouldn't you *want* to give feedback that would be positive if this other person is complaining about something? I mean, as a friend that should be priority number one; not your own agenda.

My college training had taught me that there were actual theorems out there that could explain this phenomenon of give-and-take within conversations. It's a little something called conversational analysis (not exactly an original title, but at least it gets us to the point, right?). Conversational analysis essentially says that people take "turns" in conversation. You have constructional components and allocation components. Before I lose anybody out of boredom for the topic, try and level with me. Basically, this is a learned quality where we let one person talk, and then we give feedback. Apparently some smart guy named Harvey Sacks came up with this analysis of conversation in the 1970s. I know what you're thinking though—*really*? This was discovered only 40 years ago? You would think that one of the more basic components of human life would have been analyzed by now . . . but hey, I guess not. We clearly have a failure to communicate on even our communication.

Part of that reason, I found, is in due part to the idea that casual conversation didn't have structure. Sacks must have been ticked off because he didn't believe that was true. *No*, he did not. He wanted to prove that people actually *do* have structure in their conversations (whether they be formal or informal). The creepy part is that this guy worked for a suicide counseling service, so by way of listening to people who wanted to end their lives he started coming up with this theory. Still think it's creepy? Yes, I thought so too. I don't know if I would ever feel inspired to come up with complex theorems while working at a suicide watch hotline, but hey, that's just me.

Thanks to Sacks, we have structure in our casual conversations. Think about this for a minute: you are talking to a friend, coworker, family member, whoever and you're talking about something. Let's say it's about what you ate last night. You start off with a question: "hey, what did you eat for dinner last night?" And your whoever-person answers: "I had mac and cheese. You?" And there you go. The sequential order of conversation ensues. You're getting information from them; they are getting information from you; what a grand experience we're having. And let's face it, that's what talking and communication are for. You give information to another person in exchange for their information and vice vesa.

Why do we do this though? Why do we feel the need to give away our own info when someone else is disclosing theirs? In the case of my lady friends at the coffee shop, both clearly had an agenda. One wanted to be heard, but the other one gave the impression (at least from a distance) that she wanted affirmation that her info was "better" or on par with her friend's. But was she doing that on purpose? Even so, shouldn't your compassion override your need to just give info back? Shouldn't you say something like, "Hey, I'm sorry to hear that. I wish there were something I could do. Maybe you should try to keep talking to your spouse about this?"

Those lines aren't so hard to give, are they? I suppose this may depend on the situation. Or you just don't care enough about what this other person is saying. In which case, you're a crappy friend and really need to reevaluate your social circles.

I concluded that the logical thing to do was to share relative information. You're showing interest by relating to that other person, but you're also letting them know where you stand. How nice, right? If this other person actually gave a crap about her friend's plight, she may have answered differently, but then again, I don't know all the details. Maybe she was trying to reinforce the idea to her friend that her husband needs to come home earlier. You know, the "stick-it-to'em" mentality. I wish I could say that was the case but I'll never know for certain. And I'll never know if that husband ever started coming home more often either. Ah well, I had to get back to my work anyway.

I slaved away a little longer as the two ladies went back and forth. It was during this time when more people started to file in. It was after-dinner hours so the reason for why people were getting coffee at this time was beyond me. Were they all working nightshifts? I mean, come on. I may be older now, but a few drops of caffeine in the evening and I'm going to have a hell of a time trying to wind down later. My questions were answered though as I came to understand that this was exactly what some of these folks were doing—preparing for that long night ahead. Many of them were nurses, some doctors, and others were the stereotypical truck drivers that travel cross country. Yes, even the men you'd see on sweathogs sporting that big ol' 'MOM' tattoo were stopping in for a drink. Knowing this, if I ever decide to go into the coffee shop business, I'm going to name my place the "The Melting Pot." Maybe the "The Brewing Pot" sounds better? Yeah, Brewing Pot, it is.

Considering the amount of people stopping in, it made me realize the multitude of folks working while the rest of us are sleeping. I thought that it was rough enough having an 8-5 job. You're at work all day, stuck at a desk, cranking away on your computer while the majority of the world is doing the same, but when the day ends and you head home, other people are just starting their "day." To the nurses of the world, security folks, and 24-hour workers, I commend you.

You have a shift that no one else is willing to take and you handle it in stride (at least I hope so).

You also take notice how your friends that work these night shifts suddenly begin to disappear when you have gatherings. You start saying things like "Oh, where's Maggie?" or "Did you invite Chris?" The answer that follows is either a) "I did but he/she is working the night shift and can't make it" or b) "I forgot", which means that a string of no-I-can't-make-it's made this person forget about them entirely. It's a sad thing, but nothing to lose sleep over. You either want to hang out with somebody or you don't. And if you want to see them, you'll make the time. End of story.

By now I had been there a few hours and I was starting to make some headway on this whole school research thing. Did you know that most universities offer night courses for people who *have* a bachelor's and want to change their career path? I guess this is what you'd call the "Plan B Degree" since "Plan A" didn't turn out so well. The cost of these services were just as tight as attending school for four years, but what was more shocking is how easy it could be to switch from teaching history to engineering airplanes. I can get an aviation degree in less than 2 years? No way . . . . and if I want to be a teacher, all I have to do is put in 3 hours every other night for a year and a half? That's not too shabby. Here's a better plan: How about you just give me one semester to learn, one more semester to observe and get field experience, then take $10,000 from me to call it even. That's really what we're after anyway, right? I'll either sink or swim at this new gig and what does it matter so long as you get paid. If it doesn't work out, I'll be back in six months to try again. Maybe this time I'll get licensed in scuba instruction.

The possibilities were endless with night school, but I didn't want to get lost in the sea of uncertainty once more.

I remember ending my night before 10; knowing full well that I'd done more people-watching than actual work. In addition to that, I'd spent a whole ton of time just doing the background checks on schools. I needed to actually *apply* the next time I walked in this place. When I exited, I got a farewell from the barista people and headed out. That's funny, no scantily clad bartender waving to me as if to say "maybe next time you'll get lucky." This was new to me. There were certainly no salesmen trying to recount the good old days of selling vacuum sweepers door-to-door as well. What a relief, right? All things accounted for; I decided it'd be appropriate to go back there. So I did.

My next few visits enabled me to "meet" even more interesting people. A couple of girls who were in high school (I'm only guessing by the way they were acting) were complaining about the boys in their school having tattoos. They were so turned off by it that they had a good idea to end the fad: they were going to get multiple piercings on their face and ears. *What? What a stupid idea*, I thought. So you're basically going to end one body-altering fad by way of starting another? I suppose when you're a teenager these types of things make sense, but I don't recall ever having ideas like that when I was that age. Then again, I was never a teenage girl either; that I can recall.

Close by, another man was sitting with his parents, but from the looks of it, he was receiving the scolding of a lifetime. From what I could gather, he'd been to jail at least twice in the past year and his parents were vouching that he stop "living in the past" and take responsibility for his family. The young man, who couldn't have been more than 30, shot back virulently towards his father. He even cursed his father for not helping him when he was put behind bars. The verbal assault continued until the son dropped the bombshell I could certainly see coming . . . .

"Where were you when I was younger, Dad?!"

The words weren't heavy-handed or lengthy but I won't soon forget them. For what followed was a look on Dad's face filled with sheer shock and disappointment. The father looked defeated by the comment so he bit his lower lip and stared into the ground. If he were younger, I suppose, he would have got up and smacked his son a good one for being so intolerable, but instead you could see him internally debating how to handle the situation. There was obviously a history here and the father knew he was walking on thin ice. How does one speak clearly to another when that person is so filled with anger and resentment? I didn't know the answer to that question, but to his credit, the father did a decent job of keeping his cool before he tried to do just that: answer the accusatory words of his son.

I guess it's hard to come up with a good handle on a scenario like that; especially when emotions are running high. This son clearly had daddy issues, but the father was not immune to recognizing that either. Whether he was willing to believe that he'd abandoned his son was one thing, but to face what his son stated was another. This boy wanted his father to own up to something that was larger than the apparent stay in prison.

Onward I listened as the father tried to explain that he (the son) was being irrational and needed to put things in perspective. *Ok, this is a good move,* I thought. *Try and bring things back to a state of equilibrium before they get out of control. We don't want someone to start throwing coffee around here. That's just not cool.* But instead of being open-minded like the father hoped, the son put on a full-court press of bad memories.

"You've never looked out for me!"
"I've always had to do things on my own!"
"You just don't understand where I'm coming from because you choose not to!"

I think it was at about this time that I felt more sympathetic towards the father than the son; no matter what the circumstances of old. Even if this man had been an absent father for much of his son's life, at least he was willing to be here now and talk out his son's problems. And in public of all things. Obviously his son was not willing to share in this friendly reunion. The son wanted redemption, revenge

178

even, for the times he felt were stolen or never shared with his father. What a terrible feeling to have; on both ends. A simple conversation about trying to rectify a misdemeanor had turned into what this meeting was really all about: a bitter son with a absent father who wasn't around enough when he was a boy.

Logic says that when you're older, you accept the past for what it is. You can't change it, that's for sure, and you can't go back to make new memories. If that were possible, I'm sure we'd have a lot more happy endings in the world. Sadly, the best you can do is try and make the most of the moment you're presented and move forward. That's logical, right?

People seldom behave this way, I find. We want absolution for things that have wronged us. We want there to be an answer which paints us, the accuser, as being in the right and not unjustified in feeling the way we do. It's really selfish but it's brought on by other selfish actions. Maybe this father wanted to stay young and forego his responsibilities when he was younger? Did he not come home that much to see his son because he'd rather be out with friends? Did he have some sort of demanding job? I was prepared to cringe if the son brought up some type of infidelity, but thankfully that never surfaced. This father might have neglected his son somewhere along the way and that selfish behavior inevitably lead to his son's own selfishness that he (the father) was now faced with.

I wondered whose fault this fell on the most. Without knowing the whole story, I cannot say, but I do know what needs to happen in order to end this scuffle: someone needs to stop hating. Forgiveness would be the only way to move forward lest they both be swallowed up in disdain for the rest of their days. Upon looking at the son, I could see that the journey to forgiveness had not even begun yet.

This truly angered me to my core. This was not my life or my story but I could not help but feel pain for both father and son. As adults, you'd think they would be able to press onward without an issue, but sadly, it was not. I stand firmly in the belief that once you are old enough to make your own choices, you and you alone do what is necessary to survive. If you are running late to work one day and you get cut off by some jerk to make an exit, you make a decision. You either turn that cheek the other way, or you rev that engine, flip'em the bird and fly up next to that asshole so you can get a good look at the person who wronged you. Honestly, getting revenge is what we want to do, but is that right? And isn't that the easy route? It's easy to be angry, but it's another challenge entirely to be forgiving, especially in the heat of the moment. The type of anger I was hearing between these men encompassed years and years of wronged moments, not just a one-time occurrence. Or perhaps it was more like years and years of inward hatred, stewing and brewing to a boil that was only now coming out from under the lid.

After some more jawing and finger-pointing, the son sat back in his chair. He seemed happy to have finally vented so much. He stared back at his dad who was tongue-tied and speechless. The mother, who had been doing her best to stay mum for much of this conversation, continued a silent vigil. She stared at the ground, making subtle comments under her breath that only her husband could hear. I can only imagine what she was saying, but it was probably something to the extent of "we need to leave before things get more heated." But the father wasn't having it. He'd turn away from her, look his son in the face, and carry onward about how his son needed to "grow up."

Then something really strange happened. In the midst of the verbal onslaught that the son was throwing at his dad, the father pulled an audible. The father brought up the topic of his son's wife. The son's banter stopped dead in its tracks as if he'd been hit with a stiff right hand. The father proceeded to remind his son how he'd abandoned his own wife by misbehaving; how he'd spent money frivolously; and finally how he'd left his wife squandering for cash while he was sitting in jail. The son was speechless and for the record, so was I. I didn't know whether to continue on, pretending I was listening to music on my laptop or perhaps go buy some popcorn. The son was quieted but he took a moment to gather himself. The remark from his father was fierce enough to threw him off his game. The son could possibly have been in silent agreement; recognizing his own shortcomings just like his father. I waited to find out which was which. It didn't take long, of course.

"That's my problem, not yours!"

And there it was again. The son was good at deflecting from the issue at hand, a skill he had learned from his father it would appear. Like father, like son I suppose. In all the quarreling, these two men were merely looking at mirror images of themselves, which could have been the most inherent problem therein. This comment spurred the mother into action, who stood up and asked that everyone leave right away. Then, despite all the arguing, yelling and inability to see eye-to-eye, the father and son gave each other a similar glance as if to say, "Yes, let's go" and walked out together. Or as best they could in a together-like fashion.

Oh come on, man! It was just getting interesting! You can't leave me hanging like that, can you?! Well, sadly, they did. I scanned the room and saw that other onlookers had also taken notice of the squabble. Some watched the trio exit the building while others looked up periodically as if to hide their own eavesdropping. I was not so subtle. My head had been up for much of the conversation and I swear that I probably made eye contact with the dad at least twice. Maybe that helped to keep the father in check? Who knows?

If there was one thing I took from this experience, it was this: don't bring private matters into a public coffee house. I mean, really? Everyone else is trying to have an engaging conversation or doing work, so leave the family feud at home please.

I guess the other takeaway (and could be more important) is how difficult it can be to act like the ideal parent. I look back at my parents, and though I definitely had my disagreements, I tried not to blame them for my own problems. This always seemed like an easy way to pass blame. Both my father and my mother did the best they could with what they knew. I sat and pondered my childhood a while until I came to the conclusion that I wasn't as happy as I had thought. I *had* blamed my parents for a lot in my life. At least at one point or another and I'm sure you have too. It's as if we're angry for even being born; a crazy thought if you think on it.

There's a lot of selfish behavior going on when you're young. It's only natural considering the world you inhabit: *yours*. If your parents gave a damn at all, they did their best to provide, protect, and shelter you. And yet, despite all this, you still found a way to blame them for anything that went wrong in your life. It's ok, though. It's only natural.

Freud calls it the ego in us all; the expressive portion of our inner desires and our need to establish balance in daily life (while somehow pleasing our 'id' or subconscious in the process). No easy task for sure, right? When you're a child, you seek to please only yourself. But it's your lack of responsibilities which permits this behavior. When you get older, this changes, or at least that's what we would hope for. Growing up physically doesn't always mean you grow up emotionally. And some scars run deeper than the Mariana Trench.

I decided to forego my studies and do some research on early life. What I found was pretty interesting, and tied in directly to what had just transpired. Apparently when we're kids, we have the tendency to attach ourselves emotionally to just about everyone around us. As we get older, this lessens as we become more aware of "stranger danger" and thus, look to our parents/guardians for protection and support. Now, depending upon how your parents treated you during these years, their parenting styles could affect your own attachment capacities later in life.

So wait, back up. If my parents didn't give me the right amount of attachment/detachment as a kid, then I might have major insecurities as an adult? Well, I guess I can believe that notion. The first few years of your life are considered the most important since you're the least resistant to change during this time. I wished the father/son duo were still around as I'd love to pinpoint where exactly this relationship could have gone wrong. Was it as early as the toddler years? Or was it something that happened when he was a teenager? Maybe this guy never grew out of that "sow your oats" stage? Once again, I can't answer these questions without having all the details, but it does make you wonder. What could have been so *bad* that this son just couldn't let go?

I've disliked, even loathed, my parents for various reasons throughout my life, but as an adult, what's the point in still being so upset? Shouldn't you have your own life by then? Shouldn't you be ready to take responsibility for yourself and for your own actions? And shouldn't you be mature enough so as to not blame all your problems on events that happened years and years ago? I wish it were so. If that were the case then maybe this conversation wouldn't have ever happened. Maybe instead of having this argument in the middle of a freaking coffee shop, this father and son could be at home talking about sports or reminiscing on olden days. Heck, even the weather would be a better topic. The Midwest certainly has its fair share of "weather chatter" . . . .

"Looks like rain today."
"Nah, that's snow."
"Really? It's only May . . . ."
"Yes, and it's snowing in May."

Ah yeah, gotta love the Midwest. If there's one thing we're famous for besides being the birthplace of John Glenn and singer David Grohl, it's the fantastic seasons we have year round; no, not spring, summer, fall, and winter. We have: cold season, slightly colder season, road construction season (which is still cold) and the fourth one being the mildly temperate season (which can be swelteringly hot). It's that fourth cycle that keeps people alive and well in the Midwest. I can attest to that for sure. No other place has the change in seasons quite like the Midwest. To go from blistering cold in the winter to being as hot as the Sahara Desert in the summer is a real feat that not many other locations can claim.

Still, I sat there a while wondering if this father/son duo would ever rectify their relationship. And what it would take to do so. Counseling? An apology? Maybe an act of God himself? Who can say, I suppose. But one thing was for sure—I was making absolutely no headway on this whole school thing so I stuck my nose back in a book and got to work.

I continued this routine for some time thereafter. Not the eavesdropping on quarreling families (that only happened when the exchanges toppled over into my workspace); I'm instead referring to my new evening schedule. I'd get home from work, work out, make dinner, and then walk over to the coffee shop to do my research. And as I persisted with this habitual undertaking, I took note of the more interesting occurrences around me. Notably, those that I considered to be *regulars*; a recurring visitor at an established watering hole that typically has a specified time of entry and most times has developed a personal relationship with those on staff.

This is a *regular*.

There were plenty of regulars at this coffee shop. Their personalities differed greatly, ranging from the bizarre to downright mysterious with all others in between. Over time, I recognized how each of them would arrive at different points throughout the day only to reconvene together later that evening. This type of behavior left me questioning whether or not these people were something akin to a group of superheroes. The coffee shop was merely their headquarters for checking in at the end of a long day. This was highly inconceivable but I entertained this idea. Wouldn't it be interesting if it were true?

I decided to give each of them names to further fuel this fantasy of mine. It seemed only fitting, of course. If these people were going to be moonlighting superheroes, then they needed aliases.

First, there was the Great Gigabyte Guy or Triple G, for short. This dude owned a laptop the size of a chalkboard yet still felt it necessary to plant it firmly upon his crotch. His computer may have been the first laptop in existence. He had weird emblems all over his computer and he was usually plugged in via his headphones. I figured he must be some type of a writer or worked in media due to the plethora of stickers upon his machine. He was always laughing out loud to himself, a trait I found especially funny as the people around him were often startled by his actions. Nearly 100% of the time he failed to recognize his own abrupt behavior, making it all the more amusing to me. These same people who weren't regulars would try to sneak a peek at his screen to see what was so entertaining and those who did had mixed expressions. To this day, I have yet to take a look myself. I enjoy the mystique of not knowing what gives him such pleasure. My real suspicions are his possible involvement in government espionage or an addiction to YouTube videos. Considering the stickered computer, I'm inclined to think the latter but hey, you never know.

Another individual was an elderly man who was clearly some kind of military veteran. If Uncle Sam had a father, then this guy would be it, so his name was Great Uncle Joe, or just Old Joe. How do I know he was a war veteran? Well, he always sported an old school hat with a big brim that stated "US Air Force" upon it. I suppose that's not a dead giveaway, but the man had that certain look in his eyes that he'd seen a thing or two in his day. He had a walker to help him get around which he trudged forward with despite the awkwardness of the darned thing and he did so with a rhythmic vigor that made you think he was counting his every step. This man never talked much, but every server, man and woman knew who he was. He usually grunted as he entered and exited the place and when he got a drink, it literally took him a good 10 to 15 minutes just to take a seat somewhere. The eventual location had to be a couch too. No wooden seat would do and if there weren't a couch, he'd just stand there and wait until the person sitting at his favorite location got up and walked away (No kidding). I soon learned that the couch served a more obvious purpose than sheer strategic placement: this was for nap-taking (talk about loitering!). I guess when you're a war vet you can do that sort of thing and nobody will bat an eye. Not like anybody would tell him to leave though. That'd just be rude to "Old Joe."

The third guy on the Regulars squad was Asian Chronic Study Boy, a young Asian man (as you probably figured out from the name) who was almost always studying four to five books at a time. Unlike Gigabyte Guy, ACSB really *looked* like he was doing something productive. I don't know if he ever finished a project though because he was constantly swapping between all five books at once, never letting on if he were done with one. Then again, each book could have been for the same subject, but once again, I shall never know. What I do know is that this kid is either one of the smartest people I know or one of the worst multi-taskers on the face of the planet.

Then there was Postal Worker Willie, or PWW. I know that Willie worked for the Post Office as he sported the outfit. He'd stop in at any hour of the day, grab his coffee and then sit down to crank away on his computer without fail. Sometimes he'd just show up to sit for a while before he headed off again (likely saving the world like the rest of the squad, I imagine). He had scraggly gray hair and big aviator-style glasses to go along with a thin frame. If he had long facial hair, he'd kind of resemble Gandalf from Lord of the Rings, minus the magic and sorcery. I really wanted him to get up one day and tell people "You shall not pass!" as they patiently waited in line. That would have brought a smile to my face, even if it would have freaked out the other customers.

And then there was Loves-to-Read Linda. If she had a special power, it would be an ability to read whole books in one sitting. Linda came in every night, usually after nine, with a thick book tucked under one shoulder. She had short hair to go along with her short frame and a squared face. A rather compact and little individual, she probably had neck pains from constantly looking up at other people for she couldn't have been more than 4'9." She always had a smile on her face and never ceased to have something nice to say about the people who served her, which was a refreshing thing to behold. The smiles and gestures were likely premeditated by whatever book she was reading. She'd hold the book close to her chest and glow about the wild story she was neck-deep in. Very rarely did I see her bring in the same book twice. Secretly I hoped that one day a time would come when Linda would walk in with something by J.C.L. Faltot strapped under her arm.

Ah well, maybe someday, right?

Then there was the Annoyed-That-We're-Still-Married-But-Might-As-Well-Play-Cards Couple. As the moniker suggests, these two were a riot. They not only frequented the Starbucks I went to, but other coffee shops I dipped in and out of periodically. Everywhere I went, they seemed to follow. And no matter where they went, they always did the same thing. The wife would bring in a deck of cards, carefully cut and fold them with her husband watching and then when she was done, she'd pass them out for a rousing game of what I believe was Go Fish. I kid you not. So you're probably wondering where the "Annoyed" part comes into play. Well, let me enlighten you. It seems that the husband was always "cheating" according to the wife as she'd consistently cry "BS" over and over again (I'm sure you know what BS stands for). In the beginning, I figured that this was just the card game they were playing. You know, the game of BS. But if you listened long enough, you'd realize that the husband was, in fact, a dirty cheater and the only way the wife could keep him in line was by claiming shenanigans every other turn. Funny and a tad bit sad to say the least, but a real distraction when you're trying to get some work done. I believe the most humorous part of this tale is how the games would usually end with the wife winning. A celebratory victory dance ensued shortly thereafter which likely left her husband wondering why he participated in the game in the first place.

Lastly in my group of Regulars, there was the Illegal Immigration Mafia. I suppose these guys were a separate faction from the Regulars, but their frequent appearances gave them regular status nonetheless. Nothing big to report on these guys other than they spoke little to no English at all and often gathered in groups of 10 to 12. Old, young, it didn't matter. These guys didn't segregate by age, only by what ethnicity you hailed from. And if you had to ask me what ethnicity they were, I really couldn't answer that one. It's something between Serbian, Indian, Greek, Mexican and a dash of Middle Eastern thrown in for good measure. If I had a halfway decent work ethic, I would have tried to pick up on some dialogue but I just never did. All I know is that it definitely wasn't English or Spanish. In the long run, perhaps it was better that I never knew what they were saying. Otherwise, I'd have even more eavesdropping to keep up on.

To round things out, I'd also get the occasional drifter that would leave an indelible mark on my memory. One-timers like the couples who'd sit and talk about various swingers clubs they liked to frequent (awkward) and the entrepreneurs that would sit and organize mass marketing efforts from the edge of a foamy latte (doubly awkward when the deal goes bad). Yeah, you get all sizes and shapes when you hit up the local coffee shop. I've even been witness to schizophrenics, beggars, and pimps looking to solicit young women they saw at the shop. That last one was a major bummer for me as these women were likely to never come back again. And who could blame them either?

Thanks a ton, ya jerks.

One such man was not a one-timer, but more or less a regular like the others. I didn't include him in my team of Regulars as I was unsure what the nature of his business was. He would arrive at differential intervals throughout the day, clad in trench coat and an old-fashioned derby cap. His drink of choice appeared to be a tall coffee—no food items, just the coffee. And when he visited the shop, he would take a seat near one of the corners, carefully observing everyone else around him. I didn't think too much of this until some young ladies appeared. If they were alone or in pairs, you could see him eyeing them up from a distance, mentally prepping himself to make a move; and when he did, he said something that I could only discern as being "Hello, here is my card." I had no idea what he was doing, or what he was soliciting, but the fact that he would only talk to young girls made my skin crawl. Nearly every girl I saw turned him down, their responses either of utter disgust or occasional laughter as he trudged back to his seat in the corner. I was happy to see this rejection as it kept me from intervening on the girls' behalf. For the times I was not at the shop while he was, I can only hope the same occurred for the other girls I didn't see.

Another story that stuck out transpired over the course of a year. One time in early Spring, a few friends of mine went to a local restaurant to catch up. On our way out, a well-dressed man, in a trench coat, approached us asking for gas money. His story was that he was traveling with family and he needed a few extra bucks to get to the next gas station. I looked at my friends, looked at him, and then looked at his car, which was a Rols-Royce. In the backseat were two children and a woman in front who appeared to be his wife. I gave the others a cautionary glance, but they obliged and gave him a few dollars. He thanked us for our generosity and then left. I was content to think that I'd done something well that day, regardless if this man really needed the cash.

Months later, I'm back at my coffee shop, late at night and in walks this same man. His car, a Rols-Royce, was parked out front, lights on and still running. He came into the shop, surveyed the crowd and then approached two well-to-do women sitting in the corner. What happened next I won't soon forget—he gave these women the same story he'd given me nearly a year ago. How incredibly sad, right? This man was clearly a professional. To my surprise though, the women looked at him and denied any spare change for apparently he (or someone like him) had requested the same thing, with the same story, about a month earlier! A-ha! Rebuked! The man looked frazzled and headed back to his vehicle.

I couldn't help but feel good for the two women in the coffee shop. I know it's wrong to say so, but this man was not very righteous, it seemed. He was very good at asking for handouts and probably made a good amount of money playing the role of "hapless beggar" when he needed a few extra dollars for something other than gas. What's worse is that he was likely teaching his kids the same tricks of the trade; that is to say if the children in the car really were his children at all.

It's sad, but I used to believe that bars were the only places I'd encounter the most riff-raff and wily characters. Apparently I was wrong. The coffee shop had as many strange folks coming into their establishment as the pub across the street. Alcohol; caffeine, the ingredients made no difference—people would still act estranged and untrustworthy. The reality is equipping yourself to recognize these types.

Am I saying that the world is ugly? No, I'm not. There is a silver lining in all things. And should we still look to give handouts to those in need? Absolutely. You never know when someone you encounter really does need your assistance. And whose to say that we should always be witness to our gifts we give? For once you've given something away, you've blessed that person, regardless of what they choose to do with their money. But that's always how we think, is it? I sat there at the shop that night, grinning that this man had been caught red-handed by the women in the corner. Justice had been done, I thought, but I was more hopeful that the next person these ladies encountered would not be turned away because of this other man's ill-timed request. If the next beggar really *did* need help, then I would hope these women would not turn him away.

My observations of the world through the eyes of a coffee shop were enlightening. Days went on, nights got longer, and I settled into a comfortable habit of staying for many hours. This started something that I was not yet aware of until it hit me like a stiff right punch: I too was transforming into a *regular*. How mortifying, right? I denied this fact for a long time until the day arrived where I just couldn't hide anymore.

I headed down to the coffee shop like always with my laptop hung over my shoulder and when I got there, I ordered a drink and sat next to my favorite window. I was typing away for much of the evening (like always) on my miniature laptop (like always) and sipping on that Earl Grey tea I loved so much (like always) when it happened. Closing time had drawn near and I needed to pack my things up and get moving. The barista people were sweeping the floors and the other regulars were prepping to leave their workstations (off to save the world no less) so I decided to do the same. To my right, the Bitter-Card-Playing couple was wrapping up their game of Go Fish and once again, the wife thought she was being cheated with a few cries of "Bullshit." Chronic-Study-Guy was busily cramming in any last minute info he could and Gigabyte Guy was sampling another hilarious YouTube video. When most of my things were tucked away, one of the baristas approached my table and politely offered me some leftover food. It was a simple token for sticking around so late and a nice gesture at that.

"It'll go bad anyway," he said. "You can have some on the house."

I'm not usually a late night muncher, but I grabbed two donuts and a muffin since this had never happened to me before.

Then he said it.

"Figured you could use one since you're in here so much."

If you'd like to insert brooding music at this time, then be my guest. The team of Regulars responded as though they had felt a ripple in the Force. All eyes became fixated on me. Asian Chronic Study Boy halted his feverish note-reading; Gigabyte Guy unplugged his headphones; and the Illegal Immigrant Mafia paused for a minute to observe what had transpired. It was as if they'd been waiting for my name to be called out. Now that the time had come, they were prepared to usher me into their group. Their gazes turned upon me in unison and I could feel their collective eyes saying, "You're one of us now."

The jig was up. I gasped in silent horror. I had been found out and it was obvious that I had been overstaying my welcome. But as much as I dwelled on the negative that night, I soon came to realize that this could be a really good thing. I mean, I got free stuff tonight. I could get free stuff if I stuck around long enough every night, right? So why not take advantage of that? During the weekends I'd seen plenty of pub regulars get free beer or two so I didn't feel much different. Yeah, I wasn't pounding down a fifth of Jameson at these coffee shops, but I was drinking enough green tea to make my pee smell like a rainforest. Apparently that warrants a free muffin once in a while.

And yes, I'm more than happy to receive said muffin.

Theory: Once you go without a roommate . . .

. . . there really is no going back after that.

I wasn't always living by myself. There was a brief period in time where I was living with someone else. And no, it was not someone of the opposite sex. I'm a little too old school for that type of behavior. No, I was living with another dude. And this dude didn't have an apartment at all. He had a freakin' house. A really nice one too; older in style but the type of comfy, cozy, Grandma and Grandpa home to make you feel at ease. I was in the middle of a job change and needed a place to hole up so I asked this friend of mine for a favor. To his credit, he was more than willing to let me stay and I was quick to thank him before I even moved in.

And so, let the roommate experience commence.

I hadn't lived with someone else for nearly three years. Up until then, I had stayed at two locales which were one floor only so I wasn't accustomed to having a second floor, multiple baths, or garage for that matter. These were novelties that I just didn't have. I could at least brag that I'd had a fireplace at my most recent abode, but it was a gas fireplace. And yeah, a gas fireplace doesn't exactly exude manliness. Not that I was going for an overly masculine apartment, I just wasn't going to be cutting down trees for warmth like a real man in the foreseeable future.

Speaking of real men and manliness, I'd like to refer to my now ex-roommate as 'Hans'. If you ever knew Hans, you'd understand how appropriate such a name is for this guy. Hans and I are of the same age and we were both in our mid-20s when I moved in with him. However Hans could pass for a 30something Austrian bodybuilder if he ever chose to. Aside from me calling him Hans, he's held other numerous nicknames that span from 'Marble', to the 'Terminator', to 'Granite Man'. By now, I'm sure you're getting the proper mental image as to what Hans looks like—basically, he's a stud and a prime physical specimen.

Case in point, when we first met in Cleveland, I literally thought he was some kind of freelance model hiding out in the Midwest of America. No joke. Luckily he didn't bear the same self-indulgent personality that models stereotypically possess. I applaud you, Hans, for your humility and modesty regardless of your chiseled physique and statuesque appearance. I don't hate you, Hans, but I may envy you at times.

Hans' demeanor was not a concern for me, you see. He was a good guy so knowing this would make things easier when living with him. If you're new to choosing roommates, then this should be a top priority. What's your threshold for acceptable behavior? And does this person's attitude or personality match your own? It's not about opposites attracting one another; it's more about achieving balance of work, life and everything else in between.

Hans and I would certainly mesh, but I knew this wasn't going to be an easy journey. Once one allows himself to live alone, it's very hard to revert back to the thinking of sharing the same square feet every day with another. I speak about this from the male's perspective, of course. We're territorial creatures, we men. So if I'm not sharing this house with my wife (or future spouse), then it makes the situation all the harder to conform to. True, I *could* have spooned with my same-sex roommate every night, but that'd just be weird for me. And hopefully for him, too.

We didn't necessarily resort to peeing on certain objects; you know, in order to mark our territory, but we did meet to discuss various borders and boundaries (no spooning was an unspoken rule, of course). He advised me that he wouldn't be around for any of the coming weekends, so I would likely make the move without his assistance. *No problem*, I thought. I can get the usual moving buddies to help me relocate and we'll go from there. No need to have the homeowner around whilst I move in. Yeah, I've been through this little charade before.

I arrived the next weekend with plenty of stuff in tow. I had been to Hans' domicile before, but I don't think it truly hit me that I was going to be living there until I showed up that day. And just as I was getting my things out of my trunk, another cruel realization sunk in: I looked around the block and saw that the entire street was conservative, Midwestern suburbia. There were no duplexes, no old dormitories, no young folks living in apartment complexes, none of that. Every home was the same for about two miles along Hans' street. And considering that Hans and I were likely the only twenty-something bachelors on the strip, I could already foresee the rumors flying about once I was all moved in.

That particular paranoia came to fruition very quickly. I paused during one of the couch transfers to notice a family of four watching us from afar. The look on their faces was something to the extent of "ok, why is that guy moving in that other guy?" I wish I could say I was exaggerating in this instance, but I bring the facts to the table, people. That family was likely to have Hans and me on the night watch list very soon. For as long as I was living with Hans, I was going to have to stave the discussion as to who is the big spoon and who was the little spoon.

Ah well, I thought. I shrugged off some other passing glances as the moving day came to a close. In good nature, I thanked my fellow movers with a large pan pizza and decided to get settled in. My first order of business was shutting all manner of blinds in the living room, which as I look back on this, that may have not been the best course of action. Probably should have waited a while to start doing that. I mean, if you got nothing to hide, then you got nothing to hide, right?

Yeah, I was already paranoid, it seemed.

Hans and I's time together started off well enough. I had a room upstairs (so no basement dwelling) and a closet just for me. We established an unwritten rule to never cross food items in the refrigerator and sectioned off our respective drawers in the bathroom. Not bad, eh? Hans was more of a workaholic than me so we didn't see each other that often. In fact, the first month I was there I probably saw Hans about four or five times in total. The man traveled so much that I almost always had the house to myself on weekends. This was something I was accustomed to, but not with so much empty space. Still, I could come and go as I pleased. This didn't appear to be as bad as I had initially thought.

Our honeymoon ended sooner than expected.

The first real strike (aside from lingering rumors of homosexuality) revolved around my mode of transportation. Hans' driveway wasn't wide enough to house two cars at the same time; however, you could park one behind the other if need be. Since neither one of us wanted to constantly remind the other to move, I had to park mine on the road in order to give him his space. A fair agreement, I suppose. Hans had advised me that there was no parking on the roadside after 2 am, lest one wishes to face the wrath of being ticketed. Sure enough, one of the first nights my car was out there, I was ticketed. Go figure, right? I had seen other people leave their cars out on that road and not move an inch for days so why was mine so special? If these people were getting tickets too, then they obviously didn't care. Or they were tipping off officers to try and get rid of me?

I checked a few other vehicles that I had seen sitting there all night and saw no such ticket. *Very peculiar,* I thought but I paid my fine and then put my car in the driveway. A few days later, I left my car out there again and was met with the same result. Yes, this was my own fault but when I did another sweep of the corresponding vehicles, I saw no such yellow slip saying "get off the road, idiot." Ok, police tickets don't say that but they may as well if they're going to grant someone a parking violation. If it's a personal note that attacks my intelligence then maybe I'll take it just a little more seriously; "please pay the court $15" doesn't cut as deep.

This whole thing had the makings of a conspiracy. When I moved my car back to the safety of our one-lane driveway, I tried to catch a peek of the neighbors. Two mothers (likely housewives) were already out for their morning walk/run/jog. I saw one of them shoot me the evil eye as they passed on by. I was caught off guard but managed a dirty look of my own with a raised eyebrow and furrowed brow.

The die was cast and I knew the neighborhood was against me.

I wanted to fight this ticket but the rigmarole of battling a measly parking ticket can be as fruitful as trying to convince the Duggars to stop having children. It just doesn't come easy (unless you're Mr. Duggar). So I chewed my tongue a while, bit my upper lip and paid the crappy $15 that I owed to the community. I then had to persuade Hans to coordinate how we'd park our cars so neither of us was being left out in the street under any circumstances. We eventually came to a compromise. I would move my car onto the driveway, regardless if I were first or second. Since Hans typically woke up before me, he'd just have to move my car if I was behind him. And since he had to move my car, he'd have to use a spare set of keys (now this part is important!) to do so. He'd then leave the keys in an easily accessible location for me to find in case I didn't have my original pair.

At least that's how we planned it out to work.

You know when you come up with an idea and you think it's bulletproof? You figure there are no errors in this plot of yours and the only failsafe you need is so idiot proof that it would take a person on the level of Forrest Gump to screw it up. Yeah, we thought we had this covered.

It didn't take long for this arrangement to reveal the inherent flaw in our plan. Hans is a great guy, don't get me wrong but remembering minor details is not exactly his strongest suit. I had not been at my new job for more than three months when I awoke one morning to find no sign of my keys. My car sat idly on the side street as I checked kitchen drawers, lifted placemats and combed the commode where Hans frequented every morning. There was no such sign of my keys. It was getting late in the morning and I was beginning to feel the pinch of having to call Hans and solve this debacle. If I didn't act soon, I'd be grabbing the nearest bus or hitching a ride from a coworker.

So naturally, I called Hans first, but got no such response. This was another flaw in Hans' internal makeup. His turnaround time for answering a distress call was not the best. This could explain why he chose a desk job over coast-guarding or some other form of life-saving profession. If he had chosen the latter, I'm sure the beaches he worked would have the lowest survival rate of any in America.

When I wasn't getting a pick up, I sent a few more texts out but was still receiving nothing in return. At this point, I was getting really worried. My car was locked with no spare set of keys to be found and I was starting to craft a story in my head as to how I had to explain to my boss the dilemma of a roommate who "stole my keys." Yeah, that looks really professional. I can't even begin to describe the type of embarrassment that filled me that day. Luckily when I called in, the rings went straight to my boss' voicemail so I was allowed the opportunity to fumble through a horrid retelling of my forced living arrangement and how Hans had come to take my keys with him to work that morning (or at least I hoped that's where they were).

So as I sat in the basement looking up bus schedules, I got a phone call from my roommate. The conversation went a little something like this:

Me—"Hey, did you get my message?"

Hans—"Yeah, man. And uh . . . yeah, they're in my jacket pocket. I don't know how they got there, but they're there. Where are you?'

Me—"Well, I'm here still and I'm looking up bus fares to get to work. Where are you?"

Hans—"I'm at work. Do you need me to come get you?"

Me—"Yes, that'd be great. Can you get here in 15 minutes?"

Hans—"I have a meeting in 5 minutes. Can I come get you in a couple hours?"

To say I was shocked was a little bit of an understatement, but I handled it in stride. Hans wasn't really giving me any options so I told him that I'd catch the nearest RTA and ride into the city. Hans, to his credit, offered to pay me back for the bus fare. The cost for the emotional scars associated with calling my boss and telling him the debacle I was in is another matter entirely but I was willing to take what I could get. So I checked the bus routes in the area and to my dismay, there wasn't another one coming around for a good hour.

Well, that's just perfect, isn't it?! A few minutes later, I got another phone call from Hans.

Hans—"Hey man, it's me (Hans). I can come get you now. I'll be there soon."

Me—"Awesome. See you then."

I was relieved to hear that my roommate was coming back to retrieve me but the damage had been done. I was going to head into work and have to face my coworkers with a certain shame that said, "Yes, the dog ate my homework." Whether or not anyone truly believed me is their own agenda, but when such a thing happens to a person, the truth is often wilder than any lie you could possibly dream up.

When Hans arrived, we didn't say much to each other. In fact, I had already forgiven him for what had happened. He gave me my keys and I got in my car and headed out. And yes, my spare set was sitting in my dashboard. I smacked myself in the forehead and waved goodbye for the day. Not much else to say on the matter. Hans was a good man for skipping his meeting to rush me my keys so I thanked him later for stepping up. We then toasted brews later that night to wash away any tension we may have had.

All was right with the world.

So one would think that we learned our lessons with this little experience, right?

Well, not exactly . . . .

Just a few days later (no, I'm not even kidding), Hans' neglect to return my keys surfaced again and this time, he took *both* sets of my keys. The spares and the main copies.

So there I was, not even two days after enduring Hans' key thievery, I found myself on the phone with Hans who was busily explaining his now perfected method for swiping my car keys and leaving them in his coat pocket. And there *I* was again, frantically calling my coworkers to come get me since I couldn't bring myself to call my boss one more time. True, I had mapped out the bus routes on my computer just in case, but one would think that lightning wouldn't strike twice in such a short timeframe. Unfortunately for me, it did. To sum up the second experience of the Great Key Caper of 2011, a coworker eventually came to my aid and took me to work.

And thus, I decided that a greater action needed to be taken.

Later that night Hans and I had a discussion about our cars. Well, it was more about my car and why I had a growing concern over Hans' inadvertent method for humiliating me at work. I don't remember the full conversation but I recall a few "are-you-kidding-me's" and a couple "what-were-you-thinking"s coming into the exchange. Hans apologized thoroughly and I accepted the apology in full despite my impatience for the matter. After all, it was never done maliciously, just in error. Those things are forgivable.

We'd never have to relive these escapades again, but I soon found myself forgiving many other things about Hans. Habits like the need to wake up at 5 am every morning, regardless of day of the week, and pound an empty coffee container against the sink. This sound can only be described as the noise one hears when a burglar is trying to break into a house. Or at least that's what I thought was happening when I woke up one morning to this incessant banging resonating from downstairs. I draped myself in my bed comforter and snuck down to see what was happening. To my surprise (albeit a happy surprise), Hans was standing, coffee container in hand, smashing the darned thing against the side of the sink as if he were trying to break it. I did a shark's circle around him to see if he noticed me and when he didn't, I assumed that he was sleep-walking. I didn't want to wake him at first as I've heard that one should never wake a sleep-walker, but since he showed no sign of stopping this odd activity, I had to say something.

"Hey, man. You awake?" I asked my roommate.

Hans didn't say a word at all. He just turned towards me, eyes groggy and half-open as he continued to hit the coffee can. Then he decided to speak.

"Yeah man . . . I'm just emptying the coffee can."

If what he was doing constituted as 'emptying the coffee can', then I was most curious to see what his methods were for starting *up* the coffee maker. Since I was downstairs already, I took note of the time on the wall. It wasn't even 5 am yet. I knew I wasn't dreaming so I figured it was appropriate to bring this situation to his attention. You know, since this wasn't exactly normal human behavior.

"Ok, I can see that . . .," I said with a questioning tone. ". . . but it's not even 5 yet, man. Do you know what time it is?"

"Yeah, man . . .," he said. "I always get up this early." And without hesitation, Hans returned to banging the coffee container once more. Eyes still half open, hair unkempt and sticking every which direction, Hans was clearly content with what he was doing. The noise echoed throughout the house as I counted the times he took to smash the living daylights out of this container. I stopped after about 20.

Now, if this were my little brother or another relative, I would have tackled this guy and put an end to this. But since this was Hans and not the average Joe, I figured I would just go upstairs and try to go back to sleep. Who knew what an enraged half-awake Romanesque bodybuilder could do if he were awakened prematurely; and I wasn't about to find out. When I got upstairs, the pounding ceased and I breathed a collective sigh of relief. *Maybe he won't do that every day*, I thought . . . .

Well, as you can guess, Hans' mid-morning coffee thrashing occurred quite often so I adapted as best I could. I soon became so resilient that I didn't even hear the train in our backyard when it rolled on by either. A nuclear missile could have hit the side of our house and I wouldn't have noticed by the time I'd properly adjusted to my new environment, but it took a long while to get to that point. There were plenty of semi-sleepless nights in between that kept me right around the standard five to six hours of sleep. In hindsight, I suppose you can't really complain if you knowingly choose to live with someone who has a massive train running through their backyard. That's just a moot topic in my mind so my resolve to get over the situation turned out in my favor eventually.

In addition to the coffee-banging and train-rolling, there were other challenges Hans and I would faced. Hans was an iceman. In fact, he may have been an Eskimo in a prior life. Why you ask? Well, he liked the cold; no, he *loved* the cold. The house stayed at a steady 55 degrees throughout the fall and into the winter. When I challenged his preference, I was expecting to hear something about being frugal with the gas bill, but Hans retorted by stating he loved the frigid air. It helped him sleep at night, he said so I didn't want to argue that. I just wanted to get back to a point where I could feel my nose in the morning again. Was that too much to ask?

Hans also shared a love for short shorts and high woolen socks. An odd combo for sure, but the man sported this outfit most every night. Creature of habit? Oh, you betcha, but that's not the interesting part. The socks were a scientific marvel if I ever saw one. Not only were they as thick as a bed comforter, casting the illusion that Hans had feet the size of elephants, but these socks appeared to gather no static. I had always expected to be jolted if I walked too close to him but shockingly, (like how I did that?) this never happened. Sure, I didn't get close enough for this to occur, but the fear of penned up electrical energy made me keep a safe distance. One misplaced touch of the arm or hand and I'd be fried like a tree that's been struck by lightning. Can you just see the headline?

Man killed by roommate by way of static shock. NASA to study strength of custom wool socks. Government to employ new "Shock Socks" for war on terror.

Hans wasn't much for negotiation either. Before I moved in, I decided I would take some online courses to work towards a teaching degree. The only catch was that I needed internet access. That doesn't sound like a problem, does it? Nearly every home in America has a TV, an iPad or internet, right? Yeah, Hans had plenty of these things, but the internet was the only one I cared about. As fate would have it, Hans' internet provider (who shall not be named) billed Hans inaccurately for a service visit. This compelled Hans to call customer service and argue on behalf of what he was promised: a $15 visit.

The bill was for $25.

Hans didn't like this and neither did the customer service rep. And neither did her supervisor. And neither did the supervisor's supervisor. Hans didn't appreciate any of the answers he was getting so he threatened to cut his internet and TV package entirely should they not agree to his terms. I'll give you three guesses as to what happened next.

Ok, we don't have time for you to guess so I'll just tell you. Somewhere along the conversation, the provider made the offer of $20 to which Hans replied "cut my power." So yeah, no internet, no TV, and no way for me to do my courses at home. I attributed this to Hans' own stubborn attitude. In the long scheme of things, I could have just fronted the extra $5 but Hans would not accept. It's the principle of the matter, he'd say and my argument was shut down. As were my classes.

I pleaded with Hans to reconcile his relationship with the cable company, but when he did, the provider gave him the same treatment he had shown them: neglect. Three to four weeks worth of waiting and we still had no cable guy to come rewire the house. I then knew Hans had been blacklisted somehow and I was sharing in the brunt of his punishment.

So yes, I spent a good month hightailing myself to other friend's houses for their Wi-Fi and mooching off free internet at coffee shops. If my virtual teacher happened to call on me, I typed in the same response every time—"sorry, cannot speak on microphone. Still not in privacy of own home." This was embarrassing to say the least, but I took the hardships as a sign that I wasn't ready for my teaching degree just yet. *Perhaps I should focus on my writing more?* I thought. I didn't need the internet for that!

Hans also picked up a hobby or two while I was living there. One such hobby was his sudden desire to learn acoustic guitar. For someone who had never picked up an instrument in his whole life, I wasn't too optimistic for poor Hans. I wanted to encourage him to stick to lifting and biking, but this was something he felt compelled to do.

Now, before I go any further on this subject, I should definitely mention how Hans and I are very similar people. We're both competitive by nature and we love to challenge ourselves. I should have known I'd be asking for trouble when I brought my guitar into his house. I had taken lessons a few summers ago but I never got off the ground running so I had to give up. Sad to say, but I did. Hans had a guitar of his own too but this thing was just gathering dust. When he saw me bring my own guitar to the house, it must have inspired him because he almost immediately signed up to take lessons.

And lessons were something he definitely needed. It started out just like any student learning a trade would. Hans would take his guitar out late in the evening and he'd strum a few notes here and there. And when I say notes, I'm being as generous as I can be. The guy clearly had a long road ahead of him if he were ever going to rock out to Free Bird. In his defense, I couldn't even get past the Star Spangled Banner so touché on that one. After a while, Hans' practice schedule took larger and longer chunks out of his evening. Some of these jam sessions crept into the late hours of the night and by late, I'm referring to 11-pm-on-weekday late. That's bad if you need to get up at six the next day. Take this for example.

So there I was, sleeping in the guest room, gathering strength for another day at the desk when I begin to hear the faint sound of poorly arranged chords coming from the vents. I dismissed them at first, but the noise escalated into a string of unnoticeable melodies and tunes that were undeterminable to the human ears. I opened my eyes and looked at my clock—11:05 pm. Really, man? At *this* hour? If I had the strength, I would have gotten up and headed downstairs, but once again I stopped myself as I figured he might be sleep-walking. My experiences with the coffee smashing had left me feeling hesitant on my approach.

I suffered through the sounds a little longer as I tried to fall back asleep. When Hans' notes petered out, I got a second wind and went to check on the matter. I meandered downstairs (comforter over my head; the attire I took on for these adventures) and saw that Hans had literally fallen asleep at the wheel. His head was cocked back, mouth agape with one hand over the guitar. One would expect to find some kind of mushroom or weed present but all that Hans had by his side was a Tupperware container of half-eaten pea soup (his favorite dish). I shook my head and went back to bed.

The next night, I placed an extra pillow over my vent in case the noise returned and sure enough, it did. This time a little bit later, say 11:15 pm. If you've made it this far in the book, then you know how I've mentioned that nothing good tends to happen after 10:18 pm. Knowing this, we can officially add playing-guitar-while-your-roommate-sleeps to said list of no-no's. Nevertheless, I was impressed with how well the pillow worked as I drifted into a peaceful slumber.

One would assume that I'd beaten the odds on this one, but I decided I was going to say something to him if this persisted. When his next practice started up, I was downstairs in the basement watching TV. I walked upstairs with a purpose as I structured the argument I would make within my head. I hadn't even got to the living room when I heard Hans talking on his phone. The speaker was on so I could hear the other person pretty clearly. From what I could gather, he was apparently playing guitar over the phone for one of his nieces. She cheered him on even though his music was terrible and even asked if he'd play it again for her the next night. When I heard this, I couldn't bring myself to tell him to stop. Instead, I offered that he call her earlier the next night so that we weren't interrupting any people's sleep schedules (namely my own). Hans complied and away we went. I won't say this necessarily stopped me from plotting ways to "accidentally" smash one of his fingers in a door the next day, all I'm saying is that I agreed to let him play earlier in the day. That's about as good a contract compromise as any.

Spending time *outside* the house with Hans proved to be a demoralizing experience. I enjoyed his friendship and company but there was a catch to his friendship I was not prepared for. You already know that Hans has the appearance of a Greek god, so what does that mean when two young men go out for a drink together? Well, I'll tell you: the Greek god gets all the girls. Hanging with Hans made me feel like a little brother at a big boy's party. I was bait he could dangle at the end of a line if he felt inclined to do so, but to his credit, he never treated me that way. In fact, how he behaved was even worse—he acted like the attention he got from women was no big deal. Can you imagine what it's like when a trio of good-looking women approach you and ask what the "sharp-dressed guy behind you" is doing with his evening? Well, it's not a great feeling by any means. Old, young, unmarried, married—none of this mattered to these women; Hans was a special prize.

And hey, I'd have to agree with those ladies. Hans is a good guy who doesn't revel in taking advantage of every situation, namely people. But gosh, wouldn't it be nice to throw *this* guy a bone once in a while? I mean, come on now. I may be Zeus' kid brother at the bar but that should count for something, right?

Well, I don't want to dwell on that nonsense forever. Hans and I went on, moving past the guitar hiccup and my own insecurities; all the while enjoying each other's company for a time. We had differing schedules for sure, but we were finally starting to meld. Hans was compromising with my sleep schedule and I tried to take shorter showers in the morning. I fancy a long shower from time to time. It helps me wake up, get clean, and freshen my mind for the day. Hans did not think this was so. The guy took showers like any other person but he was none too appreciative of my longer-than-normal bath routine. And though I tried to plead with him that this was necessary to my day, he just wasn't having it. He wasn't having it so much that he decided on a house project while I was still living there. The project would involve the deconstruction of the one and only shower/bathroom/toilet in the entire house.

Yes, that's right—a complete overhaul of the only place we could keep our collective hygiene in good, working order. I was doubtful of his plans at first but Hans affirmed me that the project would only last a couple of weeks—two tops. No need to worry then, right? I was confident that Hans would uphold his end of the bargain so I didn't question him when he outlined the intended timetable. I knew that I could at least shower at the local Fitworks that I went to and if I needed to go number one or number two, I could always go at work or at the gym. Not the most appealing thing the in the world, but hey, this project was to be quick and easy, right?

Yeah, right . . .

I'm going to assume you're a smart person if you're reading this so you can likely figure out what happened next. The bathroom project would not proceed as planned and we were not going to have a bathroom within two weeks time. Could I hold it in for two weeks? Probably not. I hear that's bad for your intestines and such but I could at least not shower for a day or two if need be. Yeah, it's surprising what you can live with when you absolutely have no other options.

Our troubles really began when I saw what we were working with. Two young lads appeared one evening to start the bathroom dismantling and for all I knew, they could have been my age or significantly younger. I know it's not right for me to judge right off the bat, but I asked Hans about their authenticity. He (once again) assured me that these guys were professionals.

Things started off well enough. First, the bathroom was torn to shreds. That's pretty standard so I began my days by showering offsite. I'd get up early, go workout, shower, and then head off to work downtown. Wasn't bad at first, but this routine persisted long beyond the anticipated timetable. Weeks went by and still no in-house shower. What's worse is that the bathroom remained the same: torn up with no sign of reconciliation in sight. I asked Hans about what was going on, but he defended our dynamic duo as "hard-working youngsters trying to make a buck." I, on the other hand, was not feeling the love; especially when the pair began to tear out the downstairs toilet (the last source of relieving one's self in the house). I was worried that I may never take a private dump again.

As such, I decided to investigate.

I stayed home one day to see what these boys were up to. In all honesty, they appeared a little shocked that I was home that day, as I'm sure I threw *their* schedule off. I set up my laptop in the basement to start hammering away on some spreadsheets as the crew got to work. Within a few minutes, I could hear the pitter plop of parts being tossed around upstairs. It sounded like these fellas were playing tag or something, and when it stopped; one of them came downstairs where I was.

"Hey, we need to do something down here," one of them said to me.

"Ok?" I said quizzically. Considering how everything was *upstairs*, I wondered what these guys needed that was downstairs. I figured this had to do with the water pipes but I asked anyway to confirm.

"Yeah, we need to run some wires down through the walls. Just try to ignore me for a while."

I nodded my head and went back to it. The guy walked past me and into the boiler room portion of the basement. What happened next can best be described as a plumber's game of Marco Polo as one voice yelled to the other from two floors away. I swear I heard something to the extent of "no, don't do that, you'll make all the water go everywhere" which was swiftly followed by "I'm not gonna cut it, just chill out." The only thing missing was Moe, Larry, Curly or Shemp to complete this little exchange.

I braced for the worst, but I wasn't about to interject where I didn't know what was going on. Thankfully, no wires were cut and no water was spilled but the shouting match continued for a good 15 to 20 minutes. A few bangs here, a few knocks there and the one in the basement with me emerged from the adjacent room.

"Well, I think that's good. Thanks for putting up with that," he said apologetically.

"No problem," I said. I mean, he was quite sincere about it so I couldn't judge until the project was completed. But then again, it was nearly a month later since the start date and still no bathroom. I decided to ask the crucial question.

"Hey, when do you guys think you'll be done?" I asked. The youngster halted like he'd been hit with a freeze gun.

"Well, we were hoping to get it done last week but we had some setbacks," he said.

"Setbacks?" I asked, curiously.

"Yeah, we just didn't anticipate a lot of the plumbing that was in the walls. Had to tear some things out here and there. Nothing too major though. Should all be fine."

Dude, for your sake, I hope it really is nothing major, I thought. My first inclination was to tell Hans of the situation at hand. After all, these are the guys he was recommended so he ought to know these guys are taking liberties to rearrange his plumbing (quite literally). When the day ended, I went upstairs to take a look at what had been accomplished. And what I found was a whole lotta nothin'. I wasn't too surprised unfortunately. My patience was slowly reaching a fever pitch. That night, Hans and I had a discussion about our hired help and whether or not they were really working like they should.

"Don't worry, it'll get done," Hans assured me. "I knew that they had to change some things and it might take longer. Sorry I didn't tell you."

I promptly bantered back like a disgruntled spouse. I thought that if anyone could hear this, they'd think we were some sort of married couple. When that sunk in, I stepped away to wipe my hands of the situation. Hans must have felt the same as he too walked backwards from the room and into his place of study. That was it, I thought. It had finally happened. I needed to move out. We were beginning to become "cohabitators" and I needed to cut the strings before they became too tight. Three weeks later (and still no bathroom or shower), I told Hans I was moving out. He didn't ask me why, he just asked when I wanted to move out. I pointed to the line of pee-filled Gatorade bottles on our basement steps and said "when the pee bottles cover the top floor, it'll be time I move out." A little dramatic, yes, but I needed some way to show how peeing at home had become quite an inconvenience. If I had to sneak one more poop at the local gas station or Starbucks without purchasing something, I'd feel eternally guilty.

The next day, I went searching and found an apartment. Two days later, I found a moving van. And on the third day, I drank so much water that I filled up three whole Gatorade bottles. This was more than enough to cover the top step of the basement.

That's it, the time had come.

A month and three weeks later, the upstairs bathroom was completed. Additionally, the downstairs bathroom was furnished with a full vanity. And wouldn't you know it, the finished product actually looked quite nice. Kudos to those two knuckleheads who started the project; they actually did a decent job. Too little, too late for this guy though; I was already on my way out. My first night alone was spent with a good movie and a self-made dinner (Cast Away and pea soup, if you're wondering). The movie felt very appropriate for the occasion, as did the pea soup.

.As I settled into my new place, I was filled with mixed emotions. On one hand, I was relieved to be out but on the other, I felt as though I hadn't left on the best of terms. Yeah, we were still friends and nothing would change that, but I felt like I didn't have a good reason for moving other than I needed a bathroom again. No, it was more than just the private bathroom. It was the need to have my own stuff where I wanted it. And not worry about sharing milk. And not having to ask for him to stop playing guitar at midnight. Or pretending to be a gay couple in the middle of suburbia around Halloween . . . .

Quick sidebar, one of the funnier/embarrassing times spent at Hans' was Halloween 2010. Only a few kids came to our doorstep asking for handouts and when they did, Hans asked that I remove myself from sight completely. My retaliation for this measure took the form of me in a bathrobe while shouting out the occasional "hun, who his that at the door?"

Yes, I wasn't helping our situation but I figured I'd make it worth my while. Oh, memories . . . .

Yeah, I guess I had several reasons for moving out. Each more ridiculous than the one before it, but deep down, I knew I'd made the right decision. I took part of the day to sit and think about the times I'd spent with Hans. I called him to say thanks for everything and then he thanked me in return. I asked why the thanks and he told me that all my rent went directly to the bathroom fund (funny world we live in, is it not?). So there you have it—my rent was merely meant to pay for his refurnishing. In return, I was treated to six months of inhabiting the same space as Hans.

I suppose it wasn't a total waste. He got his bathroom and I got my own bathroom back. Done deal. Yeah, we didn't have a ton of huge parties and half the street thought we were gay, but who's to say we didn't enjoy each other? We had a good run, Hans and I, and we each got a little more insight into each other. The most notable insight being that neither of us was ready to take on a serious roommate anytime soon. Or perhaps, the bigger insight is that once you live alone, you really can't go back to having a roommate.

The only roomie I wanted from here on out would be my wife. That was the bigger issue at hand for me. If I couldn't handle a few months living with a close friend though, then how was I going to deal with a woman in the house? Sure, you get some added benefits from being married, but was I going to be able to tolerate this person? I certainly hope so. The only contingency would be that if she ever took up guitar lessons, she'd have to do it in her free time and not at home.

My thoughts then drifted to Hans' life. I wondered how he was ever going to handle it too. You know, living with a woman of his choosing. He clearly had his own schedule and did not deviate from that schedule. And his communication skills were just as bad as mine. I felt some sympathy towards him as I dozed off that night. Maybe we were both destined to lead a life alone, free from the strain of an opposite sex partner to spend time with.

Who can say really, but I wasn't about to let the thought bring me down. I quickly shifted my thoughts to my big screen television, complete with surround sound and 1080p viewing, but my night took a turn soon as I felt . . . empty. There was nobody sitting at the couch to my left. Nobody snoring, nobody dressed in knee-high wool socks (one of Hans' favorite accessories) and definitely nobody I could talk to if I was bored. Yeah, I could pick up the phone and call a friend, but that's not the same. I was fearful that separation anxiety was setting in as I made myself another bowl of soup.

Through all the trials and tribulations (small ones at that), I actually missed Hans' company. Are you really that shocked? Nothing in life is as bad as we make it out to be. The bathroom issue was a problem but it was merely an inconvenience. Were we doomed to hold our pee in for 2 months? No, absolutely not. And was I going to lose my job because my roommate stole my keys two times in the same week? No, and I would certainly pray not.

Instead, these experiences were just memories now. Memories that included the countless nights of deep discussion, brew toasts, and a comforting feeling that yes, there was another person within close proximity who just so happened to be a friend of mine. That's a really cool feeling if you ever get to experience that. Sure, Hans and I aren't *best* friends, but we're great friends; and that can be just as cool.

I didn't sob that night; I didn't even cry. I did text a message to Hans to ask him if he'd like to grab a beer after work the next day. He replied, "Sure, man." Was Hans feeling the sting of loneliness like I was? Perhaps, but he was never one to pass up a cold beer if the chance arose.

I was feeling inspired by this train of thought so I put my things aside and got up to grab my guitar. It may have been nostalgia taking over me, but I didn't mind. I felt like writing a song to chronicle the next chapter of my journey. This old girl (in reference to the guitar) was dusty from its lack of use, but when I strummed a few notes, she seemed to come back to life. I recalled chords C and G so I played around a bit, trying to make something sound somewhat appealing to my ears. As I did this, I started to sing a song. Hans, this one's for you:

I moved away,
To find my own peace.
My bags were packed,
So I signed the lease.
I thought I was better,
Away from thee.
Your bathroom was broke,
So I couldn't pee.
My keys were stolen,
More than once.
I told my boss,
That you were a dunce.

I needed to study,
For a teaching degree.
So you cut the cable,
And I still couldn't pee.
Your place was cold,
Like an icy tomb.
Yet you wore your shorts,
Like spring was in bloom.
The train in the backyard,
Made quite a sound.
But paled in comparison,
To your sink-smashing rounds.
All things considered,
You're still my good friend,
Just don't expect me to ever come back,
If you tear out your bathroom again.

To 'Hans', thanks for letting me tell these stories in such a manner. You're a good friend . . . so long as we don't live together.—J.C.L.

Downright Good Thought: If you ever join a gym, please be aware that, yes . . .

. . . people are watching you.

I like to work out in my spare time. Yeah, I enjoy getting a good lift when I can. You know, get my "swell on", so to speak. It's a habit I started halfway through my teenage years. Back then, I was just a wee lad compared to the brutes I shared the gym with. Like a modern day Rudy, I stood out because I could never stand *up* to those other gorillas. Being the smart boy that I was, I bided my time. I waited till the monsters moved from the free weights so I could get my reps in. It was all about patience, perseverance, and knowing when to take the right opportunity. And that's what I'm talking about here: watching and waiting. Even more so, watching the plethora of stereotypes that frequent our gyms and waiting for the right time to write about it.

That time is now.

To the vast majority out there, going to the gym is a casual activity. You wake up, plan to make it there after work, and depending on your workload, you may get to the gym or you may not. You're not overly concerned with two year memberships or personal training sessions; you really just want to maintain that "principle" shape that you've always wanted. I've definitely been in this category. I'm not really out to impress anyone; I just want myself to stay toned so I don't feel like a statistic. And by statistic, I mean to not contribute to the obese lifestyles Americans have today.

I saw an article a year ago that detailed which of the 50 states was the "most obese." Ok, first off, I didn't even realize that we have studies like this. I mean, how does one even calculate that type of thing? I don't recall some guy with a tape measure running around to every house asking to get waist measurements and I definitely don't remember one of those random mail surveys saying I could win "$100 bucks" just by answering a few questions. So what the heck, right? I had to investigate further.

My efforts lead me to a group that tabulates this information for a living: the CDC (Center for Disease Control and Prevention). So the Center for Disease Control and Prevention keeps record of how fat Americans are getting? I find this to be very ironic. The fact that we categorize obesity as a disease may be the reason it's the CDC's responsibility to collect the data, but isn't that ridiculous? Of all the things in the world that the CDC must concern itself with, it must first handle the task of reporting on the epidemic that is obesity.

Are you surprised though?

I doubt it considering the amount of media surrounding the topic. After all, there have been numerous television shows that take overweight people and turn them into Slender Sally's and Abtastic Adam's. I can't even begin to count the number of infomercials claiming to have pills and special diets that "guarantee weight loss" in just two weeks. And don't forget the biggest weight-losing mogul of them all: Weight Watchers. I've never done the program, but I know people who have. It's a simple enough concept. You get a daily allotment of calories per day and you have to abide by it. It's just a classic "watch what you eat" plan. Heck, I wish I'd have come up with that. If that's all it takes to lose some pounds, then why doesn't everybody do it? Heck, why not just stop eating for a while and let your fat reserves get gobbled up? I know that you can't go a few days without water so at least keep that on the menu while you're fasting. And do something else besides sitting around, thinking about the next Big Mac you want to chow down on. That's probably a good start. So come on, people. Get some self-control and start losing those pounds!

I'm talking to you, Mississippi and Alabama. You were the number one and number two states with the most obese people in America for 2011 (for a second straight year no less). Shame on you, south. Shame on you, both. We thought you were doing better since the war ended but if this is just payback for not winning all those years ago, it's time to move on and quit wallowing in your defeat by devouring deep-fried chicken. It only hurts you in the long run, my friends. But you're probably saying, what about the folks up north? I hate to admit it, but Ohio was number 13 for a second straight year. That's not cool, Midwest. Out of 51 possible contestants (including the District of Columbia), the good old Midwest was ranking somewhere in the highest percentile.

Since I don't appreciate that kind of stigma, I've made it a point to hit up my local gym at least four times a week. Five, if I'm fortunate enough to do so. At one time, I could make it seven days a week but that got old real fast. Mostly because I couldn't walk the next day and seeing as how walking is a pretty important thing to do daily, I decided against the seven-day-a-week routine.

Despite all my individual efforts, the obesity problem in America has only continued to escalate. True, our population is larger this year than what it was last. That much is a fact, but you can't ignore the issue at hand. The US is filling up (literally) with bigger people.

For instance, take a look at the "world's heaviest man": Manuel Uribe. This guy had eaten so much that he accumulated more than 1,000 pounds worth of body weight. Say what?! His sheer bulk became so much that he couldn't even get out of bed in the morning. If that wasn't bad enough, he had to be moved forcibly from his home via a crane. I'm just going to go out on a limb here and say the obvious—how the $%@# did that happen?! I mean, come on man! Maybe the biggest shocker of all is that this man eventually got married (even while being unable to move from his bed!). That's just crazy talk, but love appears to know no boundaries in reaching the hearts of all men; even if that heart is buried below several hundred pounds of excess fat and muscle.

Aside from wondering how the couple consummated their marriage, I can see others questioning just how Mr. Uribe got to this state. At first, I felt frustrated by his predicament, angry even; but then I felt some sense of sympathy for this man too. I mean, there was clearly something very wrong with him or else he wouldn't have consistently been eating that much. This man had become so incredibly large that he couldn't even move, let alone take care of himself. It makes me ask the question—when did it just become *too much*? At what point did this man wake up and say, "I need to make a change" or rather, at what point did his wife say, "You probably should seek help." This baffles me to no end. An intense ignorance to one's own preservation must have taken hold and then persisted until the body reached a breaking point. For this man, the breaking point was immobility.

In the extreme case of Mr. Uribe, there are those who lose sight of keeping that ideal shape; a secure body type that is both comfortable and rewarding for the individual. I'd like to think that most people who go to the gyms are trying to reach that plateau. This plateau may not be herculean or Xena-like, but at least it's a goal to progress towards. And that's what this chapter was intended for after all, was it not? Well, that and the allure of people-watching at the gym.

When you're a single guy, you join a gym for all the wrong reasons. Yeah, you may want to get in shape, but ultimately, you're thinking you may make some new friends while you're there—preferably of the female kind. As such, you may gravitate towards a machine that a pretty girl is using. It may not even be a work out you should be using (like that ridiculous groin stretcher thing) but you walk over anyway. You puff your chest out, hands on your hips as you conjure up a method to start conversation that's more than "Hey, are you done with your reps yet?"

This is a difficult spot to be in. When I joined my first gym, it was huge; a massive facility with hundreds of members attending there. After a week or two, I noticed a young girl arriving the same time I did and working out in the same places I did too. This was semi-encouraging so I decided to strike up a conversation. What's your name? How long have you been going here? What's your sign? You know, all the normal stuff one would ask. But that's where the innocence ended for as I was questioning her, I was expecting to hear about her job. When she told me she wasn't presently working, but was in school still, I expected to hear about the college she attended. This too, was met with disappointment.

"Wait, what school did you say you attended?"—Me.

"Um, the one down the road . . . you know, Blah Blah High."—Her.

Yes, that was awkward. I walked away from this high school acquaintance with the realization that I wasn't very good at recognizing age. At least not yet. In my defense, she looked very mature and handled herself in a mature way too. That's no excuse, I know, but it does make me wonder how bold this girl was with other guys at the gym (or just in general). Lord, I can only hope that the next guy she runs into is at least closer to her age. And that he's not some scum bag trying to score a high school girl. That's all I can ask.

By way of avoiding a possible date rape situation, I decided that I needed to assess my environment a little better before I engaged another person. And so, I turned my attention to the various peoples of the gym, naming them along the way. I like to think of the relatively fit and casual people as the Toners. They want to be in shape, but not crazily in shape. They're not prescribing to Tony Horton's P90X routine anytime soon. That would just take too much time. These are the people who walk in, sit on a bike and read a magazine for 45 minutes whilst they pedal away to their heart's desire. They're also the same people who have that tiny sliver of sweat dripping from their foreheads or down their backs when the workout gets somewhat difficult. And by difficult, I mean any workout that lasts longer than a half hour. The Toners don't want to linger in the gym; they just want their workout so they can get out and go home feeling a tiny bit better about themselves. And kudos to you guys for that. My hat is off to you for showing up to the party. That's half the battle, after all.

Then there are the Life-Changers. The ones who's New Year's Resolution told them to get back to the gym. They've resolved that they have a need for a better body and they want that body NOW. They sign up for every class the gym offers while enlisting the aid of a personal trainer in order to get the most out of their triple platinum super user membership. The pressure the Life-Changer puts on himself has got to be exhausting.

First of all, when one is making goals, you have to be realistic. Hopefully if you're a Life-Changer, then you're already aware that the possibility of losing 30 pounds in a week is not very feasible. The Biggest Loser show does it, but you're not on television with registered nurses and doctors by your side—you're at a local gym. Nor is it sensible to believe that you can grow deltoids and pecks the size of Mount Everest in a mere two weeks. It's just not in the cards. Things like weight loss and body change take time so you can't expect the impossible in such a short timeframe. I know this because I've seen people try. And guess what, it ain't pretty.

Let me tell you a quick story. When I was in high school, I worked out at a local gym. One day, a woman came strolling in with an agenda clearly in mind. She wasn't inside more than a minute before she began to pitch a fit about how she wasn't losing any weight. She wasn't really "big", per se, but she was no petite lady either. She started raising cane how she couldn't see any results, how her pants were still tight and her husband didn't notice her. That last part is still uncomfortable for me to tell to this day. One of the staff members stepped up though and asked her how long she'd been attending the gym. She responded with "four days."

Four days?! Really? Oh, come on now . . . . You have to give this fitness thing more time than that, sweetie!

The Great Wall that China built certainly won't collapse overnight. There's an investment here and you have to stick to the plan. I, for one, would probably be just as impatient though. I've always been impatient with most things I do in life (for good or bad), so when it comes to one's own body image, it's even harder to have that added patience with the matter. You always want to put your best foot forward and if we can't achieve this right away, then some of us give up. It's only human nature. That's why it's really inspiring when you see people who go through those self-transformations and develop into the individuals that they were craving to become. Like Jillian Michaels, for example or Jared from the Subway commercials. Where there's a will, there's a way.

You certainly have to admire the Life-Changer's spirit, if nothing else. Now, I think there's no problem with getting a trainer involved. That's why they're there, of course. Some people need a whip cracking at the back to get through a workout so a trainer certainly provides that extra push. Since the Life-Changer employs the aid of said trainer, others around the gym take notice. If you're walking around with an employee who has a nametag on, then you're 100% more likely to get looks around the gym. I am just speaking the truth.

I, myself, could never ask a trainer to help me at the gym. I'm far too shy and too content with my own workout to ever ask for help. If one of my buddies wants to lift with me, then yeah, I'll lift with them. If one of my friends asks me to do a spinning class with them, then sure, I'll check it out. I'm not biased against switching things up, I just don't want some jacked up guy (or gal) telling me to do some crazy lift that I'd never think of on my own. Case in point, do you ever notice how trainers want their pupils to do the most embarrassing lifts/stretches? I once saw a male trainer make a woman do a backwards lift on a hamstring machine that made her look like she was peeing like a dog. Is that really necessary, man? Or were you doing it to show off to your other fitness gurus? Either reason is plausible; just don't expect me to do the reverse cow girl on a machine anytime soon, pal.

What I'd really like to see (though it'll probably never happen) is this next group of gym nuts ask for a trainer. You know who these people are: the tanned up, decked out, muscled monsters of the facility. How do you describe such a demographic of individuals? I don't know if there is one so I'll just run with "those who are tan." I guess the acronym for that would be TWAT, but since the derogatory nature of this word is quite vulgar, I'll go with something a little less demeaning: the Bulgers (due to the "bulgy" nature of their beings).

The Bulgers, as it were, are an interesting bunch. Their overall intent, it seems, is to make every inch of their body stretch to the utmost limit imaginable; their muscles protruding with mountainous curves that push out veins resembling rivers or tributaries under their skin. I've observed several versions of the Bulger in my day: the free weights Bulger, the multi-cut off Bulger, the bulging vein Bulger, and the loves-to-shower Bulger. The latter I tend to stay away from at all costs. You never know with people these days, ya know? The differing types of Bulgers tend to overlap so you really can't segregate them too much. They're all cut from relatively the same cloth. And that cloth, typically a high school or college t-shirt, is shred in four to five sections to allow for optimal deltoid viewing. They (Bulgers) act as though everyone in the gym is checking them out (regardless if no one is) and make things especially awkward in any locker room by walking around naked for the entire world to see. Yes, Bulgers are fun folks to observe in their natural habitat (minus that last part).

I don't discriminate when it comes to the Bulger either. There are as female Bulgers as well as male Bulgers (how else would they breed?). Female Bulgers may not be as recognizable at first, but they're there. They are just less obvious because they choose very specific times to be at the gym. The female Bulger's twilight hour is between 5 am and 7 am in the morning and then it's between 6 pm and 9 pm at night. The morning species is more about the hardcore running and lifting while the nightly crew is densely populated in the yoga and spin classes. Trust me, they're there. Since I've tried out these classes at least once, I've seen them there. They may seem like they're as elusive as the Sasquatch, but if you show up at the right time, you'll find them.

Bulgers excel at more than just lifting weights; they are also adept at making the gym a very uncomfortable place for others. A Bulger's overly serious nature makes the atmosphere so tense you could cut it with a knife. I've seen guys do 500 plus pounds on the squat machine and then turn around to push 300 pounds on the benchpress, all the while jamming out on their headset with a power drink in hand. And speaking of power drinks, why do all power drinks have to be continuously shaken while you're walking around the gym? I mean, come on guys. Shake that thing up back in the locker room and leave it there. You don't look any cooler for bringing kool-aid to the party, bro. Nobody cares to know if you require rhino milk and elephant blood to supplement your workout. Everybody knows that good old fashioned H20 is a great natural resource for replenishing your fluids. So if you need something extra, then just wait till you're done lifting. That's all we ask for.

My opinion on Bulgers has changed over the years. Where I used to think these people were just muscle-brained monsters, I see them much differently these days. Maybe it's old age or just a changing of the tide? Whichever, it doesn't matter. I'm sure that inside each and every Bulger is a scared little child just crying out for attention. Somewhere in their life, lifting weights became their own utopia of power. They found power in weight lifting. People could respect them for their newfound power and so, they adopted a way of life that requires two to three hours of rigorous lifting, rigorous eating, and a rigorous wardrobe to handle their gym appointments. My only question is where does that end? Does it ever? And are these people pouring their successful lives into another soul that needs strength? I could sit here all day and mention the things *I* see, but what goes on outside the gym?

Well, that could be another story entirely.

The Bulgers are but one piece of the collective gym pie. I've mentioned the Toners, the Life-Changers and the Bulgers, but there's also the Average Joe. You know, Mr. or Miss Casual Fitness. Having a gym membership is like paying for a social experience while mixing in some physical activity. If you've ever seen the movie Dodgeball, then you know what I'm talking about. And if you haven't, then I'm by no means telling you that you should. The movie is just a nice reference tool in this scenario. Essentially the Average Joe is more interested in people-watching and shooting the bull, so to speak.

You'll find all manner of other people at the gym as well. Grannies and Grandpas who can squat more pounds than the mid-20s lifter; paranoid lifters that wipe machines down that they're not evening using and guys who sweat so much that they have to change sweatshirts halfway through their workout. Bigfoot-wannabes, whose hair covers more of their body than the clothes they are wearing, are counteracted by their antithesis, the full bodysuit members, whose clothes are so tight that you'd think they painted their clothes on that morning. Women are the biggest offenders in this department, leaving very little to the imagination with a skin-tight outfit that would make even Olympian divers blush. I'm not saying that it's always a bad sight, I'm just pointing out that not everyone is made for form-fitting attire.

By now you're probably an expert on the people who cohabitate the gym with you. With that type of knowledge, you're only halfway home to navigating your way around. That being said, here are some unwritten rules you should be aware of.

For example, if I could break down the blueprint of any gym, I would do so by explaining how there are three specific areas: free weights, suspension weights, and the treadmill/ elliptical center. I'd throw in the yoga and spin rooms for good measure too but not every gym has those. For the sake of this argument, we'll stick to the three-room arrangement and speak to it accordingly. When you venture to the gym, you have one of three locations you can populate. Bulgers tend to stick to their free weights. The Average Joes hang out by the suspension training while the I-Love-My-Legs group sticks to their run/walk machines; these folks are also known as Toners. This creates (and has created) a perpetual hierarchy at the gym; a caste system if you will. The territorial playground has been predetermined so you must decide which pack you'd like to run with.

It's no surprise that the Bulgers exhibit massive upper body strength because of their attachment to the heavy weights. The Average Joes continue on their average path due to their lack of variety in their workout. And the Toners build stamina and endurance while never truly attaining any muscle mass. Like rival gangs competing over the best hot spots, these groups attempt to establish dominion over their respective areas. Like lions and hyenas quarreling over a kill. Or packs of wolves circling a troop of bears; these are the social battlegrounds of the fitness center. There's no beating of chests or peeing on machines to mark territories, but if this gym were located in the middle of a forest, devoid of human contact, you may very well see that kind of conduct.

One might think that the Bulgers hold complete control over the gym, but interestingly enough, this is not the case. They're bigger, stronger, and more physically impressive than the other groups, but there are some key elements to be cognizant of. For one, Bulgers aren't really concerned with the "full body" workout. True, there are some who attack every able muscle in their physique, but there is a good percentage that focuses solely on the "beach muscles." Why bother with a run when you can increase your number of tricep dips? That's much more engaging to the Bulger than a walk on the treadmill. Secondly, Bulgers are typically loners by nature. They may congregate together in the free weights section, but they don't have more than two or three in their party. Like the Sith in Star Wars, "always two there are; no more and no less." The Bulgers would never, and I mean *never*, band together to overtake the suspension weights or the treadmills. Japan would sooner turn itself over to China than the former ever occur. And if there ever were an uprising at the gym, I'm sure that the I-Love-My-Legs group of women would put the Bulgers in their place. If you've seen how these women power walk, then you would watch your back before you lay claim to a vacant machine. If the Average Joes (and Janes) ever united, they could probably run the place by sheer number alone.

Inevitably, you must come to the understanding that I did: people are always watching you. Even if you're trying to stay hidden, the eyes and ears will find you. Watch what you're playing on that iPod. On several occasions I've forgotten to turn off my iPod as I pulled my headphones away from my head. How does one explain the reason for Shania Twain on his playlist? Well, you say, "Yeah, don't know what that was about" and then you ask the other party, "Well, who *wouldn't* want Shania on their iPod? I mean, come on, she's absolutely bangin' and her songs are good too. If anything, *I* should be the one getting a thumbs up for my selection of music."

Am I right?

People are constantly assessing their surroundings. We're human beings; we have a curious nature about other people, even from a distance.

This presents some major issues for anyone who is trying to go about his business. I decided to check the stats on "biggest pet peeves" at the gym. What I found in a fitness article from March of 2012, which was posted by CBS, was that workout enthusiasts have other, less noticeable reasons for being irritated at the gym. I fully expected "hate having people stare at my butt" or "really dislike it when guys hang out around the Pilates or Yoga room", but this was not to be.

Oddly enough, I didn't find any such complaint.

Nay, the number one pet peeve at the gym, according to this article, was "people who don't wipe down their machines once they're done." A whopping 44 percent said this. The list rounded out with 2) people who talk too much on their cell phones; 3) people spending too much time on a machine; 4) gym show-offs (aka the Bulgers) and 5) getting "hit on." My guess is that the ladies weighed in heavily on the fifth complaint.

Which brings me to another great truth about the gym: it's mostly full of single people. In the slim chance that you start dating someone, your whole schedule changes. You begin to plan things with the other person so getting in that timely workout doesn't always line up. When you're single and without a partner in crime, you can make it to the gym without much interference. And if you are really serious about hitting on somebody while you're there, you go at the busiest times available. That would be between 4 pm and 7 pm. That's when the singles hang out. You can scope out a hottie on the treadmill or grab a sneak peek of the yoga room. Whatever your taste may be, the gym offers plenty of good voyeurism to pick and choose who you may like to date the most. It's akin to a pool party, minus the bikinis and swim trunks. Add in some cut-off shirts, spandex and plenty of energy drinks and you've got yourself a party. So don't feel bashful about setting foot in there. Everyone else is essentially wearing the same thing too.

I can understand if you're too self conscious to get to the gym. You don't like the way you look or how your clothes wrap around that behind of yours; I get that. What I'm here to tell you is that you're already getting eye-oogled at public places, so why should the gym be treated differently? Don't be ashamed if you're thinner than a Popsicle stick and want to put on some poundage. Even world class bodybuilders had to start somewhere. Not everyone is born with a rippled bicep or flattened abs (unless of course your name is Jason Stratham—that guy is the likely exception). Keep your goals light and your progress consistent. And on the other end of the spectrum, if you're looking to lose some weight, do it in small steps. An unattainable goal is one that leaves you in want and kills any hope for future endeavors. Be realistic; don't listen to those stupid shows that promote three-hour-a-day gym visits. It's not worth the health risk and you owe it to yourself to do it in tiny doses.

There's plenty of people-watching to be done anyway and you don't want a few misnomers get in the way of doing just that.

I would encourage the gym experience to be one of adventure rather than relative paranoia. Since you are aware that people are watching, you can have fun with this fact. Go sit next to a Bulger and scream loudly as you lift your five pounds weights. Wear a leotard and high socks to the gym; show a full-bodied tattoo so that all the gawkers can wonder why a dragon is crawling your back and onto your face; and lastly, (a personal favorite of mine), pick a person in the gym and follow him/her everywhere they go, mimicking their workout to the tee. This may sound incredibly creepy but it's probably one of the greatest icebreakers for making new friends at the gym. If this individual does not give in to your mild stalking by responding with a "Hey, what are you doing?" you can always read their thoughts via the myriad of facial expressions: *What are they doing? Why aren't they using other machines around the gym? What's that smell? Is it me? I think I may report this person to the authorities* . . . .

In which case, you may want to reconsider which gym you belong to.

So the next time you're checking yourself out in the mirror, or sifting through your arm-mounted iPod Nano, know this fact: people are watching what you're doing. But hey, you probably already knew that and like the attention. Just do us all a favor and return the weights to their original location when you're finished. The staff makes "Please return all weights" signs for a reason; it's just a common courtesy. If you do not comply, then rest assured that someone witnessed your negligent behavior. And who knows, maybe that person will be following you the next machine you use? Think about it.

One Last Thought: Being alone (aka single) . . .

. . . can permit one to find one's self.

I don't want anybody to get the wrong impression with this last thought. My intent is not to enforce a concept of isolation, but rather encourage a period of self-discovery that may be fulfilling to the one who takes up such a journey. That would be far more accurate in defining the purpose of this chapter. I am no stranger to being alone but I am also no stranger to *not* being alone. There are experiences one may have personally between the two states. I'd prefer to talk about *not* being alone (single) first.

We often think that being with someone else will allow for us to gain the most growth as a person. I know you've likely heard someone tell you, "You don't know what you like until you try", but that sort of advice isn't exactly reassuring to a person who has no clue what they want out of a relationship. This can also lead a person to believe that trying *everything* is good for them. Is it a good idea to grab a cactus to know that it stings? Or is it smart to try and breathe underwater? Well, I won't know until I try it, right?

Those last two examples may appear to warrant common sense responses, but consider the dating world for a moment. Since when do people use common sense when their feelings are involved? Well? Exactly—not very many. The ones that *do* use organs other than the ones located between their thighs have a much broader scope on what it means to date. They shy away from situations where their emotions can get the better of them and they avoid conflicts that could end with personal anguish. These are the intelligent daters; the ones who value themselves as prized possessions, not generic commodities.

Whether these intelligent folk discovered their self-worth alone or with another person can vary, but they discerned this truth nonetheless. This is the single, greatest thing to recognize in life: that *your* life; no matter how strange, weird, or messed up, is worth something. When you're alone, or single, this can be a difficult concept to understand. You look at your friends and you see their happiness and you decide that you want that kind of happiness for yourself. You're tired of acting like an asexual tapeworm—you want someone to confide in, to hold, and to share some cool experiences with; you want *companionship*.

This is a wonderful to thing to aspire after, but you must be careful in your quest. For the biggest hindrance you'll have is something quite simple: *yourself*. Unless you have a solid sense of direction, a firm foothold in values, and a strong support group to lean on, you may find yourself listening to the voices of your significant others rather than yourself. This is not the fault of your main squeeze; it is merely a failure to have identity. Who am I? What am I looking for? Who can tell me what to look for? These are some fundamental questions one must ask before attempting to bond with another human being.

The challenge of mixing one's values with another can be as noncompliant as a duck trying to mate with a chicken; it just won't work. The duck may try to figure out where everything goes, but in the end, he'll just have to walk away (or waddle). I've tried like crazy to force my beliefs and my values onto the women I was with and nearly, ok 100% of the time, it never worked out. Not only did the relationship never work out, I also became confused as to what *my* core beliefs were. Isn't that a strange thing?

If my values were red paint on a canvas, then the women who challenged me in my relationships were blues, grays, and yellows; splashing and mixing their values with my own until my stark red color was no more. I haven't had an art class for a long time, but I do recall that when you blend too many colors together, you end up with something like a diarrhea brown (intriguing thought is it not?). Spend too much time assimilating yourself with that of others and you'll be left with nothing but crap. I was under this illusion that my values were ingrained like a strong oak tree, rooted deep where I stood. My reality was that of a container full of clay; on the outside I had a hard shell, but once you opened me up, I was still trying to mold myself in every way shape and form.

I've been witness to many, like myself, who experienced something very similar. Before their morals or values were confidently planted, they were eager to merge themselves with someone else; unaware of the danger in doing so. Usually, you'd think this would happen much earlier in life like, the teenage years but even adults will commit these same mistakes. I was fortunate enough to avoid all that chaos as a teenager, but I was not as lucky as a young adult. The protection I gave myself was good, but my reaffirmations of what *I* wanted were not always reinforced. There is a fine line between being challenged by life and being challenged by the person you're with. A good significant other will challenge you to improve, to better yourself, but if their challenge to you is one of competitive deceit, then you're already knee deep in a toxic relationship.

My earliest interpretations of dating made me want to stay far away from romantic relationships for as long as possible. I was much more content to go home every night, listen to music, and go to bed. I mixed in some sports, homework and the occasional hangout with close buddies but girlfriends were non-existent in my teenage life. No family is perfect; I must make that absolutely clear. Only now, in my adult life, am I fully aware of how blessed I was to have two parents to come home to every day of my young life. For so many others, this was not to be so in many ways, "dating" must have seemed like an escape. The chance to rely on another person of similar age was comforting and relieving; an opportunity to find peace in the midst of a messy world. If I had to guess, I'd say that more than 90% of the kids that started "dating" before their other classmates did were the ones who had troublesome home lives. It's so much easier to be taken down a wrong path or be led astray when you lack a model in your life that breeds protection, character, and love. You'll eventually find yourself clinging to other lost souls in hopes that they might understand what you're going through.

This is what teenage "dating" looked like to me.

Were there those who dated that *didn't* come from unhealthy home lives? Yes, absolutely, but what did their canvas look like once the dating experience was over? Was it muddied with other colors? Or was it still that strong red like mine had been? There's a good chance theirs was still red, but it probably had some similar colors showing up that hadn't been there before.

For me, I may have been avoiding all the pitfalls of my peers, but I wasn't fortifying myself either. I was in no man's land; moral purgatory, if you will. A place that was devoid of any real action and pouring out of life's good graces; this is where I resided. So when I left that black hole I was in, I was never fully prepared for what was in store: an open challenge to the model I had presented myself under. The pressure in sustaining that model when you're a lump of clay is damn near impossible. Point of fact, it *is* impossible.

The quest for "self" then begins all over again; who you *thought* you were was false, but who you *really* are is still buried deep within.

All living things believe in some form of self-preservation. My observation of early dating was merely an act of self-preservation. I saw the consequences of certain actions so I steered clear of the dating highways. When the time arrived for me to take the wheel, I was not enthused to discover just who was driving the car: an uncertain driver. Not *inexperienced*, just uncertain; there is a difference.

Many times we believe that experience will teach us what we need to know. "You won't know till you try it" is not good advice unless you're sampling food. If you're testing the "taste" of a new relationship with uncertainty, then you are making yourself vulnerable without even knowing it.

When I finally stopped gorging on the buffet that was open dating, I slowed down to reassess just what the heck I was doing. Who was I? Did I like myself? And was I enjoying the person I was when I was in a relationship? It was sobering to look back and see how I reacted to so many circumstances where I *thought* I'd keep a level head, but didn't. I came to understand that every choice I made in a relationship was a selection linked directly to my values and self-worth. Without either of these in strong stature, I was liable to crumble, become bitter, and turn bad situations into far worse ones.

I needed a getaway from others in order to become whole again, I figured. Honestly, I thought I'd return to who I was *before* I started this whole dating venture; *before* I lived with people other than my immediate family; *before* I had a conflict of character. This path to becoming strong again seemed linear and I needed to only right myself like I had so many years ago.

In hindsight, this was foolish thinking. Life teaches us that once you've had an experience, you cannot erase that memory by simply jumping back to where you were previously. The journey for self was not linear, nor was it perpendicular; it needed to be a complete 180 from where I was headed. I find it ironic, albeit strange, that when we are children we have such a better handle on who we want to be. As adults, we drift to thinking that our dreams as just dreams and if we don't become that which we're gifted in, we will accept some other fate that the world chooses for us.

I am *not* in this line of thinking (at least not any longer).

If your intent is to become the best of you, then you must evaluate your inward and outward personas. When the two become married, that's when you know you've become who you're meant to be. You are not wasting time wondering who you are or what you're asked to do. This new person is shaped by both experience and an inner calling; not the passing judgment of an acquaintance or significant other.

The time allotted for me as a single man has often felt like a prison, but ultimately, it's been a blessing. I've made some crucial observations of other people but more importantly, I've made some serious headway in my personal growth. Do I have it all figured out? No, of course not; that's what the rest of the journey is for. And let's just be honest about something too: if I had it figured out, I probably wouldn't be single any longer. Am I right? Maybe my next writing venture should be about understanding women a little better, no?

"Epiphanies, Theories, and Downright Good Thoughts . . . made while never understanding women whatsoever."

Well, the title needs some work but it's a good start. With the way things are going, I'll have plenty of time to finish it.